Mindwise

Mindwise

How We Understand What Others Think,
Believe, Feel, and Want

Nicholas Epley

ALFRED A. KNOPF | NEW YORK | 2014

To Jen, the mind I'm luckiest to know

CONTENTS

PREFACE Your Real Sixth Sense ix

PART 1 (MIS)READING MINDS

1 An Overconfident Sense 3

2 What You Can and Cannot Know
   About Your Own Mind 14

PART 2 DOES IT HAVE A MIND?

3 How We Dehumanize 37

4 How We Anthropomorphize 61

PART 3 WHAT STATE IS ANOTHER MIND IN?

5 The Trouble of Getting Over Yourself 85

6 The Uses and Abuses of Stereotypes 117

7 How Actions Can Mislead 141

PART 4 THROUGH THE EYES OF OTHERS

8 How, and How Not, to Be a Better Mind Reader 161

AFTERWORD Being Mindwise 185

Acknowledgments 191

Notes 195

Index 229

Your Real Sixth Sense

The only true voyage of discovery, the only fountain of Eternal
Youth, would be not to visit strange lands but to possess other
eyes, to behold the universe through the eyes of another.

—Marcel Proust (1922)

In the spring of 2011, my wife, Jen, and I were riding in a cramped van
with painfully uncomfortable seats in Addis Ababa, Ethiopia. We
had just left a courtroom where a judge had awarded us legal custody
of two young siblings, now our son and daughter. After we filled out
piles of paperwork and waited months to complete our adoption, it all
ended very simply. "The children are yours," she said.

Our van pulled up to the razor-wired gate that led to the adoption
center where our children were living, honked its horn, and waited for
the gates to open. My stomach was in knots. I gripped Jen's hand as if
clinging to a cliff. Our children's biological father was waiting to meet
us on the other side of the gate.

He had traveled more than half a day by foot, rusty bus, and broken-
down minivan from a cluster of mud-built homes in rural Ethiopia to
appear in court that morning. He needed to confirm, in front of the
judge, that he had lost his wife to disease and could no longer care for
his children. Our new son and daughter were so malnourished that
they were at only the second percentile on the World Health Organization's growth charts, below what is presumed necessary to live.

Their young lives had been excruciating in the ways that only crushing poverty can produce.

My mind raced as the van stopped. What will he think of us? Will he be happy or sad to see us? Does he want to meet us or was he forced to? Is he filled with regret or relief, pain or hope, or some complicated mix of all of the above? Is he keeping some horrible secret about them from us? What is it like to have decided to walk your own two children to an orphanage and let them go?

Jen and I already had two biological children of our own, ages five and ten at the time. I knew what it was like to be a father. I knew how it felt to rock your child to sleep, to hear their first "I love you," to burst with pride for their Little League home runs, to be certain you'd give your life to save theirs. I knew nothing about the kind of desperation that would lead me to walk, hand in hand, with my children to an orphanage and give them away. I deeply wanted to understand, to know, to see the world through this man's eyes so that I could someday explain it to our children, but his mind was a complete mystery to me. I had no sense of what it was like to be in his shoes.

Stepping out of the van and into the main office, we found two men sitting anxiously in worn-out chairs, wearing ill-fitting suit coats over their mud-stained T-shirts and torn jeans. One man glanced up at me. Almost instantly, tears started running down his face. I was startled by the incongruity of a hard-looking farmer sobbing. He stood, walked over, and wrapped his arms around me. We hugged tightly, almost desperately, with both of us now in tears for several long minutes. It felt like the longest embrace I'd ever received. He just wouldn't let go.

Behind that embrace was a lifetime's worth of information, of understanding into our children's pasts and his hopes for their future, of his beliefs about what was happening and his deepest feelings toward it. Behind that embrace was the mind of a man I so deeply wanted to understand, one I held so physically close in my arms, but whose mind will always remain out of reach.

YOU, MIND READER

That morning I experienced just how difficult it was to see the world through the eyes of another, to truly understand the mind of someone else. That moment was a deeply personal example of a scientific lesson I have been learning over the past two decades in my research as a psychologist, except that the scientific lesson is that we can have the very same difficulties understanding nearly everyone in our lives, from our coworkers and neighbors to our friends and family. Even your spouse is more mysterious than you would guess. Arguably, your brain's greatest skill is its ability to think about the minds of others in order to understand them better. I am going to tell you what research reveals about how that ability works, how it makes mistakes that lead to misunderstanding and conflict, and how to become wiser about the minds of others.

I am going to tell you about mind reading, but not the kind you normally associate with this term. I am not going to tell you about magic tricks that will allow you to astonish your friends at your next party. Nor am I going to tell you about telepathy, clairvoyance, or any kind of extrasensory power that creates a psychic connection with anyone. Instead, I am going to tell you about the kind of mind reading you do intuitively every day of your life, dozens of times a day, when you infer what others are thinking, feeling, wanting, or intending. The kind that enables you to build and maintain the intimate relationships that make life worth living, to maintain a desired reputation in the eyes of others, to work effectively in teams, and to outwit and outlast your competitors. The kind that forms the foundation of all social interaction, creating the web of presumptions and assumptions that enables large societies to function effectively. The kind I'll be describing as your *real* sixth sense.

Like any sense, this one can be stretched beyond its obvious limits, as it was when Jen and I met our children's biological father. When others' experiences are so different, their cultures so foreign, or their history so unknown, our sixth sense clearly fails us. But these humbling experiences are relatively rare for most of us. Far more often, our

ability to reason about the minds of others operates so quickly and easily that we hardly even notice we're using it, or even pause to consider
that our assumptions about the minds of others might be wrong.

Your sixth sense is running in high gear nearly all of the time, from
the moment you get up in the morning and dress to impress to when
you lie awake at night wondering whether others find you intelligent
or not, trustworthy or not, or really love you or not. During the day in
between, you easily recognize that your employees are clueless, but are
sure your boss thinks you're brilliant. You sense that your coworker is
lying when he calls in sick but are confident that your clients are honest when they claim to love your work. Walking home from the office,
you notice the homeless person at the end of your block and you *feel,*
just for a moment, the indignity of sleeping barefoot on icy cement
and you toss him some change. There is no magic or mysticism in
this. Our daily lives are guided by inferences about what others think,
believe, feel, and want. This is your real sixth sense at work. *You are a
mind reader.*

It's easy to understand why. You and I are members of one of the
most social species on the planet. No human being succeeds in life
alone. Getting along and getting ahead requires coordinating with
others, either in cooperation as friends, spouses, teammates, and
coworkers, or in competition as adversaries, opponents, or rivals. Does
she really love me or not? Is he being truthful or lying? How can I keep
my employees happy? What do my kids, friends, customers, or adversaries really want? Knowing the minds of others is essential for social
success because it enables you to anticipate what others are going to
say before they say it, to know what others want before they choose it,
and to predict an opponent's move before he makes it. At its best, such
mind reading can be a thing of coordinated beauty. Celebrity chef
Anthony Bourdain describes one such case in the bond between him
and his sous-chef: "In our glory days together . . . I could look across
the room at Steven, raise an eyebrow, maybe make an imperceptible
movement with my chin, and the *thing*—whatever the *thing* was at the
time—would be done."[1]

And so, with the obvious benefits that come from social understanding, you and I and nearly every other human being on the planet

have become so well practiced at reading the minds of others that our sixth sense operates almost invisibly. As philosopher extraordinaire Jerry Fodor has written, "Commonsense psychology works so well, it disappears." Only at the rare times when it is stretched beyond its limits, or is proven to be profoundly mistaken, does its existence come back into view.

ON MY MIND

My goal is to bring what I think is your brain's greatest ability out of the shadows and into the light of scientific inspection. Like thousands of other psychologists at research universities around the world, I use the basic principles of the scientific method to understand why you think, act, and feel as you do. More specifically, I conduct experiments that test your sixth sense to learn exactly how, and how well, you reason about the thoughts, motives, attitudes, beliefs, and emotions of others. This ability is one of your brain's greatest because it allows you to achieve one of the most important goals in any human life: connecting, deeply and honestly, with other human beings. Mind reading allows you to cooperate with those you should trust and avoid those you shouldn't. It allows you to track your reputation in the eyes of others, helping you to ensure that others think of you as a competent and reliable person worth befriending. At its best, being able to read the minds of others enables understanding between friends, forgiveness among enemies, empathy between strangers, and cooperation between countries and couples and coworkers. Without it, cooperative society is barely imaginable.

However, even our greatest abilities may be far from perfect. Just like vision, where most people can see reasonably well but need corrective lenses to see clearly, our ability to reason about the minds of others creates a social sense that is reasonably accurate but is also prone to systematic mistakes. My experiments over the past two decades, and far more research from many other scientists, demonstrate the many ways in which our sixth sense works well, but not nearly as well as we might think. Although it's easy to recognize our limitations when the differences are as stark as they were for me in Ethiopia, the truth is that you are likely to understand much less about the minds of your family members, friends, neighbors, coworkers, competitors, and fellow citizens than you would guess. I will cover this in chapter 1. In fact, our lack of insight even extends to the mind you presumably know the best: your own. In chapter 2, I'll describe what it appears we can—and cannot—know about ourselves. That we cannot read anyone's mind perfectly does not mean we are never accurate, of course, but our mistakes are especially interesting because they are a major source of wreckage in our relationships, careers, and lives, leading to needless conflict and misunderstanding. Our mistakes lead to ineffective solutions to some of society's biggest problems, and they can send nations into needless wars with the worst of consequences.

Fortunately for improvement's sake, the mistakes we make trying to understand the minds of others are predictable and therefore correctable. Our mistakes come from the two most basic questions that underlie any social interaction. First, does "it" have a mind? And second, what state is that other mind in?

We can make mistakes with the first question by failing to engage our mind-reading ability when we should, thereby failing to consider the mind of another and running the risk of treating him or her like a relatively mindless animal or object. These mistakes are at the heart of dehumanization. But we can also make mistakes by engaging our ability when we shouldn't, thereby attributing a mind to something that is actually mindless. These mistakes are at the heart of anthropomorphism. I cover these issues in chapters 3 and 4, respectively.

Once we're trying to read the minds of others, we can make mistakes with the second question by misunderstanding others' thoughts, beliefs, attitudes, or emotions, thereby misunderstanding what state another mind is in. Our most common mistakes come from excessive egocentrism, overreliance on stereotypes, and an all-to-easy assumption that others' minds match their actions, which I'll describe in chapters 5, 6, and 7. All of these mistakes have the same basic consequence of leading us to think that others' minds are more simplistic than they actually are. Knowing about these mistakes can obviously help you avoid them, but perhaps the best way to avoid these mistakes is to rely on another sense altogether. I'll explain this in chapter 8.

An optometrist can tell you how your eyes enable you to see the visible world, and therefore also knows how to fix malfunctions that keep you from seeing it perfectly. As a psychologist, my goal is to tell you how your brain creates a sixth sense that allows you to "see" the minds of other human beings. Perhaps more important, my goal is to describe your brain's predictable malfunctions that keep you from understanding the minds of others as well as you could. My goal is to improve your psychological vision.

IMPRESSIVE AND IMPROVABLE

Before leaping headlong into a detailed description of your sixth sense's shortcomings, it's worth taking a moment to marvel at its very existence. Others' minds are, after all, completely invisible. You've never actually seen a *belief*, smelled an *attitude*, or poked a *feeling*. No *intention* has ever walked past you on the sidewalk. You can't weigh a *want*. Like atoms before electron microscopes, minds are inferred rather than observed. They exist only as a theory each of us uses to explain both our own and other people's behavior. When your friend chooses an apple rather than an orange, the real cause of that choice involves an incomprehensible chain of electrical pulses, neurotransmitters, and dendritic connections. None of us explain other people by describing those actual neural causes because our intuitions give us a much simpler explanation: your friend *wanted* an apple. Strictly speaking, you did not see your friend's *want* in the same way you saw your friend's apple. Instead, you assumed the existence of your friend's *want* by relying on a theory that choices are caused by unobserved preferences. Like all good theories, our intuitive theory about minds both explains and predicts behavior, serving a very functional purpose even if its core principles are merely presumptions.

But what a marvelous theory it is. Human beings have been explaining one another for millennia without ever referencing a single neuron because the sense we've evolved is of such practical value. Mental concepts like attitudes, beliefs, intentions, and preferences are so highly correlated with whatever is actually going on in the brain that we can use our theory about other people's minds to predict their behavior. A person with conservative attitudes will generally vote for a conservative politician. A person with selfish intentions will usually be less generous than a person with generous intentions. And a person who claims to hate you is more likely than others to harm you. No knowledge of neuroscience is needed for this.

In fact, it is the ability to reason about the minds of others that appears to make us uniquely smart as a species. Living in large groups means that you *must* have the ability to understand other people's minds—their thoughts, beliefs, emotions, and wants—if you want to get along or get ahead. Such brainpower requires actual brain cells, which is why cerebral cortex size—the part of your brain involving thinking about the minds of others—is directly related to the size of the social groups they inhabit.[2] The bigger the social groups, the bigger cerebral cortex you need (relative to total brain size) to manage effectively in those groups. The cerebral cortexes of monkeys actually appear to grow larger when they're housed in larger social groups, presumably to manage the increased neural demands.[3] Human beings inhabit the largest social groups of any primate, explaining why your hat size is three times larger than a chimpanzee's.

You can see our species' social advantage emerging very early in life. In one particularly ambitious experiment, researchers compared the intellectual ability of 105 two-year-old toddlers with that of 106 adult chimpanzees, using tests involving both physical objects and social objects.[4] The tests involving physical objects included being able to track where food was located after it had been hidden or moved, being able to choose and then use the correct tool to get food otherwise out of reach, and being able to use sound as a cue for the location of a hidden reward (such as the sound of food rolling around inside a cup). In the tests involving social objects, another mind was involved. These social tests included being able to solve a problem correctly after watching the experimenter solve it, being able to use an experimenter's gaze as a hint to where food was located (this required understanding that where a person is looking is a cue for what he or she is thinking), and using a person's unsuccessful attempt to open a canister as an indication that there was food inside it.

The results were both clear and profound. When completing the physical tests, the kids and chimps were neck and neck: both solved 68 percent of the problems correctly. But when completing the social tests, where another mind was involved, the kids trounced the chimps, 74 percent correct to 36 percent correct. Our species has conquered the Earth because of our ability to understand the minds of others, not because of our opposable thumbs or handiness with tools.

In fact, this ability forms the backbone of all cooperative social life. This is why those with greater social sensitivity have stronger friendships, better marriages, and are happier with their lives in general. At work, leaders do better when they have some sense of whether or not their instructions are being understood. Managers motivate their employees when they have some sense of what their employees want and need. Salesmen close more deals when they have some ability to know what their customers want and can modify their pitch accordingly. Most of us avoid getting into fistfights or looking like complete idiots because we have a reasonable sense of what others think and feel, and thus can manage our relationships reasonably well. Being able to understand others is a major part of what lets you move smoothly through life.

■ ■ ■

So give your brain a hand! In a world of seven billion people, where both your happiness and your economic success depend critically on your relationships with others, it is hard to imagine a more useful ability than understanding other people. Even better, your brain comes fully equipped to do it.

With that self-affirmation behind us, let's start looking a little more carefully. As impressive and useful as your sixth sense may be, having an ability and using it perfectly are two very different things. When put to the scientific test, we're not nearly as wise about others as we think we are. Our mistakes do not mean that we are social idiots; nor do they mean that we can't all come to have the kind of relational understanding that Anthony Bourdain experienced with his sous-chef. Instead, our mistakes simply tell us that being a social savant requires practice, work, and some thoughtful strategies.

The key to improving your understanding of others is to determine where your ability falls short of perfection, so that you can work to improve it. I will explain our consistent shortcomings in great detail, but do not let this focus cause you to lose sight of the impressive ability you already have, or to believe that there's no hope of doing better. When the Marist Institute for Public Opinion conducted a poll of 1,020 Americans, asking them what superpower they would most like to have, the ability to read the minds of others tied for the top spot with the ability to travel through time.[5] The irony is that unlike time travel, mind reading is a superpower you already have. It's also one you can use more wisely to make it even more powerful.

But before we talk of improvement, I need to spend the next chapter giving you a more precise sense of the magnitude of our brains' shortcomings. At times, the size of the gap between what we think we know about others and what we actually know can be shocking.

PART 1

(MIS)READING MINDS

*The main problem is that we think we understand
the minds of others, and even our own mind,
better than we actually do.*

1

An Overconfident Sense

A lot of leaders are coming here, to sit down and visit. I think
it's important for them to look me in the eye. Many of these
leaders have the same kind of inherent ability that I've got, I
think, and that is they can read people. I can read fear. I can
read confidence. I can read resolve. And so can they—and they
want to see it.

—former U.S. president GEORGE W. BUSH

'm sure you have no trouble realizing that people occasionally misunderstand each other. Such conflict keeps newspapers and divorce
lawyers in business. Surely you can also think of times when others
have misunderstood your thoughts, emotions, or intentions. Maybe
you've sent a sarcastic e-mail that your coworkers took to be serious,
making you look like a jerk rather than a joker? Or had earnestness
mistaken for belligerence, shyness mistaken for arrogance, generos-
ity mistaken for cynical manipulation? We've all been there. In your
cooler moments, you probably realize that even you sometimes mis-
interpret and misunderstand others, including the people you should
understand the best. Not often, it might seem, but at least sometimes.

More often, though, our sixth sense leaves us feeling like George W.
Bush, with considerable confidence in our ability to understand others. Bush even had this clear sense after meeting Vladimir Putin for

the first time: "I looked the man in the eye. I found him to be very straightforward and trustworthy. . . . I was able to get a sense of his soul."[1] Whether accurate or not, our first impressions are formed quickly and easily, and are therefore held with considerable confidence. Seeing someone for only fifty milliseconds, faster than the blink of an eye, gives us enough time to form an impression of their competence.[2] These snap judgments matter. In one experiment, politicians who looked more competent than their rivals after a fleeting glance were significantly more likely to win their election (about 70 percent of the time), suggesting that those snap judgments put people into our most powerful positions.[3] Your sixth sense works quickly and is not prone to second-guessing.

So just how accurately do we understand the minds of others? For many years, psychologists have been trying to answer this question by putting mind reading to the test. We might, for instance, ask you to look at pictures of people who are happy or sad, proud or ashamed, elated or afraid, to see how accurately you can recognize each emotion.

Or we might ask a group of people to tell us how much they like you, then ask you to *predict* how much each of these people will report liking you, and then compare your predictions with the other people's actual rating to assess your accuracy.

How well do we perform on these tests? Are we as socially skilled as we think?

MIRROR, MIRROR

To get a sense of your actual abilities, let's start with what is likely to be a very common and important bit of mind reading: trying to guess another person's impression of *you*. Much of our everyday life is spent trying to understand how we're being evaluated in order to help us create just the right impression. Does your boss think you are intelligent? Do your coworkers like you? Do your employees understand your instructions? Does your neighbor find you trustworthy? Does your spouse really love you? Or perhaps more important if you are young and single, do others think you are attractive?

In fact, knowing what others think of you appears to be one of the most common things you might want to know about the minds of others. In one survey, Mary Steffel and I asked an online sample of five hundred Americans to imagine that we had invented a "brainoscope" that would allow us to see into the minds of others. We asked our respondents to imagine that this device would allow them to know what others are thinking and feeling with perfect accuracy. We then asked our respondents to tell us who they would use their brainoscope on and what they'd want to learn about. Somewhat to our surprise, our respondents were not interested in understanding the minds of the rich, famous, or powerful. Instead, the vast majority wanted to peer into the minds of those closest to them, particularly spouses and dating partners but also bosses, family members, and neighbors. Interestingly, they wanted to get a look at the minds of those they presumably knew the best. And what our respondents wanted to find out most was what these other people thought of *them*. The majority wanted their brainoscope to work like a magical mirror, Narcissus 2.0.

This isn't such a bad idea. Knowing your own reputation can be surprisingly difficult. Consider, for instance, a study that analyzed a set of published experiments all sharing the same basic design.[4] In these experiments, people working in a group would be asked to predict how the other group members would rate them on a series of different traits. Researchers then compared these predicted ratings to the other group members' actual ratings on the very same traits. The traits varied from one experiment to another and included qualities like intelligence, sense of humor, consideration, defensiveness, friendliness, and leadership ability. The groups varied in familiarity, with the members of some groups being fairly unfamiliar with one another (such as having met only once, in a job interview) and the members of other groups being very familiar with one another (such as having lived together for an extended time as roommates). If people knew exactly what others were thinking, then there would be a perfect correspondence between predicted and actual ratings. If people were clueless, then there would be no correspondence between the two. Statistically speaking, you measure relationships like these with a correlation, where perfect correspondence yields a correlation of 1 and no correspondence yields a correlation of 0. The closer the correlation is to 1, the stronger the relationship.

First, the good news. These experiments suggested that people are pretty good, overall, at guessing how a group of others would evaluate them, on average. The overall correlation in these experiments between predicted impressions and the average actual impression of the group was quite high (.55, if you are quantitatively inclined). To put that in perspective, this is roughly the same magnitude as the correlation between the heights of fathers and the heights of sons (around .5). It is not perfect insight, but it is also very far from being clueless. In other words, you probably have a decent sense of what others generally think of you, on average.

Now the bad news. These experiments also assessed how well people could predict the impression of any single individual within a given group. You may know, for instance, that your coworkers in general think you are rather smart, but those coworkers also vary in their impression of you. Some think you are as sharp as a knife. Others think you are as sharp as a spoon. Do you know the difference?

Evidently, no. The accuracy rate across these experiments was barely better than random guessing (an overall correlation of .13 between predicted and actual evaluations, only slightly higher than no relationship whatsoever). Although you might have some sense of how smart your coworkers think you are, you appear to have no clue about which coworkers in particular find you smart and which do not. As one author of the study writes, "People seem to have just a tiny glimmer of insight into how they are uniquely viewed by particular other people."[5]

But perhaps this is holding your mind-reading abilities to too high a standard? It's hard, after all, to define traits like intelligence and trustworthiness precisely, so it might not be so surprising that we have difficulty guessing how others will evaluate us on these ambiguous traits. What about predicting something simpler, such as how much other people like you? Surely you are better at this. You learn over time to hang around people who smile at you and avoid those who spit at you. You must have a much better sense of who likes you and who hates you within a group. Yes?

I'm afraid not. These studies found that people are only slightly better than chance at guessing who in a group likes them and who does not (the average correlation here was a meager .18). Some of your coworkers like you and others do not, but I wouldn't count on you knowing the difference. The same barely-better-than-guessing accuracy is also found in experiments investigating how well speed daters can assess who wants to date them and who does not, how well job candidates can judge which interviewers were impressed by them and which were not, and even how well teachers can predict their course evaluations. Granted, it's rare that you are completely clueless about how you are evaluated. Accuracy tends to be better than chance in these experiments, but not necessarily by very much.

Perhaps, though, getting these broad and general evaluations right is still too much to expect of your sixth sense. What if we tried something simpler still, something specific and concrete that you've likely spent a considerable amount of time thinking and learning about? Can you accurately predict how attractive a member of the opposite sex will find you after being shown a photograph of you? You have, after all, lived a full life with yourself, looking at your face in the mirror every morning, and getting a sense of whether people tend to find you attractive or not. At certain points in your life (perhaps you're at that point right now), you may have thought of little else. And yet when Tal Eyal and I ran a series of experiments in which we asked people to predict how attractive they would be rated by a member of the opposite sex who was evaluating a photograph we took of them, we found that people's predictions were no more accurate than chance guessing.[6] Across two different experiments, the overall correlation between predicted and actual evaluations was 0. It's not that our volunteers consistently thought they were more attractive than they were actually rated, but that their predictions of how attractive they would be considered from a single photograph simply bore no relation to how they were actually rated on the basis of that photograph. It is often said that love is blind, but our participants did not even have a chance to be blinded by any love. They were just blind to begin with.

The central challenge for your sixth sense is that others' inner thoughts are revealed only through the façade of their faces, bodies, and language. Just as human beings have evolved the ability to use cues from that façade to see what truly lies beneath—to be mind readers—so, too, have human beings developed a skill to use their façade to mislead and misdirect others—to be liars and deceivers. Anyone who has ever been on the receiving end of "Does my butt look big in these pants?" knows that what you say to someone does not always reflect what you truly believe about them. And yet, time and time again, researchers have found that our attempts to guess when another person is telling the truth and when they are lying are just that: little better than guesses. When George W. Bush met Vladimir Putin, he felt like he had learned a great deal about the inner "soul" of this former KGB agent by reading his behavior. I wouldn't bet on it. When one group of researchers evaluated decades of studies and hundreds of experiments that measured how well people could distinguish truths from lies, they found that people's ability to spot deception was only a few percentage points better than a random coin flip: people were 54 percent accurate overall, when random guessing would make you accurate 50 percent of the time.[7]

These mistakes are no laughing matter. At times, they can have deadly serious consequences. Neville Chamberlain, as the prime minister of Great Britain, believed Adolf Hitler's assurance in 1938 that peace could be preserved with Czechoslovakia and thus encouraged the Czechs not to mobilize their army. "In spite of the hardness and ruthlessness I thought I saw in his face, I got the impression that here was a man who could be relied upon when he had given his word," Chamberlain said. He was wrong. Hitler was actually lying, having already mobilized his army to attack Czechoslovakia and needing to buy just a little more time to ensure a crushing invasion. Nearly seventy years later, American officials had learned not to trust scoundrels. They were therefore certain that Saddam Hussein was lying when he said, time and again, that he had no weapons of mass destruction. But again, like the majority of American people at the time, they were wrong.[8] Americans went to war, mistakenly believing that Hussein was lying when he was actually telling the truth. It's easy to see how understanding other people can be a daunting task if you are unable to tell when they are misleading you and when they are not.

ILLUSIONS OF INSIGHT

Although it may be challenging, perhaps reading the minds of others still isn't very much of a problem in everyday life because our mind reading is finely tuned to those we know the best, such as our closest friends, relatives, colleagues, and spouses. Long-married spouses sometimes say they know each other so well that they can complete each other's sentences. Really getting to know someone puts you in sync with them, you might think, so you're able to understand each other's thoughts without even uttering a single word. There is no doubt that friends, coworkers, and romantic partners *think* they know each other's minds better than they know the minds of strangers. Is this confidence justified? Do we really know our friends and loved ones as well as we believe we do?

Again, the answer is no, but this answer comes in two parts. The first part is that you are indeed better able to read the minds of close friends and loved ones than those of strangers, although not by all that much. William Ickes, a pioneer in research on mind-reading accuracy, points out that in his experiments, "strangers read each other with an average accuracy rate of 20 percent" when videotaped and later asked to report their moment-by-moment thoughts and feelings.[9] "Close friends and married couples," he reports, "nudge that up to 35 percent." So yes, you do know what your spouse or a close friend likes and dislikes more than a random stranger would, but the gain may be surprisingly modest. The second part of this answer, however, is that the confidence you have in knowing the mind of a close friend or romantic partner far outstrips your actual accuracy. Getting to know someone, even over a lifetime of marriage, creates an illusion of insight that far surpasses actual insight.[10]

To see both of these results, imagine that you have signed up with your sweetheart to participate in an actual experiment, set up by the researchers as something like *The Newlywed Game*.[11] You sit in separate rooms, are told that your beloved will never see any of your answers, and are then given a long list of questions about yourself. Some of these concern your sense of self-worth, with questions asking how much you agree or disagree with statements like "I tend to devalue myself" and "I feel great about who I am." Other questions ask you to assess your own abilities and attributes—how you think you compare to others in terms of your intellectual ability, athletic ability, social skills, and so on. The final questions are about your preferences, specifically how much you like or dislike each of twenty-four different activities (such as playing cards, going swimming, visiting with friends, and doing the laundry). In the room next to you, your partner is *predicting* how you will answer all of these items and reporting his or her confidence that these predictions will be correct, from 0 percent likely to 100 percent likely.

Couples in the actual experiment followed exactly this procedure. The researchers then tabulated the results to see how well the partners knew each other, compared to how well they believed they knew each other.

Let's start with the good news. Partners predicted each other's exact thoughts better than would be expected by random guessing alone. These couples had been dating for up to six years, so this finding is not particularly surprising. For instance, the scale used for the self-worth questions ranged from 1 to 5, with 1 indicating strong disagreement with the statement and 5 indicating strong agreement. Because there are only five response options available, chance guessing would give you a score of 20 percent right (because you have a 1 out of 5 chance of guessing correctly for any item). Couples were significantly more accurate than this, guessing their partner's sense of self-worth correctly 44 percent of the time. This is pretty good. If you were a baseball player, this might be the equivalent of hitting a double.

Now for the not-so-good news. Bigger than the gap between actual accuracy and chance accuracy was the gap between how much partners *actually* knew about each other and how much they *believed* they knew. Remember, the participants were perfectly accurate a little over 4 out of 10 times when predicting their partner's self-worth (44 percent, on average). They believed they were right, however, 8 out of 10 times (82 percent, on average). As you can see in the figure below, the same 2:1 rate of overconfidence, or an even larger one, emerged on the other measures as well. The real problem with mind reading is the gap between the white bars and the gray bars in this figure. These couples hit a double, but thought they'd hit a home run.

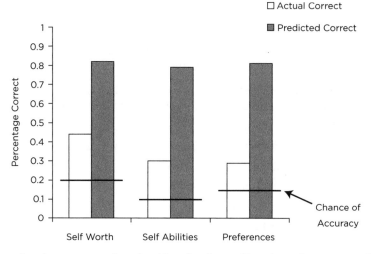

One member of a romantic couple predicted how the other would rate him or her on a series of different measures, including feelings of self-worth, self-rated abilities, and activity preferences. The lines across the bars show the accuracy rates one would expect by chance alone. The white bars show the percentage that the partners, on average, actually predicted correctly. The gray bars show the percentage that the partners predicted they answered correctly. Dating partners were more accurate than would be expected by chance alone but nowhere near as accurate as they thought they were. This figure illustrates the main goal of this book: to reduce the gap between the gray bars and the white bars in your own life, both by instilling a sense of one's limitations to reduce the height of the gray bars and by offering suggestions for how you can better understand others and thus increase the height of the white bars.

Even more surprising is that this overconfidence *increased* in proportion to how long two people had been together. The longer they had been together, the more they thought they knew about their partner. In fact, the length of a couple's relationship was not correlated with accuracy at all in this study. More time together did not make the couples any more accurate; it just gave them the illusion that they were more accurate.[12]

This illusion of insight can have dangerous consequences. In another experiment, volunteers watched videos of people either lying or telling the truth about whether they were HIV positive. People were fairly confident that they could tell if the person was lying, predicting that they had guessed correctly 70 percent of the time. In fact, they did no better than what would be expected by chance alone, correctly identifying truths and lies only 52 percent of the time (when chance is 50 percent). As people gained more information about the person in the video, they became more confident but did not become any more accurate. When, during the rise of the AIDS epidemic, U.S. Surgeon General C. Everett Koop implored Americans to "know your partner," he presumably meant accurate knowledge rather than the illusion of knowledge.[13]

The problem with our sixth sense is not that it is horribly flawed. It does fall short of perfection when we test it under challenging circumstances, but it generally performs far better than chance guessing. And compared to the mental abilities of other species on this planet, our sixth sense is what truly makes our brains superpowered. The problem is that the confidence we have in this sense far outstrips our actual ability, and the confidence we have in our judgment rarely gives us a good sense of how accurate we actually are.[14]

The main goal of this book is to reduce your illusion of insight into the minds of others, both by trying to improve your understanding and by inducing a greater sense of humility about what you know—and what you do not know—about others.

■ ■ ■

A baseball player wants to know his batting average to better assess his objective ability. When it comes to mind reading, there is no single batting average to give because the judgments we need to make about others vary so much. Some are really easy—like being thrown a pitch by a first grader—whereas others are much harder for us—like being thrown a split-fingered fastball by a major league all-star. Sometimes it's really easy to know what someone is thinking or feeling because the cues are so obvious—a person sobbing in the fetal position on your office floor clearly got fired rather than hired—and other times it's hard because the cues are so weak—your spouse has many beliefs, attitudes, emotions, and thoughts they may never have shared. The main point is that when mind reading is put to the test, it most often tells us that however good we actually are, we're not likely to be as good as we think we are.

But you can give your self-confidence one more test, because surely there's one mind that you can know with justifiable confidence: your own. You're certain that you love your wife because she's so funny, that you hate commercial interruptions on television because they're annoying, you believe that men and women should be treated equally, know that your own political beliefs are well-informed and carefully reasoned, and would find talking to strangers on a bus to be about as much fun as handling a bag of pus. You may not have a direct line into other people's thoughts, beliefs, or attitudes, but you've got an intracranial pipeline into your own mind. You can look inward and introspect, knowing your own mind quite accurately.

You're not alone in this feeling. Descartes was so certain about his introspective ability that he staked his own, as well as God's, existence on it with his famous "I think, therefore I am" bit. Leibniz also argued that introspection was a reliable sense, like seeing, that allowed you to look inward to observe the workings of your own brain. With this confidence in the powers of introspection so obvious, it is not surprising that the very first psychology laboratory ever established in the United States (by Edward Titchener at Cornell University) was set up entirely with the guideline of using introspection as the basis of all of psychology. For those early psychologists, there was no other way to understand the brain than to have people tell you what was happening inside it. "Within the sphere of psychology," wrote Titchener, "introspection is the final and only court of appeal, that psychological evidence cannot be other than introspective evidence."[15]

Yes, we can certainly peer inward. The real question is, again, whether our confidence in introspection is justified. Is the faith that you, Descartes, Leibniz, and Titchener—all very smart people, for sure—have in your ability to know your own mind justified?

Yes, and no, and I'll need the next chapter to explain that.

2

What You Can and Cannot Know
About Your Own Mind

All people unhesitatingly believe that they feel themselves
thinking. . . . I regard this belief as the most fundamental of
all the postulates of Psychology, and shall discard all curious
inquiries about its certainty as too metaphysical for the scope
of this book.

—WILLIAM JAMES, *Principles of Psychology* (1897)

William James couldn't put off inquiries about introspection for
long. The scientific journey to discover how well you can read
your own mind began just over three decades after James penned the
above quote, in a beat-up station wagon driven nearly ten thousand miles
by a Stanford sociologist named Richard LaPiere. The trip was inspired
by an experience LaPiere had while traveling with a young Asian couple
through a tiny town known "for its narrow and bigoted attitude towards
Orientals."[1] Such attitudes were sadly common in much of the United
States during the time between the two world wars. So with some trepi-
dation, LaPiere went to the town's nicest hotel to get lodging for all three
of them. Much to his surprise, he had no trouble at all. The clerk, he
wrote, "accommodated us without a show of hesitation." Apparently,
this clerk wasn't as bigoted as the town's reputation suggested.

Just by happenstance, LaPiere found himself in the very same town not two months later. Out of curiosity, he called the very same hotel, told the clerk that he might be traveling through town again with a "very important Chinese gentleman" in the near future, and asked if the hotel would be willing to accommodate them. Again without a show of hesitation, the clerk emphatically said, "No." This discrepancy intrigued LaPiere. Could it be that a person who thinks like a racist would not act like one? Might someone fail to know his or her own mind?

LaPiere couldn't answer these questions with this single instance, but he figured he could learn something important if he asked hundreds of similar clerks—251, to be exact—the same questions. So for the next two years, LaPiere enlisted his two Chinese friends in an epic road trip that crisscrossed the United States, seeking service at 184 restaurants and 67 hotels. As part of the experiment, LaPiere varied his friends' clothing from one place to another, sometimes asking for service himself but letting the couple negotiate for service or accommodations whenever possible. He recorded the reactions they received meticulously. This must have been a puzzling journey for LaPiere's friends, because he never informed them that they were part of an experiment—"out of consideration for their feelings," as well as to keep them from influencing the experiment's results.

Now, out of their 251 attempts, how many times do you think they were refused service?

Before you answer, you should know that LaPiere was traveling through pretty hostile territory. Six months after visiting each location, he sent a letter to each place he'd been to, asking, "Will you accept members of the Chinese race as guests in your establishment?" Nearly every person who responded said no: 91 percent of the time at the hotels and 92 percent at the restaurants. Americans lived up to their bigoted reputation.

Now again, how many times do you think the Asian couple was *actually* refused service? Ninety percent of the time? Ninety-two percent? No, not even close. LaPiere and his friends were refused service only once, "in a rather inferior auto-camp into which we drove in a very dilapidated car." Only *once*! Over 90 percent of people at the establishments contacted in this experiment believed they would act like bigots, but less than half of 1 percent actually did.

UNKNOWING THYSELF

This experiment has its flaws, but it inspired decades of research that revealed a startling message—that there can be a significant disconnect between what people think about themselves and how they actually behave. This disconnect has been found so many times since LaPiere's road trip that you would think psychologists study little else. For instance, racial attitudes in the United States have shifted dramatically since LaPiere's journey, but people still seem unable to foresee how they'll behave in a racially charged situation. The overwhelming majority of Americans now endorse egalitarianism over discrimination. It's not surprising, then, that people in one recent experiment predicted that they would be outraged by any display of overt racism, in particular by a racist comment or joke. But when actually confronted in this same experiment with an obviously racist comment, the overwhelming majority of these egalitarians sat by and did nothing. They also reported feeling less disturbed when confronted with the actual racist comment than another group who only imagined the comment predicted they would feel.[2] The same goes for blatant sexism. In one experiment, people who imagined seeing an instance of blatant sexism thought they would be outraged. When people actually saw this very same act, however, they felt virtually no rage at all.[3] Do people not know their own minds?

The list of similar scientific demonstrations is long. One of the most famous series of experiments in psychology's history is Stanley Milgram's research on obedience to authority. Most of us believe we're independent thinkers with kind hearts, so if we were told to deliver enough electric shock to kill another person in an experiment, most of us would believe that we'd refuse immediately. Indeed, when Milgram surveyed different groups of people, nobody predicted that they would be willing to deliver more than 300 volts of electricity to another person, and most believed they would stop far sooner. And yet when Milgram set up an experiment in which people were asked to do just that, he found that in his experiment *everyone* was willing to deliver 300 volts of electric shock to another person and a full 62.6 percent pressed a switch that they were told would deliver 450 volts, long past the point where it appeared that the other person might have died from the experience.[4]

Results like these are interesting but, in my experience, rarely convince anyone that their powers of introspection are weaker than they would guess. Experiments put *other* people's conscious attitudes and beliefs about themselves to the test, but because *you* did not take the test yourself, it's easy to imagine that you would know yourself better than these hapless participants did. Not so with this next example, however, because it's one you've experienced many times. We can even put it to the test right now.

What I'd like you to do is think of an important task you have to complete in the next few weeks. Maybe you need to write a paper for school, or put together a presentation for work, or finish reading a book (like this one!). The more important the task, the better. Got one?

Now write down in the space below or on some scratch paper—honestly, please—your most accurate prediction of when you are going to complete this task. Be specific. Write the date and even the time by which you think you will have completed the task. Yes, honestly:

Once you're done with that, spend a moment thinking about when you might complete this task in a best-case scenario, if everything goes as quickly as possible. Write that down here:

Finally, use another moment to estimate how long it will take you to complete this task in a worst-case scenario, if everything involved in completing it goes as badly as it possibly could. Yes, write that down, too:

_____

Now I'd like to place a bet with you. Not that you won't make your best-case prediction; I'm going to bet that you won't get your project done even by your *worst-case* scenario. I know, I sound depressing. I'm actually a very optimistic guy, but I've seen some evidence. So have you, because you've experienced it yourself many times before. People so habitually underestimate how long it will take to get tasks done that psychologists have come up with a name for it: the *planning fallacy*.

The evidence I've seen comes from a group of psychologists who asked their honors thesis students to do exactly what I asked you to do with regard to their theses.[5] If you've ever written an honors thesis, then you know it's a major project that typically serves as a capstone to an undergraduate education. These students were midway through their projects, with about two months left to go. They were asked to predict how many more days it would take them to complete the project in a best-case scenario, a realistic scenario, and a worst-case scenario. Predictions were twenty-seven days in the best case, thirty-four days in the realistic case, and forty-nine days in the worst-case scenario.

How many days, on average, did it actually take these students to complete their theses?

Fifty-five.

A majority of the students failed to complete the thesis in the time they'd predicted it would take "if everything went as poorly as it possibly could." Researchers have replicated this result time and time again.[6] In another experiment, only 45 percent of projects were done by the time people had predicted, with 99 percent certainty, that they would be completed. Even worst-case scenarios tend to be overly optimistic. I'll lose my pessimistic bet with some readers but win it enough times to come out ahead, just like casinos.

The interesting thing about the planning fallacy is not that people commit it. I'm sure you've experienced it over and over again in your own life. I certainly see it over and over in mine, from this book, which took a year longer than promised, to the list of weekend projects that remains undone almost every Monday morning. No, the interesting thing about the planning fallacy is that despite having so much experience committing it ourselves, we so consistently think that our own mistakes are things of the past rather than the present. This only ensures that we'll keep making the same mistake over and over again.

When you think one thing about yourself and the truth is another, what are you failing to know about yourself? One word: construction. You are consciously aware of your brain's finished products—conscious attitudes, beliefs, intentions, and feelings—but are unaware of the processes your brain went through to construct those final products, and you are therefore unable to recognize its mistakes.

Let me explain what I mean.

HOUSE OF MIND

In the mid-1800s, physicians and psychologists began studying the accuracy of people's perceptions of conscious experiences and found them to be woefully uninformed, leading to the familiar metaphor of the human mind as an iceberg. "We have sought the real ego in the intellect," wrote G. Stanley Hall. "It is not there. Its nucleus is below the threshold of consciousness. The mistake of ego-theorists is akin to that of those who thought icebergs were best studied from above the surface and were moved by winds, when in fact about nine-tenths of their mass is submerged, and they follow the deeper and more constant ocean currents."[7]

The iceberg metaphor is common but also misleading. First, it creates the myth that we only use 10 percent of our brains, a myth adored by psychics because it suggests that you'd be able to perform extraordinary mental feats if only you could tap into that subterranean brainpower. "Our minds are capable of remarkable, incredible feats, yet we don't use them to their full capacity," argues Uri Geller, self-proclaimed psychic. "In fact, most of us only use about 10 percent of our brains, if that. The other 90 percent is full of untapped potential and undiscovered abilities."[8] Our minds are indeed capable of extraordinary feats, but it is false that 90 percent is untapped potential. These unconscious processes are tapped every second of your life, governing nearly all of your behavior in a reasonably adaptive fashion. Consciousness is involved in only a small sliver of what you do from one moment to the next. That doesn't mean that the rest of your brain is unused potential.

Second, the iceberg metaphor misleads by suggesting a solid connection between conscious and unconscious mental processes, with the unconscious processes somehow giving rise to the conscious ones, or at least being firmly bonded to them in some direct way. In fact, there need be no connection at all between conscious and unconscious processes. Unconscious processes seem largely responsible for much of what we do habitually in daily life, and conscious processes seem largely responsible for making sense of what we do so that we can explain it to ourselves and others.

A better metaphor for the human mind is a house: you can know its finished form quite accurately, but its construction is hidden from view. My own home, for instance, was originally built in the 1920s and has been modified several times since. Upstairs we have three bedrooms, two bathrooms, and an office. Our kitchen is on the main level, facing the street, and our master bedroom looks out on our garden in the backyard. You can trust my description. I have an inside view. I see it every day with my own two eyes.

Our house is also a puzzle. Some interior walls have brick behind the drywall instead of wooden studs. There is a steel beam in one wall for no apparent reason, and a hidden walkway behind a cement wall in the basement that calls to mind Al Capone's home. We have bits of exterior siding in our attic, old sections of roof that are now beneath the existing roof, a light-switch-sized hole in the middle of the house that blows freezing cold air from some unknown pathway all winter long, and bricks with rounded corners on the front side of our house but bricks with sharp corners on the back. How our house was constructed in this way, from start to finish, and who was involved in this construction process and when is a complete mystery to me.

Every day I can look at our house and see the finished product. What I am unable to do, even with careful inspection and archeological investigation, is figure out the construction process that made it this way. I can describe in great detail *what* our house looks like, but I can only guess *why* it looks that way.

The human brain is not like an iceberg; it's like a house. We are consciously aware of finished mental products, from sensory experiences of pain and pleasure to feelings of conscious control and free will to strongly held beliefs and attitudes. We feel in conscious control of our behavior when choosing to watch one movie instead of another, we feel unbiased when telling teachers just how smart our children are, and we know we adamantly prefer one political candidate over another. But we can only guess at what's going on inside our heads to construct those conscious experiences. We can report feeling happy but are only guessing when explaining why. We can report loving our spouse but are guessing when explaining why. And we can feel ourselves thinking through important decisions that lead to an important choice but are again guessing when trying to explain why we chose option A rather than B. Introspection is blind to construction. This does not mean that our introspective guesses are never accurate, just as you might guess the correct answer to a multiple choice question. It means that you should be skeptical about their accuracy.

MINDFULLY UNAWARE

To see just how limited our introspection can be, let's start with one of your brain's most important functions: vision. A full third of your brain is dedicated to sight, not because it is so complicated to convert waves of light into neural pulses but because the waves of light you take in are so ambiguous that your brain has to do a lot of constructive work to produce a sensory image. Every introductory psychology textbook I have ever seen contains a chapter on vision, and each of those chapters includes a figure similar to the one below, depicting how your brain allows you to see the world.

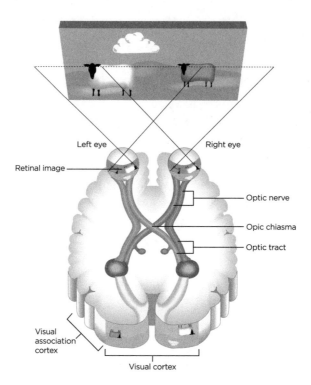

This figure portrays sight as a process in which some visual image is taken in through the lens of your eye, converted into neural signals that pulse through your brain, and eventually projected upside down and backward onto your visual cortex as a faithful representation of the world *out there.*

These are great figures. The problem is that they are only two-dimensional. What they miss is the big fat part of your head—your frontal lobes and the rest of your visual cortex—that sticks out from this figure and interprets the waves of light that hit your retina. This figure suggests that what you see is purely a function of what is out in the world in front of you. In fact, what you see is a product of invisible construction inside your brain that renders—*poof!*—a complete and finished image to your conscious experience. It seems that your vision is a realistic reflection of the way the world is *out there,* when it is actually a constructed product that exists *in here.*

To see this constructive process in action, look at the figure below. What is it?

Yes, an elephant. Good work. Now look more closely. Did it take you a moment to notice its legs? How fast could that thing run? If vision was simply a reflection of the world *out there,* then you would notice its legs at first glance. But vision is actually a construction that starts with information you already know—such as what a normal elephant looks like—to save you the trouble of having to examine everything in detail to actually see it. So most people notice the legs only on a second glance.

Now, how about this one, below? Who do you see?

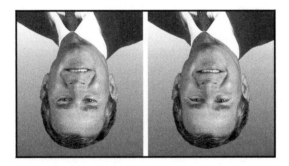

Yes, another good answer. It's a former U.S. president, a face so familiar that you can even recognize George W. Bush upside down. But now take your book or e-reader and turn him right side up. Go ahead. . . .

Whoa! What happened? Bush before his first term and then after his second? Notice how Bush's freakish features on the left were not obvious to you, no matter your political views, when the image was upside down. That your perception of a face is so dependent on its orientation simply shows that there's much more to what you see than the image in front of your eyes.

In fact, the amount of constructive work your brain does without your awareness is stunning. Your brain contains in the neighborhood of one hundred billion neurons, with each neuron making anywhere from a thousand to ten thousand connections with its neighbors through synapses. "Given these figures," writes neuroscientist V. S. Ramachandran, "it's been calculated that the number of possible brain states—the number of permutations and combinations of activity that are theoretically possible—exceeds the number of elementary particles in the universe."[9]

Of course, your neurons aren't connected randomly. They are connected in a pattern that reflects how often two neurons are typically activated in conjunction with each other. The more often one fires at the same time as another, the more their connection is strengthened in an associative network. Once they're connected in this way, the activation of one neuron will activate its associate. This is why whenever two things commonly occur together in your world, thinking of one tends to trigger thoughts of the other. Yin and _____. Dr. Jekyll and Mr. _____. Peanut butter and _____.

Not only are thoughts associated in this way, behaviors are as well. Read the following list of words for me:

> Vomit
> Puke
> Barf
> Moist
> Snot
> Slobber
> Mucus

If your upper lip is now curled ever so slightly into an expression of disgust without any *actual* barf or snot in front of you, then you get the point. Thoughts can activate the behavioral responses commonly associated with them, like an expression of disgust to go along with the feeling triggered by these words. Once thoughts of gross bodily fluids are activated, the associated behaviors they elicit follow naturally, without any conscious intervention on your part. Psychologists know that consciousness is not required to guide behavior because you get the very same reactions even if those words are flashed in front of you so quickly that you can't recognize that you have seen any words at all.[10]

WHY I LIKE THEE, DOCTOR FELL

Understanding the associative nature of your brain is absolutely essential for understanding why it's hard to know some aspects of your own mind. Over the course of evolution, your genetic code has inherited certain associative networks that help keep you alive long enough for you to pass along your genetic material through children. These associative networks need not be consciously accessible. The clearest example comes from the mysterious feeling of attraction. Some people are hot and others are not. You know it in an instant. But *how* do you know? You can introspect and come up with some guesses—"I like blondes" or "he looks fit"—but you're likely to miss a more fundamental cause.

Despite what you've been told, beauty is not really in the eye of the beholder. People around the world, and even one-day-old infants, generally agree about who is hot and who is not.[11] One of the primary determinants of attractiveness is a signal that has proven useful over millennia for finding healthy and fit partners to have babies with. Do you know what it is? Big muscles? Big smiles? Big breasts? Yes, for some, but there's one that's far more consistent around the globe: bilateral symmetry. That is, the degree to which the left and right sides of your body are identical.[12] I know: it sounds hot, doesn't it? It doesn't get much conscious attention because your brain is so good at assessing symmetry that it constructs your feeling of attraction almost instantaneously. Introspection misses this constructive process entirely. And so if you ask why someone finds a supermodel attractive, I can promise that nobody other than trained evolutionary psychologists will say "symmetry."

Attraction is a powerful feeling that we can report on quite clearly, but our conscious understanding of its construction is empty. An old nursery rhyme captures this dumbfounding well:

> I do not like thee, Doctor Fell,
> The reason why I cannot tell;
> But this I know, and know full well,
> I do not like thee, Doctor Fell.[13]

BRAINFULLY MINDLESS

If evolution sculpts neural networks through genetic inheritance, then everyday life sculpts them through practice and repeated exposure until they produce unconscious habits that guide our behavior without us knowing why. When your coworker asks how you're doing on your way to the elevator, you may have already answered, "Fine, how about you?" before even thinking about how you're really doing. You stand almost exactly two feet away from your friend without the aid of a ruler because that distance just feels right—any closer would be creepy and any further would be cold. Stepping into the elevator, you instinctively face toward the door, instead of the back or the side, without hesitation. Neural associations create habits that guide our actions like invisible hands, behaving brainfully but mindlessly.

My favorite example of this comes from an experiment examining the routine scripts we follow when asking others for help.[14] You know these scripts already. When you ask someone for help, you first have to state your request—"I need you to stay late at work today"—and then give a reason for your request—"*because* we're way behind on an important project." If you need something, you can't just ask. You have to ask *and* give a reason. If this association has become so well learned that it runs unconsciously, like riding a bicycle, then virtually any reason given for a request should unconsciously trigger a compliant response. You go along without even thinking about the reason.

You can see the importance of this request-plus-reason association by considering an experiment in which people waiting in line to use a copy machine were given a request by an experimenter. In particular, the experimenter asked if she could budge ahead in line by requesting, "Excuse me, I have five pages. May I use the Xerox machine *because* I'm in a rush?" That script follows the routine and, sure enough, 94 percent of people granted the favor and let the experimenter budge ahead in line. In a second condition, the reason was dropped: "Excuse me, I have five pages. May I use the Xerox machine?" Hmm . . . that breaks the normal routine because there's no reason. As expected, far fewer—only 60 percent of people—granted the favor. The third condition is the most interesting one, the request-plus-dumb-reason condition. Here, the experimenter asks, "Excuse me, I have five pages. May I use the Xerox machine, *because* I need to make some copies?" That's right, *because I need to make some copies.* This follows the standard script but includes a nonsensical reason. Of course you have to make copies. What else are you going to do with the copy machine, make sandwiches? But because the request follows the well-learned routine, it automatically triggers compliance. So sure enough, a full 93 percent of people granted the favor, statistically identical to the good-reason condition.

These associative networks can not only guide our behavior toward others without our conscious awareness, they can also guide how we think about ourselves. Most people around the world live their lives in ways that create positive associations with their own selves. For instance, show people the word "me" and most are then likely to complete the letter string "g o_ _" with "good" rather than with "goat," because "good" is more commonly associated with oneself than is "goat."

These positive associations, however, can make it hard to know yourself accurately. In fact, they can even make it hard to recognize your very own facial image. Erin Whitchurch and I discovered this in one experiment in which we took photographs of people and blended their facial image, in 10 percent increments, with either a highly attractive face or a highly unattractive face. This blending had the effect of making people's own faces look increasingly more or less attractive than they actually are. You can see the blended images of Erin and me in the figure on the next page. We then showed people all eleven versions of their own faces—their actual face, the five blended with the highly attractive face, and the five blended with the highly unattractive face—in a randomly ordered lineup and asked them to identify which face was their own. We found that people tended to select attractively enhanced images of themselves, thinking they were more attractive than they actually were.[15] The image you carry of yourself in your mind's eye is a function, at least in part, of the associations you have formed about yourself rather than simply of the image that appears in the mirror. Now you know why most of the pictures taken of you seem to look so bad.

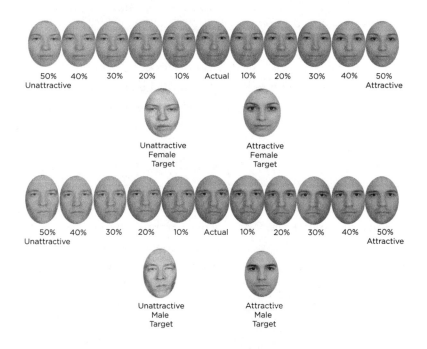

Decades before psychologists made any of these discoveries about the full reach of unconscious processes, Carl Jung said, "In each of us there is another whom we do not know."[16] Jung didn't know the half of it. We are in some ways, as psychologist Timothy Wilson puts it, "Strangers to ourselves."[17] When you think one thing about yourself and the truth is another, what are you failing to perceive about yourself? We now know the full answer. You are missing the contextual triggers and unconscious associations that are actually responsible for much of what you think and do. LaPiere's hotel and restaurant clerks (whom I described at the beginning of this chapter) knew their conscious attitudes toward Asians, but they missed the behavioral responses that would be triggered automatically when a smiling, friendly, and *real* Asian human being actually asked for a room. When thinking about how you would respond if asked to deliver electric shocks to another human being in the Milgram obedience studies, you know your conscious aversion to harming another person, but you miss the difficulty you would have in saying no to a clear and reassuring authority figure in the heat of the moment after having lived much of your life following orders from authority figures. You are missing the construction that happens inside your own brain: the triggers and intervening neural processes that make you do what you do and think what you think. We don't understand ourselves perfectly well because we have access to only part of what's going on inside our heads.

TELLING MORE THAN YOU KNOW

If some of our brain's activity is hidden from conscious introspection, why don't we feel like Weiners more often? That is, feel like Anthony Weiner more often? Weiner was the U.S. congressman for the 9th district of New York State when a self-administered photo of his groin region appeared on his Twitter account for all of his followers to see. Weiner quickly claimed that his account had been hacked. But after a week of intense grilling from reporters and increasingly implausible denials, Weiner admitted to having taken the photo himself to send to a woman in Seattle. He'd posted it on Twitter by mistake. Whoops. When a reporter asked what he'd been thinking, his introspection came up empty: "I don't know what I was thinking. . . . If you're looking for some kind of deep explanation for it, I simply don't have one except that I'm sorry." For the first time, Weiner was telling the truth. If we are merely guessing at the way our brains work, then why don't we find ourselves stumped about ourselves more often?

The reason is that we introspect about our own minds in the same way we do about the minds of others: by using a theory that makes sense of our own behavior even when we lack direct access to the actual causes of it. It works quickly and automatically, and it simply doesn't account for what you don't know. When you don't know the actual facts about yourself, your consciousness pieces together a compelling story, much in the same way it does when you're trying to read the minds of other people to make sense of why they act as they do. Blind to the constructive processes that actually guide our thoughts, feelings, emotions, and choices, we're left with the illusion that we know more about own minds than we actually do.

Consider a simple experiment where mall shoppers were asked to explain their choices. These shoppers were first shown four pairs of stockings and asked to pick the best. In fact, the stockings were identical. The researchers found that the ordering mattered: shoppers preferred whichever stocking was on the far right (thereby evaluated last) four times more often than whichever stocking was on the far left (thereby evaluated first). Nevertheless, when these shoppers were then asked to explain their choice, not a single person said anything about the ordering of the display. The researchers reported that, when asked directly if the ordering had influenced their choices, "virtually all subjects denied it, usually with a worried glance at the interviewer suggesting that they felt either that they had misunderstood the question or were dealing with a madman."[18] The order of the stockings created shoppers' preferences, but these shoppers seemed unaware of this influence on their own minds.

A long list of experiments like this one have changed the way psychologists do their work. No psychologist asks people to explain the causes of their own thoughts or behavior anymore unless they're interested in understanding storytelling. You can ask people *what* they are thinking or feeling or wanting—the finished product of some mental processes—and expect to get a solid answer, but asking *why* they think or feel or want invokes nothing but theoretical guesswork.

What's surprising is how easily introspection makes us *feel* like we know what's going on in our own heads, even when we don't. We simply have little awareness that we're spinning a story rather than reporting the facts. For instance, you spend all day at the car dealership looking over cars, pitting one in your mind against another, ultimately choosing the one that all of your thoughts point to most clearly. And driving away, you know why you're sitting in this car and not another one. Don't you? It's the shiniest, or feels the best, or has the most horse-power. Aren't those explanations justified?

Not necessarily. It is rare that the world plays devilish tricks on you, and so most often when you intend to do something—like grab a soda from the fridge for lunch—your action is perfectly in line with your intention: you want a soda and so you grab one. This consistency between intention and action makes it seem like whatever reasons you offered for wanting a soda might also be reasonably accurate. But what if the world was more devilish? While you're reaching for your soda, the devil in your fridge puts a beer in your hand instead. When your spouse asks why you're having a beer for lunch, you'd be startled, wouldn't you? You'd say, "No, no, I meant to grab a soda" or "The devil made me do it." Wouldn't you?

Given what psychologists know about the dramatic limits of intro-spection, one group of researchers thought you probably wouldn't notice but that you'd come up with a good story to explain yourself anyway. They didn't swap beers for soda; instead, they played a little magic trick on their participants who had been asked to look at pic-tures of two very different people and choose the person they found more attractive. Here's where the magic happened. After the partici-pant had chosen the more attractive person, the experimenter put the photographs facedown on the table and pushed the selected photo back to the participant. The experimenter then asked the participant to explain why he or she found that person to be more attractive. In some cases, the participant turned over the picture, and there was the person he or she had actually chosen as more attractive. But in other cases, the experimenter's magical sleight of hand instead substituted the photograph of the *other* person, the one chosen to be *less* attractive, and asked the participant to explain why they found *this* person to be more attractive.

Two interesting things happened. First, surprisingly few people (only 27 percent) noticed that the experimenter had slipped them the wrong photograph, even when given unlimited time to choose between very dissimilar photographs. When going to pick up your date next time, you might want to bring along a picture from home, just in case. Second, when asked to explain their choice, there was no difference in the reports given by those who were explaining the photo they'd actually chosen as being more attractive and those given the one they had not actually chosen. People who were shown the card they had *not* chosen nevertheless told a completely compelling story explaining why they *had* chosen that photograph. They failed to notice the card switch and so they devised a perfectly good explanation for a choice they had not actually made.[19]

The important point here is that the stories we tell about the workings of our minds rely on the same mind-reading abilities we use to make sense of the minds of other people. If you see someone smiling at a cartoon, you will assume that they find it funny. If you find yourself smiling at a cartoon, even if you are smiling only because you've been asked to hold a pen in the corners of your mouth so that it makes a smile, then you are likely to report finding the cartoon funny as well.[20] If you see someone hunched over, you will assume that they are not feeling very proud. Find yourself hunching over in the same way, even if only because you're filling out a survey on a table with very short legs, and you may report being less proud of yourself and your accomplishments, too.[21]

The only difference in the way we make sense of our own minds versus other people's minds is that we know we're guessing about the minds of others. The sense of privileged access you have to the actual workings of your own mind—to the causes and processes that guide your thoughts and behavior—appears to be an illusion.

I'M OKAY, YOU'RE BIASED

Illusions matter not simply because they are interesting but because they are consequential. The ability to introspect—"to feel ourselves thinking," as William James put it—creates an illusion that we know our own minds more deeply than we actually do. This illusion has one disturbing consequence: it can make your mind appear superior to the minds of others.

To see how, let's go back to vision. If you are perfectly sighted, then when you look out at the world, you automatically and instantaneously see a brilliant array of colors—a silver computer monitor, a neon green jacket, a bright red apple. All of the work your brain does to perceive color happens magically, completely outside of your conscious awareness. Color is not in the object being seen; it's inside our heads, in the way our brains interpret particular frequencies of light. We know this because some people, such as those who are color-blind, interpret the very same waves of light differently and therefore see very different colors. But without awareness of all of the constructive processes going on in your brain that allow you to see color, it seems to you that color exists *out there* in the world, rather than inside your own head—that the color red is actually on the apple in front of you, rather than simply appearing red to you because of the magic done by your neural connections. This creates what psychologists refer to as *naïve realism*: the intuitive sense that we see the world out there as it actually is, rather than as it appears from our own perspective.[22]

If a person thinks he or she sees the world as it actually is, then what happens when he or she meets someone who sees the world differently? When your friend tells you that the red apple is brown, who do you think needs to visit the eye doctor? Naïve realism suggests an answer: *they* do. It calls to mind a famous line of George Carlin's: "Have you ever noticed that everyone driving slower than you is an idiot, and anyone going faster than you is a maniac?"

Arguing about the color of an apple or speed on the highway is relatively trivial, but arguing about abortion rights, religion, same-sex marriage, gun control, or any other important issue on which opinions diverge is a serious matter, with conflict inflamed by the fuel of naïve realism. If the illusions you hold about your own brain lead you to believe that you see the world as it actually is and you find that others see the world differently, then *they* must be the ones who are biased, distorted, uninformed, ignorant, unreasonable, or evil. Having these kinds of thoughts about the minds of others is what escalates differences of opinion into differences worth fighting (and sometimes dying) for.[23]

The fingerprints of such naïve realism are at the center of almost any difference of opinion. When Bill Clinton was impeached, he claimed a vast right-wing conspiracy was the cause. When Sarah Palin was called out for making questionable statements at political rallies, she blamed the "lamestream media" for its biased coverage. This is not an isolated issue limited to one political stripe; people on both the right and the left tend to see the moderate media as biased *against* their own position simply because moderate opinions differ from more extreme ones, a phenomenon referred to as the "hostile media bias." When commentator Juan Williams was fired from National Public Radio for making ambiguously racist remarks, conservative Senator Jim DeMint tweeted, "The incident with Juan Williams reminds us the only free speech liberals support is the speech with which they agree."

When other people don't share your views, the all-too-common sentiment that comes straight from naïve realism is "I'm right and you're biased."[24] My hope is that these last two chapters have opened you up to the possibility that your own sixth sense can be quite mistaken. A more accurate understanding first requires the recognition that your judgment could be wrong, or could at least be wrong more often than you might think. The most useful perspective to take on our own mistakes is one that one of my MBA students, Debbie Lovett, described perfectly after a few weeks in my class: "One plus to learning that one probably isn't as great as they thought they were is also learning that others probably aren't as wrong as I thought they were, too. While I perceive that I've always been typically humble and kind—I've also undoubtedly been internally frustrated. . . . How nice to be able to gain some true humility and cut others more slack."

■ ■ ■

If I've convinced you that some humility about your own judgment is in order, then it's time to press on. Understanding how your sixth sense works is critical for understanding its mistakes. The very first mistake is failing to engage that sense when you should—a bit like needing to see what's in front of you but failing to open your eyes. Understanding the mind of another person first requires engaging your ability. Like closing your eyes and failing to see, failing to engage your sixth sense can keep you from "seeing" the minds of others. Under certain circumstances, as I will describe in the next chapter, it can even lead to a sense that others may have little or no mind at all.

PART 2

DOES IT HAVE A MIND?

The mistakes we make in trying to understand the minds of others come in two varieties. The first are mistakes of engagement. Sometimes we fail to engage our ability when we should, and other times we engage it when we shouldn't.

3

How We Dehumanize

The worst sin towards our fellow creatures is not to hate
them, but to be indifferent to them. That is the essence of
inhumanity.

—George Bernard Shaw

One of the most amazing court cases you probably have never
heard of had come down to this. Standing Bear, the reluctant
chief of the Ponca tribe, rose on May 2, 1879, to address a packed audience in a Nebraska courtroom. At issue was the existence of a mind
that many were unable to see.

Standing Bear's journey to this courtroom had been excruciating.
The U.S. government had decided several years earlier to force the
752 Ponca Native Americans off their lands along the fertile Niobrara
River and move them to the desolate Indian Territory, in what is now
northern Oklahoma. Standing Bear surrendered everything he owned,
assembled his tribe, and began marching a six-hundred-mile "trail of
tears." If the walk didn't kill them (as it did Standing Bear's daughter),
then the parched Indian Territory would. Left with meager provisions
and fields of parched rock to farm, nearly a third of the Poncas died
within the first year. This included Standing Bear's son. As his son lay
dying, Standing Bear promised to return his son's bones to the tribe's
burial grounds so that his son could walk the afterlife with his ances-

tors, according to their religion. Desperate, Standing Bear decided to go home.

Carrying his son's bones in a bag clutched to his chest, Standing Bear and twenty-seven others began their return in the dead of winter. Word spread of the group's travel as they approached the Omaha Indian reservation, midway through their journey. The Omahas welcomed them with open arms, but U.S. officials welcomed them with open handcuffs. General George Crook was ordered by government officials to return the beleaguered Poncas to the Indian Territory.

Crook couldn't bear the thought. "I've been forced many times by orders from Washington to do most inhuman things in dealings with the Indians," he said, "but now I'm ordered to do a more cruel thing than ever before." Crook was an honorable man who could no more disobey direct orders than he could fly, so instead he stalled, encouraging a newspaper editor from Omaha to enlist lawyers who would then sue General Crook (as the U.S. government's representative) on Standing Bear's behalf. The suit? To have the U.S. government recognize Standing Bear as a person, as a *human being*.

The case lasted several days, during which the government lawyers attempted to portray the Poncas as savages, more like thoughtless animals or unfeeling objects than rational and emotional human beings. Perceiving the Poncas as mindless, after all, is what had made it possible for officials to treat them as property under the law rather than as persons. This perception was clear from the government attorney's opening question: he asked Standing Bear how many people he had led on his march. "I just wanted to see if he could count," the attorney explained.

After several days of testimony, the trial drew to a close. Judge Elmer Dundy knew that Standing Bear wanted to address the audience in his own words, as was customary in Ponca tradition, but direct statements at the end of a trial were not allowed under U.S. jurisprudence. Respecting Native American tradition and violating his own, Judge Dundy called the bailiff to his desk, whispered that "the court is now adjourned" to secretly end the official proceedings, and then allowed Standing Bear to rise and address the court.

So it had come down to this. At about ten p.m., at the end of a very long day, Standing Bear rose. Illiterate, uneducated, and with no time to prepare an address, he stood silent for a minute to survey the room. Finally, he spoke: "I see a great many of you here. I think a great many are my friends." Then he tried to reveal that he was, in fact, much more than a mindless savage. He explained his tribe's difficulties in the Indian Territory, stated that he had never tried to hurt a white person, and described how he had taken several U.S. soldiers into his own home over the years and nursed them back to health. Then, in a stunning moment that channeled Shylock's monologue from *The Merchant of Venice*, Standing Bear held out his hand. "This hand is not the color of yours. But if I pierce it, I shall feel pain. If you pierce your hand, you also feel pain. The blood that will flow from mine will be the same color as yours. I am a man."[1]

Standing Bear was a man intelligent enough to lead his tribe along a six-hundred-mile journey in the dead of winter and back again, a man who felt love so deeply that he carried his son's bones around his neck to fulfill a promise. Yet he found himself pleading with people from far-off places who had failed almost completely to see his mind and instead viewed him as a piece of mindless property. Facing those unable to recognize a sentient mind before their eyes, Standing Bear had been forced to show his to them.

DISENGAGED

Standing Bear's case is an extreme example of a surprisingly common failing of our sixth sense. Like closing your eyes and then concluding that nothing exists, failing to engage your ability to reason about the mind of another person not only leads to indifference about others, it can also lead to the sense that others are relatively mindless. Most extreme examples typically involve some kind of hatred or prejudice that distances people from one another. The Nazis, building on centuries of anti-Semitic stereotypes, depicted the Jews as greedy rats without conscience or as gluttonous pigs lacking self-control. The Hutus in Rwanda depicted the Tutsis as mindless cockroaches before killing them by the hundreds of thousands. Exceptions in these extreme cases typically came from those who actually knew the targets of prejudice directly. General Crook had interviewed Standing Bear and his tribesmen in his office; they'd told him directly of their pain and suffering, of their hopes and dreams, of their beliefs and memories. He did not think of the Poncas as mindless savages, and so was willing to orchestrate the legal case in which he was named as the defendant. From these examples, we begin to learn important lessons about what it takes to recognize the existence of a fully human mind in another person, as well as the consequences of failing to recognize one.

Of course, Standing Bear is neither the first nor the last human being to have his mind overlooked and underestimated. The cross-cultural psychologist Gustav Jahoda catalogued how Europeans since the time of the ancient Greeks viewed those living in relatively primitive cultures as lacking a mind in one of two ways: either lacking self-control and emotions, like an animal, or lacking reason and intellect, like a child.[2] So foreign in appearance, language, and manner, "they" did not simply become *other* people, they became *lesser* people. More specifically, they were seen as having *lesser minds,* diminished capacities to either reason or feel.[3]

Similar evaluations play over the course of history like a broken record. Martin Luther King Jr. was assassinated in Memphis while supporting a labor strike by sanitation workers whose rallying cry was "I am a man." In the early 1990s, California State Police commonly referred to crimes involving young black men as NHI—No Humans Involved.[4] In 2010, thousands of immigrants protested extreme immigration laws in Arizona while carrying signs saying, "I am human." When people around the planet demand human rights or claim they have been treated inhumanely, the central issue is their oppressors' failure to recognize their mind. This may be why Article 1 of the Universal Declaration of Human Rights puts a person's mind front and center: "All human beings are born free and equal in dignity and rights. They are endowed with reason and conscience and should act towards one another in a spirit of brotherhood." Apparently, it can be easy to forget that other people have minds with the same general capacities and experiences as your own. Once seen as lacking the ability to reason, to choose freely, or to feel, a person is considered something less than human.

The essence of dehumanization is, therefore, failing to recognize the fully human mind of another person. Those who fight against dehumanization typically deal with extreme cases that can make it seem like a relatively rare phenomenon. It is not. Subtle versions are all around us. Even your refrigerator may hold an artifact of one example. When the French began making champagne for the British, the champagne makers quickly learned that the Brits preferred much drier champagne than the French did. In fact, the French found this version to be unpalatable. They named this inferior champagne *brut sauvage,* poking fun at the seemingly unsophisticated Brits. The joke was eventually on the French: *brut* is now the most popular variety of champagne in the world.

Our sixth sense's shortcomings in these cases arise partly from our failure to engage it when in the presence of someone so different or distant from ourselves. It may feed off prejudice and hatred, but it does not require either. Disengagement can come anytime there is a distance between two minds that needs to be bridged. For instance, when team owners in the National Football League proposed extending the season from an already punishing sixteen games to a grueling eighteen, Ray Lewis, one of the most fearsome players in the NFL, protested that the owners had overlooked the players' experience and were thinking of them only as moneymakers. "[I know] the things that you have to go through just to keep your body [functioning]. We're not automobiles. We're not machines. We're humans." There's no reason to think that any kind of prejudice or animosity was involved here. The owners may well have been focused on their own finances rather than on their players' minds, a focus that would make it easy to overlook or underestimate their players' pain.

Even doctors—those whose business is to treat others humanely—can remain disengaged from the minds of their patients, particularly when those patients are easily seen as different from the doctors themselves. Until the early 1990s, for instance, it was routine practice for infants to undergo surgery without anesthesia. Why? Because at the time, doctors did not believe that infants were able to experience pain, a fundamental capacity of the human mind. "How often we used to be reassured by more senior physicians that newborn infants cannot feel pain," Dr. Mary Ellen Avery writes in the opening of *Pain in Neonates.*

"Oh yes, they cry when restrained and during procedures, but 'that is different.'"[5] Doctors have long understood infants as human beings in the biological sense, but only in the last twenty years have they understood them as human beings in the psychological sense.

Your sixth sense functions only when you engage it. When you do not, you may fail to recognize a fully human mind that is right before your eyes. It is comforting to imagine that such "mindblindness," as psychologist Simon Baron-Cohen describes it, is just a chronic condition or personality trait for some people, a condition that neither you nor I have. Indeed, for some it is. This is a comforting story because it makes the inhumanity that can stem from dehumanization, from overlooking the mind of another person or being indifferent to it, seem like something that is likely to exist in *other* people, not in you. Although it is indeed true that the ability to read the minds of others exists along a spectrum with stable individual differences, I believe that the more useful knowledge comes from understanding the moment-to-moment, situational influences that can lead even the most social person—yes, even you and me—to treat others as mindless animals or objects. Engaging with the mind of another person depends not only on the type of person you are but also on the context you are in. None of the cases described in this chapter so far involve people with chronic and stable personality disorders. Instead, they all come from predictable contexts in which people's sixth sense remained disengaged for one fundamental reason: *distance.*

DISTANCE MAKES MINDLESS

For psychologists, distance is not just physical space. It is also psychological space, the degree to which you feel closely connected to someone else. You are describing psychological distance when you say that you feel "distant" from your spouse, "out of touch" with your kids' lives, "worlds apart" from a neighbor's politics, or "separated" from your employees. You don't mean that you are physically distant from other people; you mean that you feel psychologically distant from them in some way. You've developed different beliefs than your spouse over time and have "grown apart," your kids' generation is so different from your own, or you work in a large corporation with more employees than you can name. These two features of social life—the magnitude of the gap between your own mind and others' minds, and the motivation to reduce that gap—are critical for understanding when you engage your ability to think about other minds fully and when you do not.

Distance keeps your sixth sense disengaged for at least two reasons. First, your ability to understand the minds of others can be triggered by your physical senses. When you're too far away in physical space, those triggers do not get pulled. Second, your ability to understand the minds of others is also engaged by your cognitive inferences. Too far away in psychological space—too different, too foreign, too *other*—and those triggers, again, do not get pulled. Understanding how these two triggers—your physical senses and your cognitive inferences—engage you with the mind of another person is essential for understanding the dehumanizing mistakes we can make when we remain disengaged.

TRIGGER NO. 1: SENSING OTHERS' MINDS

Not long ago, I took my three sons camping and ended up in the emergency room. My oldest son was whittling an impossibly large branch with a ridiculously small pocketknife when the blade slipped and sliced into his hand. I had my back turned, tending our campfire, but when I heard him cry out, I instantly spun around to see him hopping up and down with blood dripping out of his hand, looking me squarely in the eyes with a mixture of pain and fear. In a split second I knew exactly what he had done, was wincing in pain right along with him, and was equally worried about what we were going to do. In that split second, our minds merged.

My brain came equipped with exactly the same operating system that yours did, one that allows our brains to synchronize with another's automatically, under the right circumstances. There is no magical psychic connection in this; it follows three perfectly natural steps. First, you and another person have to be sharing attention, to be looking at or thinking about the same thing. As human beings, you and I are exceptionally good at this attention detection. When my son cut his hand, I instantly glanced at his face and could tell, from twenty feet away, that he had cut his palm rather than his wrist. I couldn't measure the angle of a roof if I had an hour and a handful of protractors, but both you and I can sense the angle of a person's eyes down to decimal points within a split second, and can therefore easily figure out what someone else is looking at. Once two or more people are focused on the same thing, their minds start to merge, because they are reacting to the same event. You are disgusted by vomit. So am I. Cute babies make you happy. Me, too. Slicing your hand with a knife hurts, *a lot*. I'm with you. Although we all like to think of ourselves as unique, by and large our brains respond to events very similarly. When two people are evaluating the same event, they are setting the stage for thinking and feeling the same way as well.

Second, once our eyes are attending to the same event, our faces and bodies may synchronize. "When we see a stroke aimed," wrote Adam Smith in *The Theory of Moral Sentiments*, "and just ready to fall upon the leg or arm of another person, we naturally shrink and draw back our leg or our own arm." When I saw that my son had cut his hand, I winced in pain just as if I had cut myself. A similar thing happens at my kids' soccer games, where I have to keep the row in front of me clear, to allow room for empathy kicks. Other parents kick along with their kids, too. Almost any event can provoke such imitation. See someone yawn and it's hard not to yawn yourself. Laugh and at least some in the room will laugh with you. The same is true of smiles and startles and frowns, all of which are contagious in crowds. Pay attention the next time you're in a group and you'll be startled by how often you catch yourself adopting similar gestures or postures, a similar pace of speech, or even a similar accent as others. It's as if you've become a puppet on someone else's strings.

Finally, once eyes and bodies are merged, our minds tend to merge as well. Thoughts and feelings come from what we're looking at and how our bodies are reacting to it, so when two people are watching something and reacting similarly, they are likely to be feeling and thinking similarly as well. Adam Smith thought imitation reflected your understanding of another person's experience—your body shows what you think another person feels. In fact, the reverse is also true: you feel what your body shows. When you see a pained expression on a friend's face, your face may also contort into a pained expression, thereby making you feel a touch of pain yourself.[6] Sit up straight and you'll feel more proud of your accomplishments.[7] Smile and you will feel happier.[8] Even furrowing your brow, as if you are thinking harder, can lead you to *actually* think harder.[9] This link from imitating another person's actions to experiencing the other person's emotions is a critical link for understanding the minds of others. If a researcher disables your ability to imitate another's facial expression, such as by asking you to hold a pen pursed between your lips[10] or by injecting your face with Botox,[11] your ability to understand what another person is feeling drops significantly. Botox dulls your social senses right along with your wrinkles. Buyer beware.

This three-part chain—sharing attention, imitating action, and imitation creating experience—shows one way in which your sixth sense works through your physical senses. More important, it also shows how your sixth sense could remain disengaged, leaving you disconnected from the minds of others. Close your eyes, look away, plug your ears, stand too far away to see or hear, or simply focus your attention elsewhere, and your sixth sense may not be triggered.[12]

The importance of physical distance for engaging our sixth sense is perhaps best illustrated by a surprising problem for military leaders in times of war: soldiers in battle find it relatively easy to shoot at someone a great distance away but have a much more difficult time shooting an enemy standing right in front of them. George Orwell described his own reluctance to shoot during the Spanish Civil War. "At this moment," he wrote, "a man, presumably carrying a message to an officer, jumped out of the trench and ran along the top of the parapet in full view. He was half-dressed and was holding up his trousers with both hands as he ran. I refrained from shooting at him. It is true that I am a poor shot and unlikely to hit a running man at a hundred yards. . . . Still, I did not shoot partly because of that detail about the trousers. I had come here to shoot at 'Fascists,' but a man who is holding up his trousers isn't a 'Fascist,' he is visibly a fellow-creature, similar to yourself, and you don't feel like shooting at him."

Orwell is far from alone. Interviews with U.S. soldiers in World

War II found that only 15 to 20 percent were able to discharge their weapons at the enemy in close firefights.[13] Even when they did shoot, soldiers found it hard to hit their human targets. In the U.S. Civil War, muskets were capable of hitting a pie plate at 70 yards and soldiers could typically reload anywhere from 4 to 5 times per minute. Theoretically, a regiment of 200 soldiers firing at a wall of enemy soldiers 100 feet wide should be able to kill 120 on the first volley. And yet the kill rate during the Civil War was closer to 1 to 2 men per minute, with the average distance of engagement being only 30 yards. Battles raged on for hours because the men just couldn't bring themselves to kill one another once they could see the whites of their enemy's eyes. Even General George Crook's men had this difficulty. At Rosebud Creek on June 16, 1876, his men shot 25,000 musket balls but hit only 99 Native Americans, wounding just 1 person with every 252 shots. Modern armies now know that they have to overcome these empathic urges, so soldiers undergo relentless training that desensitizes them to close combat, so that they can do their jobs. Modern technology also allows armies to kill more easily because it enables killing at such a great physical distance. Much of the killing by U.S. soldiers now comes through the hands of drone pilots watching a screen from a trailer in Nevada, with their sixth sense almost completely disengaged.

All of this research highlights how our sensory experiences make it possible to understand the minds of others. General George Crook was able to recognize Standing Bear's suffering, appreciate his plans, and understand the injustice because he saw the Poncas' pain right before his eyes and listened to their stories as told through their own voices. Government officials too distant and disconnected to use their senses remained disengaged, making it more likely for them to think of the Poncas as mindless savages. You consider the minds of others, at least in part, when your other senses lead you to.

TRIGGER NO. 2: INFERRING OTHERS' MINDS

Other people obviously do not need to be standing right in front of you for you to imagine what they are thinking or feeling or planning.

You can simply close your eyes and imagine it. You can imagine that someone who got fired is deeply unhappy or know that being cut by a knife is painful without having to see a pink slip or blood. When company executives think of their customers, husbands think of their wives, or politicians think of their constituents, there is no need to have a customer or wife or constituent on hand to trigger these people's physical senses. They can rely on their inferences based on what they already know (or think they know) and work from there.

You can see this distinction between senses and inferences working clearly in the minds of doctors. Over time, doctors naturally become desensitized to the distress and pain of their patients, just as you habituate to any repeated experience, yet doctors retain the ability to know when their patients are in pain and when they are not. Far from being a bad thing, dulling their empathic sense is essential to the practice of medicine. You and I would be physically crippled trying to give another person an injection.[14] A doctor may not feel it when another person is in pain, but can infer that the other person is in pain without any difficulty. There seem to be two different routes to understanding the mind of another person.

In fact, scientists can now pinpoint these different routes in the brain. In one experiment, physicians who practiced acupuncture lay on their backs in an fMRI machine and watched videos of people being poked with needles. Some videos showed people getting poked in the foot, others in the hand, and others in the lips. These are painful to watch, I promise, at least if you're not a physician. Nonphysicians who watched these videos had the same reaction I do, with the neural regions that are active when actually experiencing physical pain firsthand also being active when watching other people experiencing pain. It quite literally hurts to watch someone else being hurt. The physicians, however, showed virtually no response in these physical pain regions at all. Instead, the physicians showed activity in a very different part of the brain, most notably a relatively small spot in their medial prefrontal cortex (MPFC). This spot is located about one inch above and behind the inside part of your eyebrows, on each side of your brain. For the good of your social life, try not to get injured there.[15]

More important for you than its location is the MPFC's function: it is involved in making inferences about the minds of others.[16] When you wonder, "What on earth are they thinking?," your MPFC is engaged. When you are mulling over what your mom wants for her birthday, you're using your MPFC. And when you are calmly noting, "That person is in pain," your MPFC is engaged. When the physicians in this experiment saw someone getting poked in the face with a needle, they did not feel the person's pain. Instead, their engaged MPFC indicated that they calmly inferred the other person's pain. Most of us might wish that our doctors were more sensitive, perhaps better able to feel our pain, but what we really want is for them to *know of* our pain. We do not want a doctor's empathy; we want a doctor's MPFC.

The MPFC and a handful of other brain regions undergird the inferential component of your sixth sense. When this network of brain regions is engaged, you are thinking about others' minds. Failing to engage this region when thinking about other people is then a solid indication that you're overlooking their minds. Research confirms that the MPFC is engaged more when you're thinking about yourself, your close friends and family, and others who have beliefs similar to your own. It is activated when you care enough about others to care what they are thinking, and not when you are indifferent to others. It is significantly less active when you're thinking about the minds of those who are psychologically distant from you. When Republicans think about what fellow Republicans believe, they are using the MPFC. When Republicans think about what Democrats believe, they are using their MPFC a bit less. Democrats do the same thing, of course, just with the opposite groups.[17]

This neural activity is important because it tells us something critical about how people think about one another. Those who are close to us are considered mindful human beings, "like me." As people become more and more different from us, or more distant from our immediate social networks, they become less and less likely to engage our MPFC. When we don't engage this region, others appear relatively mindless, something less than fully human.

A neuroimaging experiment shows this most clearly. In this experiment, American university students lay on their backs in an fMRI scanner and looked at pictures of relatively close in-group members—fellow college students and "Americans"—and more distant out-group members—the elderly and rich people.[18] Most interesting were these students' responses to pictures of homeless people, a group that was seen as being the most different from the students themselves. In the scanner, pictures of homeless people triggered the MPFC significantly less than photos of any of the other group members, and instead produced activation more similar to that seen when participants looked at disgusting objects, such as an overflowing toilet or vomit. Outside the scanner, these participants rated the homeless people as more disgusting than any of the others. More tellingly, the volunteers also rated the homeless as being less mindful—less intelligent, less articulate, and less emotional.[19] The homeless were seen more as mindless objects than as fully mindful people.

You don't need to look deep into a person's brain to see the consequences of failing to engage your MPFC. You can hear it in the impressions people share about the minds of others. In calling for welfare reform in 2010, for instance, South Carolina's lieutenant governor, André Bauer, likened the poor to "stray animals" whose government assistance should be curtailed. "You know why?" he said. "Because they breed. . . . They will reproduce, especially ones who don't think much further than that. . . . They don't know any better." Bauer's sixth sense appears to have been disengaged, as is true for many people when they think about the poor, the homeless, the most disadvantaged and distant of social groups. Distance—a sense of dissimilarity, of difference, of otherness—can keep your MPFC uninvolved, leaving you to think about other human beings as something less than fully human.

LESSER MINDS

The mistake that can arise when you fail to engage with the minds of others is that you may come to think of them as relatively mindless. That is, you may come to think that these others have less going on between their ears than, say, you do.

This may sound too abstract, but there are many subtle examples of it in daily life. Let me start with one from the most basic and fundamental experience you have of your own mind: your sense of free will. Although many scientists have little patience for explanations of behavior based on free will, there is no doubt that you and I feel like we have it. It seems that we can freely choose to eat another doughnut or not, move our fingers or not, keep reading this book or not. But what about the minds of others? Are others as free to choose as you are, or do they have *less* free will? Are they more beholden to their circumstances or their environments or their rigid ideologies than you are?

The finding from careful research is that most people answer these questions by claiming that they have more free will than others do.[20] For instance, having free will means being independent, free to choose any of a number of different options regardless of the surrounding circumstances, in accordance with one's own interests and desires. In one experiment, college roommates were asked to report how predictable their past decisions in life were and how predictable their future decisions will be. Each person did the same for his or her roommate. These students rated their own past and future as considerably less predictable than their roommates' past and future, as if their roommate had less free will—a lesser mind—than they did.

Free will also requires being able to choose between different options—"life is what you make it," as the saying goes. In another experiment, employees at two different restaurants were given a list of things they might be doing over the next ten years, from where they could be living (for example, the East Coast, the West Coast, the Midwest, an apartment in the same town) to where they could be working (in the same job, in an exciting job, in a boring job, having no job) to what their lives would be like (same lifestyle as now, more family-focused lifestyle, more carefree lifestyle). They circled all the possibilities that seemed likely, then did the same for a coworker they knew well. At the end, the researchers counted the number of genuine possibilities people had circled, and there were markedly more circles for one's own future life than for the well-known coworker's life. Having free will allows you to make wonderful choices, but it also allows you to make terrible choices. If you ask people to chart out their futures compared to others', they don't simply report having more freedom to end up with good options, such as owning a great house or having an exciting job. They also report having more freedom to end up with terrible options, such as owning a crappy house or having no job at all.

It's not only free will that other minds might seem to lack. This *lesser minds* effect has many manifestations, including what appears to be a universal tendency to assume that others' minds are less sophisticated and more superficial than one's own.[21] Members of distant out-groups, ranging from terrorists to poor hurricane victims to political opponents, are also rated as less able to experience complicated emotions, such as shame, pride, embarrassment, and guilt than close members of one's own group.[22] One series of experiments even found that apologies from distant out-groups, such as Canadians being asked to forgive Afghan soldiers for a friendly-fire incident, are relatively ineffective because those distant others are seen as relatively unable to experience remorse. Their apologies therefore seemed disingenuous.[23]

When the mind of another person looks relatively dim because you are not engaged with it directly, it does not mean that the other person's mind is actually dimmer. Standing Bear was seen as being less than fully human—as being unsophisticated, unintelligent, and unfeeling—and today this seems like a relatively rare instance of extreme prejudice. Perhaps it is, but it is also an example of how being disengaged from the mind of another human being can make them appear relatively mindless, as having less going on between the ears than you and your close friends do. More subtle versions of that disengagement are common, and the mistakes they create can lead us to be less wise about the minds of others than we could be.

SOCIALLY UNWISE

Many African traditions speak of a concept known as *ubuntu:* "a person is a person through other persons." Your humanity comes from the way you treat others, the idea goes, not the way you behave in isolation. Humanity comes from treating others as human beings, not in the biological sense of having a fully human body but in the psychological sense of having a fully human mind. I have spent the last fistful of pages explaining how good people like you and I can, under the right circumstances, remain disengaged from the minds of others and thereby treat them as relatively mindless. By failing to engage our capacity to understand the minds of other people, we not only become indifferent to them, we risk losing some of our own humanity.

But this is not a book about social justice; it is a book about social understanding. Engaging more directly with the minds of others can not only make you behave more humanely toward others, it can make you behave more intelligently in the presence of others as well. Let me offer examples from three areas: being a smarter fighter, leader, and neighbor.

SMARTER FIGHTERS. For many Americans, thinking that the terrorists responsible for the September 11, 2001, attacks on the United States might have had minds with capacities like our own, that they could feel compassion and empathy and remorse, might seem wrong, even offensive. Simply trying to imagine the terrorists' perspective may be repulsive. And yet government and military leaders around the world are charged with diminishing these threats as effectively as they can. What are they to do? Diminishing threats requires understanding the minds of those who threaten. Might a failure to recognize terrorists as fully human have diminished our ability to combat them?

In *Wired for War,* Peter Singer describes how the shock and awe strategy that opened the Iraq War was intended to terrify the enemy in the hopes of scaring them into submission.[24] Led by drones and long-range aircraft, U.S. forces sought to establish fear of an eye in the sky that could see everything and kill anywhere. If you believed that your enemies were unfeeling savages, then you would need something really terrifying in order to make them feel enough to give up their fight and surrender. You'd need something really shocking and awe-inducing in order to have any effect at all. Even President Barack Obama seemed to think of the terrorists as unable to feel, writing in *Dreams from My Father* that his powers of empathy could not allow him to understand the "stark nihilism" that guided the 9/11 terrorists.[25]

These views mischaracterize the typical mind of a terrorist. Suicide bombers, for instance, do not come from exceptionally poor backgrounds.[26] They are not psychopaths, unable to feel the pain of others. Instead, they have families, and some have children. They love those who are close to them. What distinguishes the violent actors from the nonviolent ones are fully human emotions and motives that are very familiar to you: a deep connection to a social group, intense empathy for others who have suffered for a cause, and a passionate commitment to defend a livelihood under attack. The violent actors are overwhelmed by empathy for their own group, which all too often naturally leads to disdain for competing groups. They act out of *parochial altruism,* a strong commitment to benefit one's own group or cause without regard for the consequences for oneself.[27] It is the very motive that John McCain, while campaigning for president of the United States, said all people wanted: "to serve a cause greater than their self-interest." Parochial altruism motivates us to help those who are close to us and to fight those who threaten us. It uses the language of family, of brothers and sisters, of brotherhood and sisterhood. One suicide bomber's father said, "My son didn't die just for the sake of a cause, he died . . . for the people he loved." Love is not a motivation commonly attributed to terrorists.

It's easy to see how mischaracterizing the minds of terrorists can lead to faulty military strategies. If the enemy is like an unfeeling animal, then a truly terrifying display of strength is needed for them to be sufficiently afraid. But if the enemy fights out of empathy for their own group members and a cause that is greater than any one of them, then "shock and awe" may inspire them as much as it terrifies them. That seemed to be precisely what happened after the United States invaded Iraq in 2003. "The concept of 'shock and awe,'" said retired Pakistani general Talat Masood, "could drive moderate and uncommitted civilians toward anti-Americanism." One of the most popular songs in Pakistan in 2007, in a region being hit by ten drone strikes per week, included the lines "America's heartless terrorism,/Killing people like insects,/But honor does not fear power."[28] Shock and awe seems like a poor strategy for fighting warriors who love their cause as much as we love ours.

The American military followed up with efforts to "win the hearts and minds" of Afghans and Iraqis, but the reality of parochial altruism means that this strategy came too late. You fight parochial altruism by weakening boundaries between in-groups and out-groups, between us and them. Far from being weak or soft, winning hearts and minds is the very thing that could turn empathic enemies into allies.

Would conflicts be solved more intelligently if our political leaders recognized members of the other side as fully human rather than as savage animals or mindless objects? If we, as the public who supports or opposes such actions and elects officials, thought about them with our MPFCs fully engaged? I think so.

SMARTER LEADERS. Every business leader is charged with getting things done through people. This requires understanding what actually motivates people in their jobs. This is an obvious mind-reading problem: What do my employees really want?

Leaders have two kinds of incentives at their disposal: intrinsic and extrinsic. Intrinsic incentives are any inherent to the job itself, such as the pleasure of accomplishing something worthwhile, learning new things, developing skills, or feeling proud about your work. Extrinsic incentives are outcomes that are separable from the job itself, such as getting paid, earning fringe benefits, getting a bonus, or having job security. Notice that the effect of extrinsic incentives on other people can be observed directly because it involves an obvious exchange of goods for services, whereas the impact of intrinsic incentives can really only be felt and experienced on the inside. You can see that both you and others work harder when money is at stake, but the metrics of pride and meaning and a sense of self-worth are emotional states that you feel rather than see. As a result, you can recognize intrinsic motivations more easily in yourself than in others.

Think for a moment about your current job. Look back at the list of extrinsic and intrinsic incentives in the last paragraph. How important are these different motivators to you? How about the intrinsic motivators of accomplishing something worthwhile, learning new things, developing skills, or feeling proud about your work? How important are the extrinsic factors of money, fringe benefits, praise from others, and job security? Now, how important are these different motivators to your coworkers? How about your employees, if you have them?

Every year I ask my MBA students at the University of Chicago to answer these questions in an anonymous online survey. Every year they give me the same result, one that shows subtle dehumanization of their classmates. My students think all of these incentives are important, of course, but they judge that the intrinsic motivators are significantly more important to them than they are to their fellow students. "I care about doing something worthwhile," their results say, "but others are mainly in it for the money."

My students' beliefs are not unique. A survey of 242 former U.S. junior military officers produced similar results. This survey tried to assess why these officers had left their positions before serving a full military career.[29] Like my MBA students, military officials generally assume, according to the report, that the pay gap between military and civilian jobs is a major reason why officers leave. They assume that officers are mainly motivated by money, and therefore leave because they can make more money in a civilian job. But when actually interviewed, 73 percent of the officers reported that compensation was their *least* important reason for leaving. Only 3 percent said it was the most important reason. Instead, most officers said that the job was not intrinsically motivating enough. They complained about stifling bureaucracy, the inability to be creative, and difficulty developing themselves beyond their narrow job descriptions.

Both my students and these military officers are replicating an experiment that Stanford psychologist Chip Heath first conducted with customer service representatives and their managers at Citibank. Heath asked both the customer service representatives and their managers to state the importance of different motivators. He found that managers reported being more motivated by intrinsic incentives than extrinsic incentives but that they believed that their own employees were motivated in precisely the opposite direction: that their employees cared mainly about money and little about the intrinsic incentives. When Heath had those employees fill out identical questionnaires measuring their own motivations, he found that they reported caring as much about intrinsic motivators as extrinsic ones, just like the managers claimed about themselves. The gap that emerged in this study was in the importance of the intrinsic motivators—people thought their own interest in pride, self-respect, and doing something worthwhile was relatively unique.[30] This seemingly chronic tendency to ignore or underestimate intrinsic motivation has created a market for books with titles like *Why Pride Matters More Than Money* and *Drive,* which show precisely how powerful intrinsic motivators can be for everyone.[31]

By thinking that their employees have simplistic motives, bosses overlook the actual depth of their employees' minds and therefore fail to offer their workers what really motivates them. To see how bosses could do better, consider the pseudoexperiment accidentally conducted at a General Motors plant in Fremont, California, in the late 1970s. The Fremont plant was the worst-performing plant in the GM system, and its poor performance reflected long-standing conflict between management and labor. The GM managers designed plant operations to reflect their belief that their employees were, in the words of one plant worker, "no-mind idiots" who were in it only for a paycheck. Employees had no control over their jobs, were told nothing about how their work fit into the broader production process of the car, worked as isolated cogs doing the same job day after day, and were given nothing but financial incentives for performance. The GM managers got exactly the kind of mindless employees they expected. Absenteeism was rampant, beer bottles littered the parking lot, drugs and sex were available on the factory floor, and the cars had more defects than those produced at any other GM plant. In 1982, GM gave up on their workers and shut down the plant.

Not long after, GM began a partnership with Toyota called NUMMI (New United Motor Manufacturing, Inc.) in an attempt to learn the "Toyota way." Toyota reopened the Fremont plant and hired back more than 90 percent of its former workers. In contrast to their GM predecessors, the Toyota managers designed plant operations to reflect their belief that employees had fully human minds—that they not only wanted to make a good salary but *also* wanted to take pride in their work, would embrace opportunities to learn and improve, and were smart enough to give useful input about plant operations. Workers were educated on the entire production assembly system, were given the power to improve that system and reduce defects by stopping the line if necessary (using the now famous "Andon cord"), and were put in teams that worked together as a single unit, among other changes.

The turnaround was incredible. In just one year, the plant went from having the most defects in the GM system to having nearly perfect ratings. Estimates were that it would take roughly 50 percent more manpower at a typical GM plant in Fremont, California, to produce the same number of cars as NUMMI. The worst plant had become arguably the best, using nearly all of the very same employees. What was the secret? According to industry analyst Maryann Keller, it was "no secret at all, and it was as old as history: Treat both white- and blue-collar workers with respect, encourage them to think independently, allow them to make decisions, and make them feel connected to an important effort."[32] That is, treat employees like mindful human beings who care about doing a good job instead of like mindless idiots who care only about making money.

Would bosses be smarter managers if they recognized their employees as fully mindful human beings who care about doing a good job instead of seeing them as lesser minds who care only about getting a paycheck? I believe so.

SMARTER NEIGHBORS. Aristotle said that "man is by nature a social animal," but Aristotle never rode the train with me to work each morning. At seven forty-five a.m., I board the train that takes me from my home on the South Side of Chicago to my office in Hyde Park. The loading ritual is consistent: most passengers board alone and sit as far from one another as they can, facing forward in single file along the windows leaving an open seat next to them in the two-seat arrangement. At the next stop, more people get on and fill up the second set in each row along the aisles. People are then sitting mere millimeters (or less) from their new neighbors, at which point they completely ignore each other. With their faces glued to their books or iPhones or other tools of disengagement, these purportedly social animals spend thirty minutes within fifteen feet of three dozen people without ever engaging their MPFCs. I've observed the same drill in trains around the world, as well as in airplanes, break rooms, and doctors' lobbies. In each case, people in the presence of another mind ignore it, treating others the same way they do a nearby lampshade. *Social* animals? Really?

By remaining disengaged from other minds in this way, we neglect a chief source of human happiness: engaging relationally with other people. In one large survey of happiness, for instance, having positive relationships with friends and family members was the only necessary ingredient for being very happy.[33] Surveys of Americans also consistently show that isolating activities like commuting are some of the least pleasant of any day. Not only is isolation unpleasant, it is bad for your health as well. Social isolation is a greater risk factor for cardiac arrest and death than even cigarette smoking.[34] But every morning on my train, and in countless other contexts like it, people neglect an opportunity to turn an unpleasantly isolated experience into a pleasantly engaged conversation simply by connecting with the mind sitting next to them. What if you engaged more with the minds of your nearby neighbors instead of ignoring them like mindless objects?

I believe I know what you're thinking, because we also asked people to tell us what they thought of this idea. That is, Juliana Schroeder and I asked Chicago train commuters to fill out surveys asking how positive they thought their commute would be if they (a) sat alone and "enjoyed their solitude," (b) talked to the person sitting next to them on the train, or (c) did whatever they normally did. Consistent with the behavior I see every day, these commuters predicted that they would have the *least* pleasant commute if they talked to someone but would have the most pleasant commute if they sat in solitude. These predictions, however, look to be completely mistaken. We know this because we actually conducted another experiment on the very same train line with the very same population of commuters. In this experiment, we asked people from the same group of train commuters, based on random assignment, to either (a) sit alone and "enjoy their solitude," (b) talk to the person sitting next to them, or (c) do "whatever you normally do." In direct contrast to what people predicted, those who were asked to talk to the person sitting next to them actually reported having the *most* pleasant commute, whereas those who "enjoyed their solitude" reported having the least pleasant commute. The benefits of connecting did not appear to come at a cost to productivity because there were no differences in how productive people reported being across these conditions. Nor were our effects restricted to only certain personality types. Using personality scales to measure traits like extraversion and openness to experience, we found that people had a more positive experience when they connected with their neighbor regardless of whether they tended to be outgoing or shy, open or reserved.

My fellow train commuters are not unusual. We have found the same effects when people commute on buses and in taxicabs. In fact, the positive effect of talking to one's taxi driver is particularly large.

Perhaps because taxi drivers come from interesting and varied backgrounds, they seem to make especially pleasant conversational partners, at least for the length of your ride. Knowing this, I've now talked to cabdrivers from Ethiopia in Washington, D.C., from Afghanistan in Philadelphia, from Sierra Leone in New York, and from tough urban neighborhoods in my own Chicago. The stories I get are fascinating, the conversations are almost always interesting, and my experience is consistently better than if I had simply stared out the window instead. The same goes for airplanes and office lobbies and now my own commuter train. Your ability to engage with the minds of others is one of your brain's greatest abilities. You'll be happier if you actually use it.

It's easy to see how engaging with distant others, being civil toward strangers, is a benefit to other people. But our research suggests that it's likely to benefit you as well. Jen and I observed this firsthand when picking up our adopted children from Ethiopia. We were driving back to the village where they grew up, along dirt trails better suited to donkeys than cars. People stared blankly at us as we drove by; we were probably the only Westerners they had seen in weeks or months. Occasionally, someone would shout something. "Foreigners," our driver translated. At one point I stopped staring blankly and instead looked one of the boys directly in the eyes, smiled, and waved. It was like I flipped a switch in him. I suddenly wasn't just a foreigner; I was a human being. He flew into a wide-eyed smile and a big wave. I did the same to the next person, and the next. What had been indifferent stares turned into friendly waves and wide smiles. Our ride, and their brief moment with us, became instantly better. Nobody waves, but almost everybody waves back.

Would your life be more pleasant if you waved more often, trusting that people would wave back? Would you be happier if you engaged the minds of others more routinely instead of treating nearby neighbors as mindless objects? I encourage you to find out for yourself.

. . .

Judge Dundy deliberated for ten days after Standing Bear's closing remarks. He resumed the trial by beginning with a personal note: "During the fifteen years in which I have been engaged in administering the laws of my country, I have never been called upon to hear or decide a case that appealed so strongly to my sympathy as the one now under consideration. . . . But in a country where liberty is regulated by law, something more satisfactory and enduring than mere sympathy must furnish and constitute the rule and basis of judicial action." Dundy then carefully refuted each point made by the government's attorney and decided that Standing Bear and all Native Americans must now be considered persons under the law. General Crook got his wish—he lost his case. Standing Bear was not a mindless savage, he was a man.

This chapter has detailed how a brain as brilliant and capable as ours can, at times, fail to recognize a mind standing right before our eyes. Our sixth sense, this amazing ability each of us has to understand the mind of another, must be engaged, up close and personal. When distance keeps it disengaged, we may see other human beings as lesser minds and, thereby, as lesser persons. The capacity for mindblindness is not limited to only a select few. Such mistakes can afflict any of us, rendering us less socially intelligent than we could otherwise be.

But if failing to engage our ability creates one set of mistakes, then engaging our ability when we should not creates another set, which I'll describe in the next chapter. In particular, once our sixth sense is engaged, it is all too easy to see other minds almost everywhere we look. Just as we can fail to recognize the mind of a human being standing right before our eyes, we can also recognize a mind where none actually exists.

4

How We Anthropomorphize

Give me one minute—just one minute—inside the skin of
this creature. Hook me for just sixty seconds to the perceptual
and conceptual apparatus of this other being—and then I
will know what natural historians have sought through the
ages. But . . . I am stuck with a panoply of ineluctably indirect
methods.

—STEPHEN JAY GOULD (1998)

Hurricane Katrina barreled into New Orleans on August 23, 2005.
It was the costliest natural disaster in U.S. history, causing over
$100 billion in property damage. Approximately eighteen hundred
people died. Eighty percent of the population evacuated. Many never
returned. Trying to come to terms with the disaster several months
later, New Orleans's mayor, Ray Nagin, had an explanation: "Surely
God is mad at America. Surely he's not approving of us being in Iraq
under false pretense. But surely he's upset at black America, too. We're
not taking care of ourselves."

It's likely that you think Nagin's explanation is ridiculous. He recognized this as well, after some reflection, and tried to retract it several
days later. But sometimes ridiculous statements can give us a glimpse
into how the human mind works. Nagin, after all, is certainly not
the first person to have thought of a mindful god when considering

a natural disaster; nor will he be the last. There was something about this particular hurricane that engaged Nagin's sixth sense and led him to see an intention behind a completely mindless weather event. Once engaged, Nagin spotted a mind where no mind actually existed.

Similar examples are all around us. Stock market analysts routinely describe the market as "angry" or "pleased," say that it's *flirting* with 10,000," or "*trying* to recoup its losses," and then base their trades on the market's presumed emotions and intentions.[1] Shortly after September 11, 2001, people reported seeing the face of the devil in a photographer's image of smoke billowing out of the World Trade towers.[2] And we all think of our nonhuman pets as thoughtful and caring and loving, granting them mental capacities that are in serious scientific dispute. Marketers take ruthless advantage of this tendency. Believe it or not, research shows that a car can appear friendly or mean because its front end resembles a face, with the headlights appearing as eyes and the grille as a mouth.[3] Car designers use this to nudge you into buying. "A mean face is what we're going for," reported the Dodge Charger's designer, Ralph Gilles.[4]

Apparently, the face of the devil in the smoke billowing from the World Trade Center towers.

For all of my talk in the last chapter about failing to engage our ability to reason about the minds of other people, it can be surprisingly easy to catch the glimmer of a humanlike mind almost anywhere we look, from the weather to computers to cars to gods. At times we seem to be experts at anthropomorphizing the world, spotting humanlike minds all around us, even in places where no mind actually exists.

GRAY MINDS

Claiming that we sometimes attribute a mind to the mindless quickly leads to a reality problem. Few will argue that a rock has a mind and that another person does not, but the enormous gray area in between these extremes of mindless objects and mindful persons is the subject of intense debates over beings that *might* have a conscious mind, complete with intentions and thoughts and emotions like pride or guilt or anger. These debates over gray minds are where societies fight their culture wars. Does an unborn fetus have feelings? Should chimpanzees be held captive for use in medical research? Do the animals we eat suffer when kept in tightly confined cages? Are corporations persons, with rights to free speech that must be protected? Is the universe controlled by an omnipotent God who knows your sins and answers your prayers?

Everyone wants to understand the reality of these gray minds, to settle these debates, to determine some point where each can be placed along the spectrum between "me" as the prototypical mind haver and "rock" as the prototypical mind lacker. Usually there is no objective answer anyone can give, which is why people argue endlessly and convince nobody.

Sometimes scientists can try to pinpoint a mind. Consider, for instance, a dog's guilty look. If you own a dog, you've seen it many times: head down, tail low, with eyes averted in a submissive approach. When I was in graduate school, the first time I took our puppy (Solomon) to the office, he stood at my adviser's feet and peed on his carpet. Bad, very bad. Solomon seemed to *know* that peeing on my adviser's carpet was wrong, lowering his head and skulking to a corner, just like my kids do when they know they've done something wrong. But was Solomon's awareness of wrongdoing in his head or only in mine?

By one scientific test, it was only in my head. In this experiment, the appearance of a dog's guilty look came in response to an owner's disapproval, regardless of whether or not the dog had actually done something wrong.[5] Dogs are deeply social, but they seem clueless about their own morality.[6]

This example makes three crucial points about the minds we attribute to nonhumans. First, it suggests that the search for reality about nonhuman minds often misses the point. Recognizing another mind anywhere—whether in another person, pet, gadget, or god—is a psychological process that happens inside your own head, regardless of whether or not there is actually another mind in front of you. You have a belief that your dog has a mind, that it can *know* when it's been bad or good. Like any belief, this one may be right or wrong. In this case, it seems wrong. You've been tricked. But when your spouse gives you the same guilty look after eating the last piece of your birthday cake, you'd be right in thinking that the guilty look also reveals a guilty mind. This does not mean that you have actual insight into your spouse but not into your dog. Instead, it means that the very same capacity that allows you to think about the minds of other human beings is also used to think about nonhumans. The interesting point is that the triggers that engage your sixth sense when you think about your spouse are also the same that engage it when you think about your pet, a hurricane, a god, a car, or a computer. No psychologist, or anyone else, can explain what it's *actually* like to be a dog or cat or bat,[7] but we can explain when you might think something has a mind and when you might not. This means that attributing a mind to a nonhuman agent is the inverse process of failing to attribute a mind to another person. Anthropomorphism and dehumanization are opposite sides of the same coin.

Second, if you and I can believe that a nonhuman has a mind, then not all beliefs are held with equal conviction or even conscious endorsement. When you plead out loud with your car to encourage it to start on a cold winter morning, you are treating it *as if* it has a mind. You would not say, if questioned by a passenger, that your car really has a brain and can think or hear you. Nevertheless, you are caressing it all the same, with your sixth sense engaged just enough so that it appears to matter. In one experiment, people who were subtly led to anthropomorphize their car by rating its personality, such as how creative or irresponsible it was, reported being less interested in trading it in than did people subtly led to think of their vehicle as an object by rating its mechanical attributes, such as the smoothness of its ride or its versatility. You may not consciously believe that your car has a mind in the same way that you believe your child or even your dog does, but your subtle inferences may lead you to treat it like one anyway.

Finally, if you and I can be tricked into seeing a mind where no mind actually exists, then the really interesting question is not whether some things *really* have minds or not but, rather, what are the tricks? These tricks matter because they help explain why people seem so completely inconsistent in their mind reading from one moment to the next. How is it that a hunter who kills deer routinely is aroused to great sympathy when asked to care for one that has been hit by a car on the road?[8] Why is nobody bothered by the thought of killing carrots but many are bothered by the thought of killing cows?[9] How was it possible for California residents to vote, in the very same election, to treat gay people less humanely by denying them the right to marry but to treat animals more like people by requiring farmers to house their pigs in more humane conditions?[10] How is it possible, at times, to treat our pets as people and other people as animals? The answer is that sometimes we are triggered to engage with the mind of another and other times we are not.

Is being tricked to see the face of the devil in smoke rising from the burning World Trade Center towers caused by the same trigger as being tricked to see God's wrath guiding a hurricane, or the same trigger as being tricked into forming a personal relationship with your car or cell phone or pet? No, these are all different. The way you recognize a mind in these nonhumans is the same as the way you recognize a mind in another human: through your senses and by your more deliberate and thoughtful inferences. This means that there are actually three triggers here that can lead you to recognize humanlike minds in nonhuman agents: it looks like a mind, can be explained with a mind, or is closely connected your own mind. That is, minds can be triggered by your perceptions, by your need for an explanation, and by your social connections. To understand when people might recognize a mind where no mind exists, we have to understand how each of these tricks can trigger our sixth sense. Let me describe each, in turn.

MINDS FROM PERCEPTION: IF IT LOOKS, WALKS, AND TALKS LIKE A MIND . . .

Nature is filled with fakes. Lithops are deliciously succulent plants that look like completely inedible rocks. The praying mantis is a perfectly deadly predator that can look like a completely harmless plant. You don't need a PhD in evolutionary biology to understand fakery. Pretending to be something you're not can sometimes help you succeed as whatever you are.

This makes it seem easy to understand how the owl butterfly got its spots. Take a look at the picture below. If you were a bird, would you try to eat an owl's face? Of course not. Surely butterflies that look like an owl's eyes are less likely to be eaten than butterflies that look like butterflies. It's not even worth questioning: "Eyespots on the wings of giant silk moths and other Lepidoptera undoubtedly mimic eyes of mammalian predators," writes one group of evolutionary biologists.[11]

Apparently, eyes in nature: the owl butterfly (left) and spicebush swallowtail caterpillar (right).

How about the spicebush swallowtail caterpillar pictured to the owl butterfly's right? This caterpillar takes things one step further, having evolved not only the yellow eyespot but also a triangular pupil within it that seems to be glaring right at you. "Their stare was uncanny," writes Cornell University ecologist Thomas Eisner. "My guess is that the confrontation works and that predators may be reluctant to press their assault on an intended delicacy that holds its ground and dares to stare back defiantly." It's a bug with Mona Lisa eyes. Who knew? In *For Love of Insects,* Eisner describes how he confirmed that the apparent pupils were responsible for the caterpillar's stare by showing pupils of different shapes to thirty students. These students overwhelmingly agreed that the triangular pupils created the strongest sense of being started at.[12] The conclusion, according to the Biomimicry Institute, is obvious: "Eyespots of the spicebush swallowtail butterfly caterpillar protect it from predators because their tear shape creates an illusion of movable, watchful eyes."[13]

Fake eyes are a great trick in nature, but this trick looks like it might be fooling us rather than the birds. University of Cambridge zoologist Martin Stevens and his colleagues were not fooled. They speculated that these spots might deter predators because they are so conspicuous rather than because they look like eyes. Of course, they look like eyes to you and me, but human beings are hypersensitive to eyes. Maybe birds' brains aren't as sensitive to eyes as we are? Maybe they just care about sharp visual contrasts?

To find out, Stevens and his team placed mealworms on little bird-feeders. Some feeders were outfitted with eyespots in the background, whereas others had equally strong color contrasts made of squares or rectangles. The control bird feeders had neutral backgrounds. His team found that predators were deterred by any conspicuous visual contrast, whether they looked like eyes or not. The spots on the owl butterfly and spicebush swallowtail caterpillar look like eyes to you and me and Thomas Eisner's students, making it easy to tell an "undoubtedly true" story of how birds are tricked in the same way.

Fake eyes are a trick we fall for almost every time, one that can dupe us into seeing a mind where no mind exists. As a member of one of the planet's most social species, you are hypersensitive to eyes because they offer a window into another person's mind. Remember from the last chapter how easily we can track people's gaze to monitor their attention and understand their mind? Seeing where someone is looking gives you a reasonable sense of what they are thinking, and may then give you some advanced warning of what they are likely to do next. Given the obvious benefits of attending to others' eyes, it makes good sense that we would be hypersensitive to anything that even vaguely resembles them.[14]

What's surprising, though, is how hypersensitive we actually are. Some years ago, I built a chicken coop for my small flock with a single door centered below two small windows. In the springtime, I put a red heat lamp inside to keep my chickens warm at night. The resulting image of a glowing-red devil's face has startled me an embarrassing number of times. Some saw the face of the devil in the smoke billowing from the World Trade Center towers. I see it for a split second at dusk in my yard, devouring my hens, which walk into its open mouth, and watching me with its blazing eyes. The illusion of a mind behind those "eyes" is hard to ignore.

I'm not alone. Very subtle cues that one is being watched, such as eyespots similar to those on the owl butterfly's wings, can make people behave as if they are actually being watched by a mindful—and apparently judgmental—observer. In one experiment, Boston residents were 30 percent more generous when there was an image of Kismet—an MIT-designed robot with big, watchful, eyes—on the screen in front of them than when there was no image of Kismet.[15] In another study, psychology professors at the University of Newcastle had the tables turned when they were unknowingly enlisted in a psychology experiment themselves.[16] In their department, professors paid for their own tea and coffee in the mailroom, using an honesty box. Over a period of ten weeks, the notice above the honesty box showed either a picture of flowers or a picture of human eyes, on alternating weeks. These professors paid, on average, three times more when the notice had eyes than when it had flowers. Nobody was really watching these professors, of course, but the eyes were enough to trick them into acting as if they were being watched by a thoughtful mind.

Eyes can lead people to act as if they are being monitored, but they are often not enough of a perceptual cue to create anything more than a fleeting glimmer of another mind. For a stronger sense, you need more. In particular, you need movement, some motion that distinguishes the mindful from the mindless. *The Guardian*'s Philip Hoare had seen, like many of us, hundreds if not thousands of still images of whales, including pictures of a whale's eye. Coming eye to eye with a moving, attentive, living whale, however, was an utterly different experience: "Silhouetted against the blue, the whale turned and looked at me, eye to eye. It was the most disconcerting moment of my life. . . . That night, I couldn't close my eyes. Every time I did, the whale swam into my head. It has yet to leave my dreams." It is the ability to turn, to move, to focus attention, to interact, to follow your movement with its own eyes that makes the inanimate become animate and, in turn, makes the living become mindful.

If motion is so critical for recognizing another mind, then what kind of motion is the most mindful? Is more motion better? It doesn't seem so. Hummingbirds move a lot, but don't they look a bit scatterbrained? Darting from here to there without taking a second to think about anything at all, too manic to be mindful. Maybe slower is better? That doesn't seem right, either. Consider one of the slowest creatures in the animal kingdom, the sloth. The first person to study them in detail, the eighteenth-century French naturalist Georges Buffon, actually heaped derision upon their apparently impoverished mental life: "Whereas nature appears to us live, vibrant, and enthusiastic in producing monkeys; so is she slow, constrained and restricted in sloths. . . . Slowness, stupidity, neglect of its own body, and even habitual sadness, result from this bizarre and neglected conformation."[17] Pity the plants who writhe in pain so slowly, so imperceptibly, that even vegans feel nothing when killing them.[18] No, slower does not seem more mindful. In fact, research suggests that the motion has to be just right, more like the speed of *your* movement.

Evidence for this conclusion comes from a few experiments that manipulate the speed of a nonhuman's movement, such as a robot's.[19] Too fast or too slow and the robot in these experiments was recognized as a mindless machine, but at just the right speed, closer to human speed, the robot seemed more mindful. It started to look like it might be thinking or planning or feeling something. You can see this for yourself with videos of people. Speed up normal human actions in a video, and the person seems thoughtless. Try watching the manic movements in early still-photo films, like those featuring Charlie Chaplin, and you'll see what I mean. When you can follow a person's, or an animal's, or even a robot's apparent thoughts with your own, your senses may also tell you that it has a mind like your own.[20]

The basic principles of perception described here are simple, based almost entirely on similarity: "if it walks like a duck and talks like a duck, then it must be a duck." This similarity principle works almost flawlessly in the simple world of duck perception, but it is subject to false alarms in the more complicated world of mind perception. Military forces are now using these perceptual cues to make war robots particularly frightening to anyone who sees them, from outfitting robots with eyes and faces to adorning robots' hands with human-like skin. Microsoft Word users in the 1990s got furious with Clippy, the program's avatar assistant, precisely because his anthropomorphic features and behavior made him seem like an overly helpful colleague who barges into your office with absolutely no social skills.[21] And some people keep pet chimpanzees, so easily seen as nearly human if judged by their appearance alone, only to find out that our closest human relatives do not have such humanlike minds after all when they rip off a friend's face[22] or mutilate a visitor's genitals.[23] Appearances, after all, can be deceiving.

MINDS FROM EXPLANATION: MAKING SENSE BY MAKING SENTIENCE

Eyes, movement, and other humanlike perceptual cues explain only a small number of minds that people recognize in objects, animals, or events. Perceptual cues like eyes and faces can explain why Disney can make millions by causing you to cry over animated fiction, or why suicide prevention groups got so angry at General Motors for airing an ad during the 2007 Super Bowl in which an anthropomorphized robot committed "suicide" by rolling itself off a bridge.[24] They cannot explain the more interesting cases where minds emerge apart from bodies or any other humanlike cues. They cannot explain why people might attribute minds to financial markets or to hurricanes or to the design of a randomly evolving universe. They cannot explain why the vast majority of people on the planet find it so easy to imagine the mind of a god, or gods, responsible for pulling nature's strings. And they cannot explain why the Tevatron from time to time seemed to have a mind of its own.

Let's start with the Tevatron. A massive supercollider located at Fermilab, in Chicago, it was named for its ability to generate up to one tera-electron-volt (TeV) of energy. The Tevatron worked twenty-four hours a day, seven days a week, for nearly thirty years, until it was shut down in 2011. It was run by hard-core physicists, who have as much patience for hearing about feelings in their machines as you have for fingernails on a chalkboard. There was no face or body or any perceptual cue to a mind anywhere along the Tevatron's nearly four-mile length. And yet one reporter who spent a day with its director, Todd Johnson, found a surprisingly humanlike relationship. "They tend not to see the Tevatron as cold machinery," he noted. "It has moods and character. They call it the Tev." According to Johnson, "Everything goes like clockwork, and all of a sudden you get a failure, and something else breaks, and then something else breaks, and it's hard not to apply anthropomorphic personality traits to the machine. You hear people say, 'Well, it's not really happy with us today.'"[25]

Johnson's description makes it clear that the Tev does not seem mindful—with moods and character—all of the time, just when "you get a failure." Why does the Tev seem mindless when all is working well but then suddenly has a mind of its own when it fails? Mark Del Giorno, chief scientist at General Dynamics Robotic Systems, reports a very similar experience with his company's warbots (robots used in war): "You start to associate personalities with each of them. Their personality comes from, say, the steering being a little loose." Why not when the steering works perfectly? Have you ever noticed that the same thing also happens with your car? When your car starts up just as planned on a cold winter morning, it's nothing but perfectly functional steel. But when it *fails* to start on that cold morning, then . . . what?

Instead of making this ending up, let's go to some data, this time from a survey of nearly nine hundred listeners of NPR's *Car Talk* show.[26] Among other questions about their cars, these respondents answered a few that surely seemed unusual, namely questions about how much their car appeared to have a mind, including beliefs, desires, and a personality. Respondents also reported their car's reliability—specifically, how often it needed unscheduled service and how frequently it malfunctioned for unknown reasons. Like the Tev and the warbots, the more unreliable the car, the more people reported that it appeared to have a mind. Another survey of computer users showed the same result.[27] The more a computer malfunctioned, the more the user reported that their computer had a mind of its own. These correlations suggest that unexpected behavior engages our sixth sense, whether the agent is a car or a computer, a particle collider or a person.[28]

Stronger evidence for this link comes from some experiments my collaborators and I conducted where we turned to four easily anthropomorphized gadgets for inspiration. One of the gadgets was Clocky, an alarm clock with a humanlike face and wheels that spin when you press the snooze bar too much, sending Clocky "running" away until you get out of bed to turn "him" off.[29] We asked people to evaluate each of the four gadgets. For some, we described the gadget as being very predictable, saying, for example, "You can program Clocky so that when you press snooze, it runs away from you, or you can program it so that when you press snooze, it will jump on top of you." For others, we described the very same gadget as inherently unpredictable, saying, "When you press snooze, Clocky either runs away from you, or it jumps on top of you." We then asked how much the gadget appeared to have "a mind of its own," to have "intentions, free will, and consciousness," and the extent to which it could "experience emotions." Our volunteers reported that the unpredictable gadgets seemed more mindful than the predictable gadgets.

This turns out to be more than just a metaphorical way of speaking; it appears to be a literal way of thinking. When we had people evaluate these same gadgets while lying on their backs in an fMRI scanner, we found that the same neural regions involved in thinking about the minds of other people—particularly the MPFC, which we discussed in chapter 3—were also engaged when thinking about these unpre-

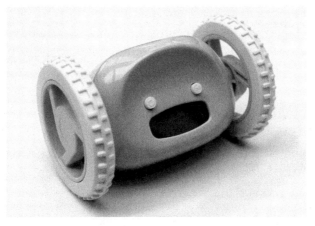

Clocky, the alarm clock who runs away from you, mindfully.

dictable gadgets. Metaphorically talking about a car or a computer or an alarm clock's mind may involve more literal neural processing than you might guess. The more unpredictable an object, the more mindful it appears. Why should this be?

The answer lies in a video of animated shapes—in particular, a video designed in the early 1940s by two psychologists.[30] The video is nothing more than a big triangle, a small triangle, and a small circle moving around the screen, yet what you recognize almost instantly when trying to explain what's going on is that you're dealing with a lovers' quarrel. The shapes quickly take on motives, feelings, intentions, and desires. When the researchers played this film to a group of thirty-four people, all but one described these shapes as if they had minds. The reason is simple: without thinking of the shapes as mindful, you would find the video nearly impossible to understand. As the authors write, "As long as the pattern of events shown in the film is perceived in terms of movements as such, it presents a chaos of juxtaposed items. When, however, the geometrical figures assume personal characteristics, a unified structure emerges." Unpredictable objects get a mind because a mind makes sense of action. When something needs to be explained, mind reading is engaged.

Notice that in order to explain the action of any self-propelled agent, from a billiard ball to a hurricane to a human being, you need concepts that explain why the agent starts and stops, the intensity of the action, the direction of the action, and the specific nature of the action. Physics and meteorology and neuroscience provide actual explanations for the behavior of billiard balls and hurricanes and human beings, but the presence of a mind provides an intuitive explanation for all three without any advanced degrees. Desires and goals describe why an agent starts and stops ("He ate the cookie because he felt hungry and stopped because he felt full"), and their strength describes the agent's intensity ("He ate like a pig because he felt *really* hungry"). Beliefs, attitudes, knowledge, and emotions all help to describe the direction and nature of an action ("He ate the cookie because he *believed* it would taste good, because he *likes* cookies, he *knew* it would fill him up, and that he would *feel* better once he had eaten it"). Neural explanations quickly get so complicated that you could never explain anything. The language of intentions and motives and other mental states avoids this complication altogether by using the same set of concepts to explain all actions. That this mentalistic language is both imprecise and inaccurate matters nothing for providing a functional explanation for almost any behavior, one that uses a language that everyone can easily understand.[31] Even five-month-old children treat self-propelled objects as if they have intentions.[32]

Because it is both imprecise and oversimplified, scientists have fought hard against the use of mentalistic (or anthropomorphic) language to explain behavior. Psychology also went through a roughly forty-year period dominated by behaviorism in which researchers disavowed talk of mental states altogether, attempting to gain scientific credibility by explaining people using only their observable actions. All mentalistic language was strictly forbidden, as an entirely new language was created to describe even the most basic behavior. A person no longer ate chocolate because they *liked* it, *felt* hungry, or *trusted* their spouse who'd said it was tasty. Instead, you had to explain why a person ate chocolate in terms of reinforcement contingencies and verbal operands and controlling stimuli, using a language that was nearly impossible to understand. Behaviorism failed not only because a person's inner mind and experience really do matter for human behavior but also because mindless explanations of behavior make little sense to anyone.[33]

Some behaviorists tried very hard. Donald Hebb, a pioneer in neuroscience, described his own best efforts to avoid using mentalistic language to explain the behavior of the chimpanzees used in his research: "A thoroughgoing attempt to avoid anthropomorphic description in the study of temperament was made over a two-year period at the Yerkes laboratories. All that resulted was an almost endless series of specific acts in which no order or meaning could be found. On the other hand, by the use of frankly anthropomorphic concepts of emotion and attitude one could quickly and easily describe the peculiarities of individual animals. . . . Whatever the anthropomorphic terminology may seem to imply about conscious states in chimpanzees, it provides an intelligible and practical guide to behavior." Lacking any other suitable explanation, the concept of a mind can explain the behavior of almost anything.

This functional purpose of mentalistic language, of describing something as if it has a mind, tells us two very important things about when minds emerge in both humans and nonhumans. First, they tend to emerge when someone has explaining to do. When the Tevatron behaves exactly as it's supposed to, it is mindless machinery. But when it acts up, then it is "not happy with us." And when a robot moves unpredictably, it starts to look like it has preferences and plans and intentions and moods. It's no wonder that 60 percent of people who own a Roomba, the vacuum cleaner that drives itself randomly around a room, report giving it a name. Ever name your upright vacuum cleaner, which does absolutely nothing on its own? I hope not.

Unexpected events like the rise and fall of the stock market look mindful in ways that predictable objects like normally functioning computers and cars do not. When a hurricane strikes *your* hometown with unusual force and catastrophic consequences, it's just the kind of capricious catastrophe that requires an explanation, something that might trigger you to think—as Ray Nagin did—about the mind of a god. After a similar trigger hit the small island of Haiti—in this case, a devastating earthquake in 2010—Haitians also flocked to God. "A lot of people who never prayed or believed—now they believe," said a twenty-four-year-old clerk, Cristina Bailey. From a self-appointed preacher at a refugee camp: "We have to kneel down and ask forgiveness from God." It is surely no accident that such natural occurrences are often referred to as "acts of God." A normal, mundane, exactly-as-expected day does not trigger thoughts of a divine mind.

Second, minds emerge from our attempts to explain a phenomenon when no other obvious explanation exists. Hume understood this when he argued that the universal tendency to anthropomorphize nature stems from our nearly universal "ignorance of causes." This is a fairly intuitive explanation for anthropomorphism. Ask a friend why people might believe that God causes earthquakes or floods or other catastrophes, and you are likely to get some version of "because they don't know any better." The interesting point is that the explanation that remains when someone "doesn't know any better" is one that relies on our sixth sense, using our intuitive theory of minds. This has profound implications. In one set of experiments, those who tended to reason by relying on their intuition were also more likely to report believing in the existence of a mindful god, whereas those who tended to reason more deliberately reported significantly less belief.[34] Religious beliefs are intuitively compelling because minds—in this case, the mind of a god—are intuitive explanations for the behavior of almost anything. In a completely different domain, research has revealed that urban children are more likely to anthropomorphize animals such as cows and pigs and deer than are rural children.[35] Why? Because rural children are likely to have considerably more knowledge about these animals, knowledge acquired through direct experience. Urban children are more likely to have learned about animals through Disney animation or by glimpsing them out the window of their parents' cars. Urban children "don't know any better," someone might say.

Minds can emerge through our explanations.

MIND AS CONNECTION: LOVE MAKES YOU REAL

There is another finding from the survey of *Car Talk* listeners that I didn't tell you about, a finding that reveals the third important trigger for engaging your sixth sense. In addition to reporting their car's reliability, respondents also reported how much they liked their car. Recall from the last chapter that people seem less likely to consider the mind of a distant person, thereby making that person seem more mindless. The opposite side of this coin is that you're more likely to engage with the mind of someone you are close to, or are trying to get closer to, thereby making them seem more mindful.[36] The same thing seems to happen with cars.[37] The more people in this survey liked their car, the more they reported it appearing to have a mind, beliefs, desires, and a personality. Liking was actually the strongest predictor of a car's apparent mind in this study, nearly double the magnitude of the correlation with reliability, which we've already discussed. Does liking something, feeling a connection to it, or even wanting to establish a connection with something give that thing a mind?

Frankly, this sounds a bit silly, like something out of a children's book. In fact, it is something right out of the *Velveteen Rabbit:*

"What is REAL?" asked the Rabbit one day. . . .

"Real isn't how you are made," said the Skin Horse. "It's a thing that happens to you. When a child loves you for a long, long time, not just to play with, but REALLY loves you, then you become Real." . . .

"Does it happen all at once, like being wound up," [the Rabbit] asked, "or bit by bit?"

"It doesn't happen all at once," said the Skin Horse. "You become. It takes a long time. That's why it doesn't often happen to people who break easily, or have sharp edges, or who have to be carefully kept."

Although she'd be a bit embarrassed to admit it, my wife has a similar stuffed animal, one she's kept ever since she can remember. "He" is Packy, an elephant-like creature that now sits in our oldest son's room (and is noticeably less real to him). My wife obviously doesn't think that Packy is *really* "real," but every bone in her body would rally to save Packy if I were, say, to throw it in the garbage, or let our kids use it for experimental dissection. Children are less embarrassed about expressing their intuitions than adults, and psychologists have no trouble getting them to say that a loved stuffed animal seems alive, can talk, can feel, and can think. This looks to be another childhood habit that adults never truly outgrow. You just have to search a little harder in adults to find it.

One pair of psychologists did this hard looking by asking university undergraduates to think about their favorite television character and their least favorite character on the same show. They reasoned that college students might not be willing to talk about their favorite stuffed animals, but all of them are experts at talking about television shows. When asked directly, the students seemed to think that their favorite character was more "real" than their least favorite character. That is, they were more likely to report that their favorite character "seems like a real person to me" and to admit to occasionally talking to him or her during the show. This difference occurred, as in the car study, because people liked their favorite character considerably more than their least favorite character. But is the favorite character *really* real? Surely these college kids are "just talking." They don't seriously mean it, do they?

Actually, it looks like they do mean it. To find this out, the researchers took advantage of a very reliable scientific result. It's called the mere-presence effect. If you are doing something simple, such as easy math problems, you're likely to perform better if you have a real person watching you than if you're alone. But if you're doing something difficult, such as very difficult math problems, you are likely to perform worse when you have another person watching you. This same effect emerged when research volunteers had a picture of their favorite TV character in front of them, as if it were a real person. They did not, however, show this mere-presence effect when sitting in front of a picture of their *least* favorite character from the same TV show. Only pictures of people's most loved characters produced the same effect that another real, live, mindful human being would. The Skin Horse may be wise after all.[38]

How this happens is not particularly mysterious. Think about how you try to relate to another person. To make it easy, let's imagine a fledgling romance. On your first date, you are extremely sensitive to how you are coming across to the other person. You carefully track the other person's likes and dislikes, doing your best to keep him or her suitably impressed. It is often a guessing game, but you spend a lot of time and effort trying to intuit the other person's emotions and thoughts and feelings. Forming a connection requires you to consider another person's mind, to adopt his or her perspective, to do your best to get into his or her head. Trying to connect with another person requires engaging your sixth sense. This is true with nonhumans as well. Musicians, for instance, often speak this way about the kind of connection they form to an instrument they're playing, a connection that also likely explains why they so often end up humanizing their instruments. Stevie Ray Vaughan played Lenny, Eric Clapton played Blackie, and B. B. King played Lucille. Willie Nelson says, "I don't know what I'd do without Trigger," the love-worn and bodyguarded guitar he's played for his entire career.

Understanding this may help to explain when people might be especially prone to identifying minds where none actually exist. In particular, it may be those who are trying hardest to create a connection with others who are most likely to do so. Remember Tom Hanks in the movie *Cast Away*? Hanks plays Chuck Noland, who gets stranded on a deserted island after his plane crashes in the South Pacific. Cut off from any human contact whatsoever, Noland is so desperate for social connection that he makes it up by creating a mind out of a volleyball. Given a face drawn out of a handprint with his own blood, the volleyball gets a name (Wilson), gets spoken to (mainly for dramatic effect in the movie), gets argued with, and then nearly gets Noland killed in an attempted rescue at sea. Desperate to form a connection with someone, Noland made up a mind that allowed him to connect with something. This idea for Wilson came to the mind of screenwriter William Broyles Jr. after he'd spent only a week in isolation on an island in the Sea of Cortez; it was also based on his own experience clinging to a picture of his family during the Vietnam War.[39] Although taken to extremes for dramatic effect, the idea is not far-fetched. Many prisoners in solitary confinement routinely have hallucinations in which they hear voices, carry on conversations with imaginary visitors, or believe that TV characters are speaking to them.

The isolation need not be so extreme. In one series of experiments, my colleagues and I found that those who felt chronically lonely, and therefore more interested in connecting with others, were more likely than those who are not lonely to rate easily anthropomorphized gadgets like Clocky as having a mind, more likely to see a sense of purpose or intentions in the universe, and more likely to rate their pets as mindful (such as thoughtful and considerate).[40] Making people feel lonely in experiments also at least momentarily increased their belief in God—a mind watching us from above.[41] It is surely no accident that many deeply religious people, from Francis of Assisi to Buddhist monks, go into extreme isolation in order to connect with the mind of an invisible God. Nor is it an accident that people report feeling a closer connection to God when they pray alone than when they pray in a group of people.[42]

Minds can appear through our close connections with others, as well as through our attempt to connect with others.

MINDS IN SOCIETY: TOO MUCH OR TOO LITTLE?

The Brookfield Zoo, in Chicago, has an enormous primate house consisting of three large rooms connected by short hallways. The human visitors walk along narrow sidewalks perched halfway up the wall, where they can look down into the enclosures. The mountain gorillas are in a unique setting, perched atop a concrete island that keeps them close to the visitors and yet safely separated.

I visited for the first time several years ago, with my family. Looking into the enclosure, I could see the most famous gorilla in the exhibit, Binti Jua, leaning against a cement tree. In 1996, Binti picked up a three-year-old boy who fell into the concrete enclosure and was knocked unconscious, defended the boy from an aggressive female, and then cradled the boy in her arms just like she had her own infant. Binti then carried the boy to an exit, where she waited for a caretaker to pick him up. On the day of my visit, Binti sat at the base of the tree, arms folded at her belly, looking up at *us* while we looked down at *them*. I couldn't help but wonder what she was thinking: Is she irritated by the people making ridiculous monkey sounds, just as I am? Is she bored? Depressed? I asked my oldest son if he thought Binti ever wished that she could step outside or go to the jungle. "Not if she was born in the zoo," he said, doing his own mind reading without a moment's hesitation.[43]

My eyes wandered from Binti, who looked contemplative at the base of her concrete tree, to the winding row of people standing just above her, gawking down, some sounding ridiculous. The nameless mass of people, one following another, herdlike, along the cement path, seemed more mindless to me than Binti did. Other minds are like smoke. They can appear clearly one moment and disappear the next. This is true whether the other mind belongs to a human or an animal, a gadget or a god. Minds emerge when others are close to us—when they look and act like us, need to be explained by us, or are in some way connected to us. Sometimes this leads us to make mistakes. Objects that look humanlike, weather events that act unpredictably, and deeply loved pets can be awarded minds they do not have. Would most people have been triggered to think of Binti Jua's mind had she not acted so much like a human mother trying to protect a child? No. Does Binti have the same mental capacities whether you and I are triggered to think of them or not? Of course she does, whatever those capacities are.

Our ability to read the minds of others is one of our brain's greatest tools, absolutely essential for navigating our complicated social lives. The mistakes we can make engaging this ability are of two different kinds: failing to recognize a mind in something that actually has one, such as a human, or recognizing a mind in something that is actually mindless, such as a hurricane or a computer or random evolutionary processes in nature. These mistakes come from failing to engage our sixth sense in some cases and from failing to disengage it in others.

It is reasonable to question whether or not the trigger that engages our sixth sense is set correctly. Do we attribute mental states to other beings, objects, and events too much or too little? There is no clear answer to this. We seem to do both. But for centuries, our willingness to recognize minds in nonhumans has been seen as a kind of stupidity, a childlike tendency toward anthropomorphism and superstition that educated and clear-thinking adults have outgrown. I think this view is both mistaken and unfortunate. Recognizing the mind of another human being involves the same psychological processes as recognizing a mind in other animals, a god, or even a gadget. It is a reflection of our brain's greatest ability rather than a sign of our stupidity. Stamp out ignorance and error wherever you find it, of course, but not all mind-reading mistakes are equally egregious. Treating a mindless gadget as mindful can sometimes look a bit silly, but neglecting the mind of a sentient human or a potentially sentient animal is the essential ingredient for inhumanity.

■ ■ ■

Scientists work slowly to reveal the reality of other minds. After many scientific tests, psychologists and biologists now know that chimpanzees have impressive mental capacities. Our dogs do as well, even if they are not as smart as we think they are, largely because we have subjected them to "anthropomorphic selection" pressures by breeding them for generations to be good human companions.[44] Even ravens try to comfort each other after a fight.[45] Our sixth sense, however, works much more rapidly to reveal the minds of others. When triggered to engage with the minds of others through our perceptions, explanations, or connections, minds may appear almost anywhere we look.

Once our sixth sense has been triggered and we are actively trying to understand the minds of others, how do we do it? After you recognize another mind in front of you, how do you know what it's thinking or feeling or wanting?

The most obvious starting point is the mind you know the best: your own. This can work exceptionally well because minds more often tend to operate similarly to each other than they do differently. If you think onion ice cream tastes horrible, believe anarchy is a terrible idea, and feel cold when you walk outside in the winter, then it's likely that other people will feel the same way. The problem is that "likely" is not "certainly." This tool works wonderfully when reasoning about the mind of a person who thinks and feels just as you do, but it works decidedly less wonderfully for thinking about minds that are truly different from your own. Egocentrism is therefore a great place to start when reasoning about the minds of others, but is a terrible place to stop. Unfortunately, the research I'll describe in the next chapter shows how easy it is to jump to egocentric conclusions and how hard it is to correct them later. This produces one consistent mistake: overestimating the extent to which others will see, think, and feel the same way you do.

PART 3

WHAT STATE IS ANOTHER MIND IN?

The second variety of mistakes we make in trying to understand the minds of others are mistakes of inference. When we're seeking to understand another's mind, we rely on at least three strategies. We project from our own mind, use stereotypes, and infer a mind from a person's actions. Each strategy provides insight but can also lead to predictable mistakes.

5

The Trouble of Getting Over Yourself

You will become way less concerned with what other people think of you when you realize how seldom they do.

—DAVID FOSTER WALLACE, *Infinite Jest*

Pity poor Ashley Todd. Eleven days before the 2008 U.S. presidential election, Ashley traveled to Pittsburgh with the College Republican National Committee on a recruiting mission. While withdrawing money from an ATM late in the evening, Ashley claimed, she was robbed at knifepoint by a six-foot-four black man. After she handed over the money, she said, her assailant saw the McCain bumper sticker on her car, threw her to the ground, and carved the letter *B* onto her face with a knife, to mark her as a "Barack supporter."

Chilling.

Major news organizations, including Fox News and CNN, picked up the story immediately, but the police were suspicious. Exhibit A: Ashley's face. There, carved into her right cheek, was indeed the letter *B*. The problem? It was *backward,* as if Ashley would be able to read it herself, from her own perspective, by staring through her cheek or by looking in the mirror. It was as if she carved the letter into *her own face.*

In fact, that is exactly what she did. The backward *B* was self-inflicted. Ashley later admitted to fabricating the entire story.

Awkward.

Ashley was a good enough mind reader to know that her story would make headlines, but not good enough to overcome the first trap that could catch any of us trying to understand others.[1] That first trap is getting over yourself—your own experiences, beliefs, attitudes, emotions, knowledge, and visual perspective—to recognize that others may view the world differently. Ashley was being self-centered, or egocentric. This is such an obvious trap that surely one would think that only the thoughtless, the übernarcissistic, or the borderline psychopathic would get caught in it. Not so. Galileo may have removed the Earth from the center of the universe, but every person on this planet is still at the center of his or her own universe. As Galileo knew, to see the world accurately, you need to look in the right place and then view it through the right lens. These are two pieces of wisdom that you and I can easily forget.

GETTING OVER YOURSELF

Here's a joke. A man on one side of a river shouts to a man standing on the other side, "Hey, how do I get to the other side of the river?" The other man responds, "You *are* on the other side of the river."

This is funny because it violates a skill so basic in social interaction that you take it almost completely for granted. When talking to another person, you have to adopt that person's point of view. Failing to do so makes you a joke.

This wasn't always so obvious to you. Understanding that others have different points of view is a realization you grew into rather than one you grew up with. This is why young children are so notoriously self-centered. "Going back to the starting point of the life of thought," writes Jean Piaget, the founding father of developmental psychology, "we find a protoplasmic consciousness unable to make any distinction between the self and things." When Piaget would sit young children on one side of a model composed of three mountains and ask what a doll sitting on the other side could see, he found that most children said the doll could see exactly what they could see. I'm afraid my own children are no different. My oldest son used to love playing hide-and-seek with me when he was little, even though he was terrible at it. His favorite way to hide was sitting on the couch with a pillow over his face. He couldn't see me, and therefore he assumed I also couldn't see him. My son is now much better at hiding because growing up means learning, sometimes painfully, that your own perspective on the world may be unique.

Although Piaget's general insight that children are more egocentric than adults was correct, psychologists now believe he was mistaken in at least one critical way. Piaget thought that developmental changes reflected a kind of metamorphosis. Like diapers and pacifiers, egocentrism was something adults had grown out of and only rarely, if ever, revisited. This stage-based thinking about development is incorrect, however, because it implies more permanent changes in the way aging minds work than actually exists. In fact, many of the reflexes observed in children that look to be outgrown are still present in adults. Childhood instincts are not outgrown so much as they are overcome by more careful and reflective thinking.[2]

You can see our childlike tendencies for egocentrism if you watch adults, particularly their eyes, very carefully. Consider one experiment in which my colleagues and I asked parents and their children who were visiting the Boston Children's Museum to take a break and play a communication game with us. In this game, one person—the instructor—sat on one side of the grid of boxes shown on the next page, and the other person—the mover—sat on the other side. The instructor—always played by an experimenter—was given a picture of the objects in different locations and was supposed to instruct the mover—either a parent or child—sitting on the other side to move the objects to their new locations. Imagine yourself in the mover's shoes. As the mover, you can see all of the objects, but some are covered so the instructor cannot see them. For example, from your point of view on the left side of the figure on the next page, you can see three trucks: a large and a medium truck in the second row from the top, and a small truck in the third row. The instructor, however, sees two trucks, one large and one smaller in the second row. You're the only one who can see the smallest truck in the third row.

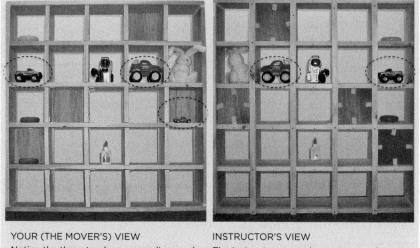

YOUR (THE MOVER'S) VIEW
Notice the three trucks: one medium and one large truck on the second row, and the smallest truck on the third row. The video camera located in the middle of the second row records your eye movements.

INSTRUCTOR'S VIEW
The Instructor can only see two trucks on the second row. The smallest truck, visible to you as the Mover, is hidden from view.

Now, here's the trick. The instructor at one point asks you to move the "small" truck. Which do you grab? The smallest truck, which only you can see, or the medium-sized truck, which would be "small" from the instructor's perspective? You're nobody's joke, so you'd most likely grab the medium-sized truck, the one you know the instructor must be referring to, rather than being egocentric and grabbing the smallest truck, which only you can see. Indeed, the adults in our experiment grabbed the object suggested by an egocentric interpretation only 25 percent of the time. Their children, however, were more egocentric, grabbing the egocentric object roughly 50 percent of the time. If you looked only at our participants' hands, you would see what Piaget predicted.

Look carefully at our participants' eyes, however, and you see a very different picture. Notice the video camera in the middle of the second row in the figure above. That camera allowed us to catch where our children and their parents were looking in three-millisecond increments, and those eyes revealed equally egocentric reflexes between the children and adults. In particular, the video footage showed that nearly all of our participants, children and adults equally, were reflexively

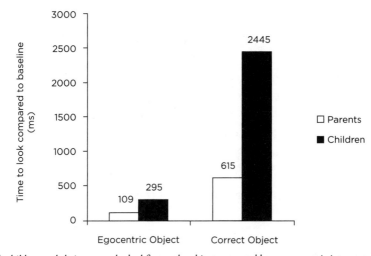

Both children and their parents looked first at the object suggested by an egocentric interpretation, as shown in the faster reaction times in the left two bars than in the right two bars. However, children and their parents differed in the speed with which they corrected that initial moment of egocentrism and looked at the correct object, as seen in the difference in the time needed to look at the correct object, shown in the right two bars. The difference between children and adults was not in the likelihood of being egocentric but in the speed with which they corrected that mistake.

egocentric, looking first at the smallest truck, both at the same time and with the same frequency. That is, adults and children were equally egocentric, at first. The only thing that differed is what they did next. The adults were better able to get over their egocentric reflex with more careful thinking—*Oh, he meant THAT truck*—than the children were.

A carpenter who built a house based on his own preferences and only later reassembled it to match his client's preferences would be out of business in short order. A brain that makes inferences about the minds of others based on its own viewpoint and only later reassembles them to match another person's perspective, in contrast, works better than a self-centered carpenter as long as its egocentric default is generally accurate and its corrections are well-timed and sufficient. The problem is that corrections are routinely poorly timed and insufficient, meaning that our default tendencies leave traces in our final judgments and decisions.

For example, when buying a gift for your partner, you know that you need to consider what he or she likes rather than what you like, but research shows time and again that people's own preferences nevertheless shape the gifts they pick for their loved ones.[3] Barack Obama (or, far more likely, his staff) might have fallen victim to this on his first presidential visit to the United Kingdom in 2009, when he gave Prime Minister Gordon Brown a DVD set of the best American movies ever made (something every warm-blooded American would love). The problem? Gordon Brown is almost legally blind.[4] Being unaware that one's own perspective is unique or lacking the time, training, or inclination to think more carefully about the minds of others can leave even the most thoughtful among us at risk of becoming the butt of others' jokes.

The good news from these findings is that our minds remain, at least in this respect, forever young. The bad news is that childish mistakes can linger well into adulthood.[5] In fact, they linger in two subtle forms, and you can understand each by thinking carefully about the ways in which your own perspective differs systematically from others' perspectives. First, you and another person may be paying attention to different things. You may look at, think about, or reflect upon different information than others do because you're focusing on different aspects than they are. When I lecture to students, for instance, I am very sensitive to my mistakes, wishing I could get a second chance at every flubbed joke or poorly answered question. If my students aren't as sensitive to those mistakes as I am, then I wind up thinking I'll be judged more harshly than I actually am because I'm more focused on my flaws than my students are. Ashley Todd made a similar mistake, looking at her cheek from her own perspective instead of an observer's perspective. Your own perspective rests atop a neck that attends to the world from your unique location in it. When two different necks are pointing their heads in different directions, they are attending to different information and basing their evaluations on fundamentally different viewpoints. To reflect the idea of two people looking at, or attending to, different information, we'll call this class of egocentric biases the "neck problem."

Second, you and another person may be attending to the same

thing but evaluating it very differently. An Al Qaeda member look-ing at the burning World Trade Center towers will evaluate that event in a completely different way than an American citizen will. Your self not only provides a unique vantage point on the world; it also provides a lens made up of beliefs, attitudes, emotions, and knowledge that you interpret the world through. Your interpretive lens may differ from others', causing you to look at the same object or event and interpret it very differently. Conservatives are likely to eval-uate a liberal policy more negatively than liberals do, because of their existing beliefs. Fans of opposing sports teams are likely to interpret the very same "questionable call" by a referee differently because of their existing allegiances. Or consider the common family dynamic captured in the *Onion*'s satirical newspaper headline "Majority of Parents Abuse Children, Children Report."[6] You can look at the same night sky but interpret it very differently when peering through the lens of a telescope versus the lens of your naked eye. To reflect the idea of two people looking at the same thing using different lenses of interpretation, we'll call this class of egocentric biases the "lens problem."

WHAT YOU SEE: THE NECK PROBLEM

All of the examples I've discussed in this chapter so far—Ashley Todd, the other side of the river joke, the instructor and mover experiment, and my son's favorite hiding place—are variations of the neck prob-lem. Each represents a failure to recognize that what you are looking at, attending to, or thinking about may be different from what others are perceiving. These examples work as illustrations because they are such obvious mistakes, but the neck problem is more subtle and per-vasive than they suggest.

Consider a pair of questions that reveal one of the subtler versions. Answer them as we go along. Compared to others, are you:

• more or less likely to live past fifty?
• more or less likely to live past one hundred?

If you just answered these two questions by thinking first and fore-most about yourself—your own health and likely longevity—and thinking relatively little about others' health and longevity, then you've reflected the self-centered feature of all variations of the neck problem. Of course, whether you are more or less likely than others to live past fifty depends not only on your likelihood of living that long but also on the likelihood that others will live that long. But when researchers ask people to compare themselves with others, the answers they get seem to be based more heavily on themselves than on others.[7] And so respondents end up reporting that they are more likely than others to experience common events that are likely to happen to everyone (such as living past fifty) but *less* likely than others to experience uncommon events that are unlikely to happen to anyone (such as living past one hundred).[8] Obviously, you can't be both more likely than others to live past fifty but less likely than others to live past one hundred, and yet that's precisely the pattern documented in research.

Researchers report similar self-centered findings for emotions. How happy are you, for instance, compared to others? The answer often depends on the responder's current happiness rather than on his or her beliefs about others' happiness. Because most people report being happy most of the time—about 85 percent, according to a survey of 450,000 Americans—most people also report being happier than others most of the time.[9] Being happy doesn't make you happier than others, if most others are happy as well. Researchers find similar results for any relatively common and intense emotion, showing that people think they are more emotional than others. For instance, following the Kennedy assassination in 1963 and the terrorist attacks on New York City on September 11, 2001, most Americans were distressed.[10] When called by a national survey group immediately following each of these events, respondents consistently reported feeling more distressed about the event than others were. This gap was especially pronounced follow-ing September 11 in New York City, where people were most immedi-ately threatened and, therefore, were the most distressed. You are well aware of your own emotions and less aware of others' emotions. That doesn't make you more emotional than others; it makes your sense a prime example of the neck problem.

LARGER THAN IN LIFE

One consequence of being at the center of your own universe is that it's easy to overestimate your importance in it, both for better and for worse. Consider a classic psychology experiment that asked married couples to report how much each of them was personally responsible for a variety of household activities.[11] These included relatively desirable tasks, like cleaning the house, making breakfast, and resolving conflicts, but also undesirable actions, like messing up the house, irritating their spouse, and causing arguments. Husbands and wives were separated from each other and then asked to indicate, out of the total amount for each activity, what percentage they were personally responsible for. The researchers then simply added the spouses' estimates together for each item. Logically, this sum cannot exceed 100 percent. If I claim that I make breakfast 80 percent of the time and my wife claims that she makes breakfast 60 percent of the time, then our kids are apparently eating breakfast 140 percent of the time. Not possible, even for the fattest families. But psychologically, if I can think of the times I made breakfast more easily than the times my wife made breakfast, then by extrapolation, there will be a lot of reportedly overstuffed families out there.

This is exactly what the results showed. The couples' estimates, when added together, significantly exceeded 100 percent. Surely you've experienced this self-centeredness before. It's even made its way into jokes. Here's one: What's a woman's definition of barbecue? Answer: You bought the groceries, washed the lettuce, chopped the tomatoes, diced the onions, marinated the meat, and cleaned everything up, but *he* "made the dinner."

Don't get too smug. The really interesting result is that researchers find more consistent evidence for overclaiming, albeit to a lesser extent, for negative activities as well. In this experiment, spouses tended to claim more responsibility than is logically possible even for activities like "causing arguments between the two of you." Being self-centered also means being uniquely aware of your faults and shortcomings, knowing when you needled your spouse after a tough day at work or broke the dishes and scuttled them into the trash can before anyone else noticed. It's harder to notice your spouse's bad intentions or unhandy dish work.

This finding can be surprising. When researchers asked married couples to *predict* how much responsibility their partner would claim for positive and negative activities, they found very cynical predictions but again found very self-centered overclaiming.[12] As you can see on the right side of the figure below, spouses tended to assume that their partner would vainly accept credit for all of the desirable activities in their marriage but deflect blame for the undesirable activities. In fact, partners were again egocentric, tending to claim more responsibility than is logically possible for all activities, positive as well as negative. It's not hard to imagine how both overclaiming and overly cynical assumptions about overclaiming can lead to unwarranted discord in almost any relationship.

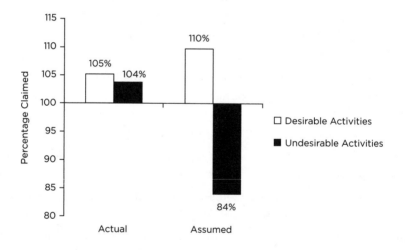

As consistent as self-centered overclaiming in marriages may be, it's likely to be even stronger outside of them, as work groups and teams get larger. In a marriage, overcoming egocentrism requires thinking of only one other person. That's not too hard. But as a group's size increases, the number of others you could be overlooking also increases, and so, too, do the consequences of being egocentric. Consider an experiment Eugene Caruso, Max Bazerman, and I conducted with 699 Harvard MBA students.[13] These students worked together in the same study groups for the entire two years of their MBA program, doing everything involved with their coursework together. The groups generally ranged from four to nine students. We asked some of these MBA students to report what percentage of the group's total work they personally contributed. We found that the amount of overclaiming increased as the size of the group increased. Groups of four or less look relatively reasonable, claiming more responsibility than is logically possible but at least being in the vicinity of 100 percent. As the number of group members increases, however, their judgments get increasingly unhinged from reality. By the time you get to groups of eight, these MBAs were claiming nearly 140 percent productivity! This brings new meaning to overachieving.

The important point is to relax a bit when others don't seem to appreciate you as much as you think they should. The mistake may be a product of egocentrism in your own head rather than others' indifference.

ON SELF-CENTERED STAGE

Thinking that others should give you more credit than they actually do is just a small part of our larger egocentric tendencies. At extreme levels, self-centered thinking can lead to paranoia, a belief that others are thinking about you, talking about you, and paying attention to you when they are not. That sounds crazy because it is, and yet all of us are prone to momentary bouts of craziness in the right circumstances. "People are insanely self-conscious," reports Elaine Miller, author of the popular interior decorating blog *Decorno*, explaining the care socialites take to convey just the right image to others with their interior decorating. "People act like they're always being watched. Even their house is a performance."

We've all been there at one time or another. Maybe you slipped on an icy sidewalk and were hurt more by the pain of embarrassment than the pain of the fall? Or said something stupid in a meeting and were certain that everyone was ridiculing you afterward in whispers? Or forgot the name of a new but important acquaintance and felt mortally embarrassed? All of the world may indeed be a stage, and it's easy to feel that we're at the center of it. Not only can this lead us to overestimate our impact in the world, it can even lead us to overestimate the extent to which others are noticing our very existence.

Consider participating in what I think is one of the most liberating experiments ever conducted—the Barry Manilow experiment.[14] Here, researchers recruited unknowing undergraduates to participate in what they believed was a standard psychology experiment. Imagine you are one of them. When you arrive at the lab, the experimenter leads you down the hallway into a small room, shuts the door behind you, and asks you to "put on this T-shirt as part of the experiment." You unfurl it before you and there, in all of its glory, is a shirt emblazoned with a large picture of Barry Manilow. You might be a big fan, but most people are not. Even fans might be a bit reluctant to bare their enthusiasm in a full-frontal exposure.

But you go along anyway, put on the T-shirt, and follow the experimenter back down the hallway; she leads you into a room where other participants are already sitting (none, of course, wearing a Manilow shirt). The experimenter explains that you're running a bit late but you can still participate anyway. So you slink into your chair, at which point the experimenter appears to have a change of heart, apologizes, and says that it's really too late and that you'll need to do this experiment another time. She then leads you out of the room.

Here comes the most important part. The experimenter tells you that the experiment is actually now over and asks you to estimate the number of people in the room who would be able to identify the person on your shirt. While you are outside the room, the experimenter asks the other people sitting in the room to identify who was on your shirt. Those wearing the shirt estimated that nearly 50 percent would notice their Manilow shirt when, in fact, only 23 percent actually did. Even in small groups, the social spotlight does not shine on us nearly as brightly as we think.[15]

The point here is that few of us are quite the celebrity that our own experience suggests we might be; nor are we under as much careful scrutiny from others as we might expect. Early on in *Casablanca,* Peter Lorre learns this lesson the hard way when he looks to Humphrey Bogart for some recognition, saying, "You despise me, don't you?" Bogart replies, "If I gave you any thought, I probably would." I think we would all benefit from having our own *Casablanca* moment.

NOT AS BAD AS YOU THINK

Fear of being under the social spotlight goes beyond simply being noticed by others. Once you're spotted, there can be the awful, gut-wrenching, heartbreaking feeling of being ridiculed as well. I once introduced a famous psychologist before a presentation to my colleagues and described his research completely incorrectly, crediting him for an experiment that someone else conducted. This is an intense moment of shame that I can't help but feel all my colleagues remember every time they hear me introduce another speaker. ("What nonsense is Epley telling us *this* time?") Not only are others noticing you, your self-centered senses tell you, but they're judging you as harshly as you fear as well.

This is why public speaking often takes the top spot on people's Most Terrifying Experiences list. But again, these self-centered fears are easily exaggerated. Over a period of several years, Tom Gilovich, Ken Savitsky, and I followed up on their original spotlight effect studies by putting research volunteers in a wide variety of embarrassing moments and measuring whether they could predict how they were being judged by others. These included being asked stupefying trivia questions in front of an audience, being introduced to a stranger as someone who has frequent "bad-hair days" and experienced "occasional difficulties with bed-wetting," singing "The Star-Spangled Banner" for an audience while chewing a large wad of bubble gum, and dancing the bossa nova in front of strangers, among others. In all of the cases we ever studied, those in the throes of an embarrassing moment consistently overestimated how harshly others were evaluating them. Even once the social spotlight was on them, it did not burn as hot as those in its glare expected it to. I think Peter Lorre's *Casablanca* moment was actually too extreme. Others may not give us much thought, but when they do, they generally cut us more slack than we'd imagine, because they're not ruminating on our mistakes as much as we are ourselves. As a bit of folk wisdom goes, "Be who you are and say what you feel, because those who mind don't matter and those who matter don't mind."[16] Indeed.

Piaget argued that becoming aware of your own perspective liberates you from it. I agree. Few experiments I've ever conducted have changed the way I live my own life as much as these. An important part of being a professor, for instance, is being able to speak in front of an audience. And yet when I first started teaching students or giving research presentations, I suffered from debilitating stage fright. I was such a wreck before my first conference presentation that I didn't sleep for two days. I lost twenty pounds in the three weeks leading up to my first academic job interview because of my anxiety (don't worry: I gained weight in college to play football, so I had plenty to lose). Although I still get nervous before speaking, it is no longer debilitating.[17] I know that almost nobody in the audience is thinking the worst thing I can imagine, that they're probably ruminating over dozens of other issues in their own life even while I'm right in front of them, and that almost no matter what happens the audience will forget about it far more quickly than I will. Before giving the commencement address at my high school some years ago, I found it reassuring that I could not recall anything my own high school commencement speaker said, even if someone offered me a million dollars to do so. In fact, I can't even recall if the speaker was a man or a woman. Think of classes you've taken, speeches you've watched, and commencement presentations you've endured. What percentage of the content do you remember? If the actual percentage is higher than your odds of being struck by lightning, I'll be shocked. Becoming aware of the power of your own perspective is the very thing that enables a broader perspective. Relax. Others likely won't notice, and if they do, they likely won't mind.[18]

HOW YOU SEE IT: THE LENS PROBLEM

If the only thing necessary for understanding the minds of others was attending to the same things, then others would be open books. But as you'll remember from our discussion of *naïve realism* in chapter 2, the problem of perspective is only just the beginning. Two people can look at the very same event and interpret it very differently, because they view it through their own lenses of knowledge, experience, beliefs, attitudes, and intentions. For instance, when major league baseball player Barry Bonds hit his record-setting seventy-third home run, driving the ball deep into the left-field stands, it was caught in the waiting glove of Alex Popov and then grabbed in the ensuing skirmish by Patrick Hayashi. Popov caught the ball first, and Hayashi held it last. Nobody disputed these facts.

The problem came when Popov and Hayashi interpreted these facts; each man naturally assumed that others would share his interpretation. Both men felt they were the rightful owners of the ball for obvious ethical reasons, and each was so certain that a judge would agree with his assessment that the two men were willing to sue each other for ownership of the ball. In fact, both men submitted the very same videotape from the very same camera as clear evidence for completely opposite conclusions. In the end, the judge agreed with neither man's interpretation fully, instead awarding joint custody of the ball to both men, with the proceeds to be split at auction. The "million-dollar ball," as it was then called, ended up selling for only $450,000, leaving neither of the two men with enough money to cover their enormous legal bills. Just because you're looking at the same thing doesn't mean that others will evaluate it as you do. Forgetting this can be costly.

LIKE ME

Popov and Hayashi aren't crazy; they're just human. In one experiment, equally human volunteers were randomly assigned to argue a hypothetical court case, either for the prosecution or for the defense. Despite being randomly assigned to these roles only moments before, volunteers quickly came to believe that their own side's case was stronger than the other side's case. More important, this wasn't just posturing; they seemed to really believe it, and they also thought the judge would rule in their own side's favor.[19] The problem with a lens is that you look *through* it rather than *at* it, and so your own perspective doesn't seem unique until someone else informs you otherwise. "I think in pictures," writes Temple Grandin, describing what it is like to be autistic. She continues, describing a natural consequence of the lens problem: "When I was a child and a teenager, I thought everybody thought in pictures. I had no idea that my thought processes were different. In fact, I did not realize the full extent of the differences until very recently."

Looking through a lens also means that it is difficult to tell when your own view is being distorted by it. A friend of mine once confided to feeling horribly embarrassed for a speaker whose slides were being presented (unknowingly) out of focus. The speaker went on and on and on, showing blurry graph after blurry graph, one fuzzy slide of notes after another. Worst of all, my friend believed that nobody else in the audience said anything because of their exceptional politeness, obviously not wanting to embarrass the speaker. It was only after the presentation that my friend realized that the lens of the projector was working just fine; the problem was with the lenses in *his own eyes*. The blurry slides were his first indication that he needed glasses.

Distortions like this are easy to find. Ever notice that "the media" are consistently accused of being biased but never found to favor those making the accusations? When your own views are one-sided, a balanced account will necessarily differ from your own perspective, and the errors in reporting will therefore seem to exist in *them* rather than in you.[20] Like the seemingly broken projector seen through the eyes of someone who needs glasses, viewers see bias *out there* in the media when the distortions exist inside their own minds. Parents do something similar. Many parents will report that the world seems to have gotten more dangerous over the years. Ask those parents to name *when* the world got more dangerous, and they will tend to give you a date very close to the birth of their first child.[21] The world has remained the same (if anything, it has gotten markedly less dangerous[22]), but having a child changes the lens through which you view it. Parents see the same events as more threatening than they once did, but they don't recognize that the change is in the lens through which they view the world rather than in the world itself.

The most natural consequence of the lens problem is assuming that others will interpret the world as you do, because you can't identify exactly how your own interpretation is being influenced by the lens you view it through. You can observe this consequence by simply asking people to report what other people believe, think, feel, or know, on topics ranging from the trivial to the critical. What percentage of other people like brown bread versus white bread? What percentage are likely to get excited about your new business model, love your artwork, or appreciate your self-published novel? How many Americans support financial regulation, are in favor of welfare, or will foreclose on their mortgage? When people are asked these questions, survey after survey finds that most people tend to exaggerate the extent to which others think, believe, and feel as they do.[23] Brown bread lovers think they are larger in number than white bread lovers.[24] Conservatives tend to believe that the average person is more conservative than liberals do.[25] Voters on both sides of an issue tend to believe that those who didn't vote in an election *would have voted* for their side, if they had chosen to vote.[26] And when it comes to morality, even those who are clearly in the minority nevertheless tend to believe that they are in the moral majority.[27]

Every year I demonstrate this to my MBA students by asking them to consider a series of questionably unethical practices.[28] These practices include dubious activities like covering meals for a friend while traveling for business and submitting the receipts for reimbursement, or taking home office supplies from work. For each practice, students report whether they think it is unethical (yes or no) and then estimate the percentage of others in the class who will agree with them. The table below shows my most recent year's results.

In the first row, you see that 86 percent think it's unethical to have your company reimburse you for a friend's meal while traveling, whereas 14 percent think it's acceptable. There's a considerable range of opinion across the other practices. The far right column shows the subjects' estimates of others' beliefs. Here you see very little range of opinion. In fact, none of the average estimates in that column fall below 50 percent. Even those in the moral minority believe they are part of the moral majority.

ETHICALLY QUESTIONABLE PRACTICE	IS THIS UNETHICAL?	WHAT PERCENTAGE AGREE WITH YOU?
You cover meals for friends while traveling and submit the receipts for reimbursement	YES - 86%	72%
	NO - 14%	60%
You pace your work to avoid getting new tasks	YES - 23%	55%
	NO - 77%	68%
You call in sick to get a day off	YES - 71%	66%
	NO - 29%	64%
You bluff about the money you currently make in a negotiation with a potential employer	YES - 53%	61%
	NO - 47%	71%
You agree to perform a task you have no real intention of performing	YES - 73%	68%
	NO - 27%	69%
You take office supplies from your office for personal use	YES - 66%	62%
	NO - 43%	65%
You pirate software from work and install it on your home computer	YES - 94%	72%
	NO - 6%	56%
You withhold information from colleagues who are competing for the same promotion	YES - 25%	69%
	NO - 75%	52%
You download copyrighted materials (songs, videos) without paying for them while working	YES - 70%	69%
	NO - 30%	66%

I asked my MBA students whether they considered various business practices to be unethical. Students differed considerably in their actual opinions, shown in the left column, with some issues being seen as unethical by a wide majority and others by only a small minority. Students varied far less in how much they thought their beliefs were shared by others in the class, shown in the far right column, where all of the percentages are larger than 50 percent.

THE EYES OF EXPERTS

Your own beliefs serve as a lens for understanding what others are likely to believe, as well as how strongly they are likely to believe it. But your mind contains multitudes, and beliefs are not the only lens that can alter your perceptions. Knowledge can also do it.

For example, read the following sentence:

FINISHED FILES ARE THE RESULT
OF YEARS OF SCIENTIFIC STUDY
COMBINED WITH THE
EXPERIENCE OF YEARS.

Now please go back and count how many *f*'s appear in that sentence. This is important. I'll wait for you.

How many did you find? More than you can count on one hand? If not, then we have just confirmed that you are a terrific reader but a terrible counter. Try it again. Look harder. I'll be patient.

Found all six yet? Don't forget that "of" has an *f* in it.

See them all now? Most people who read this sentence fail to spot all six of the *f*'s on their first pass. Instead, most see only three.[29] Why so few? This example has nothing to do with your beliefs and everything to do with your knowledge. Your expertise with English blinds you from seeing some of the letters. You know how to read so well that you can hear the sounds of the letters as you read over them. From your expert perspective, every time you see the word "of" you hear a *v* rather than an *f* and, therefore, miss it. This is why first graders are more likely to find all six in this task than fifth graders, and why young children are likely to do better on this than you did as well.[30] Your expert ears are clouding your vision.[31]

This example illustrates what psychologists refer to as the *curse of knowledge*, another textbook example of the lens problem. Knowledge is a curse because once you have it, you can't imagine what it's like not to possess it. You've seen other people cursed many times. For instance, while on vacation, have you ever tried to get driving directions from a local? Or talked to an IT person who can't explain how to operate your computer without using impenetrable computer science jargon? In one experiment, expert cell phone users predicted it would take a novice, on average, only thirteen minutes to learn how to use a new cell phone. It actually took novices, on average, thirty-two minutes.[32]

The lens of expertise works like a microscope, allowing you to notice subtle details that a novice might not catch but also sharpening your focus in a way that can allow you to miss the bigger picture and make it difficult to understand a novice's perspective. Consider the problem facing Clorox after it acquired the rights to Hidden Valley Ranch Dressing.[33] This is the most popular salad dressing on the market today and has been for years, but after purchasing the rights to it, Clorox spent ten years trying to bring it to market. What took so long?

During those ten years, the company's researchers reportedly tested many varieties, trying to make the original recipe shelf-stable. Again and again they failed to make a version that tasted as good as the original. Eventually they gave up and brought the best example they had to focus groups. To their surprise, people loved it. Like your inability to see the *f*'s because you are an expert reader, the expert food scientists had lost their ability to taste like a novice because they knew the taste of the original. Consumers had never tasted the original, and so they had no idea that the shelf-stable variation was worse by comparison. They judged it on its own merits, in isolation, and loved it as it was.

Trying to correct this lens first requires becoming aware of its influence. The problem is that it's hard to know when you are being affected by your own expertise and when you are not. Consider what is probably the most famous (as yet unpublished) dissertation experiment in the history of psychology: Elizabeth Newton's "tapping study."[34] In this experiment, carried out with pairs of subjects, one volunteer in each pair was randomly assigned to be the "tapper" and the other the listener. Tappers received a list of twenty-five songs well known to them, including "America the Beautiful" and "Rock Around the Clock." Tappers were asked to pick out three songs and then tap out each one for the listener, while they sat back-to-back. Tappers then estimated the likelihood that listeners would identify each tune correctly, and listeners tried to identify each one. The results were striking. Tappers estimated that listeners would identify the song correctly, on average, 50 percent of the time. In fact, listeners guessed correctly only 2.5 percent of the time.

It's now easy to understand the gap between tappers and listeners. The tappers were relative experts, being very familiar with the song they were tapping out and hearing it in their own minds while doing so. The listeners, however, were privy to none of this orchestration;

instead, they heard only the equivalent of musical Morse code. The important point is that the tappers were simply unable to appreciate how the rich music in their mind's stereo would sound to a listener hearing it through their finger's speakers.

None of us communicate by tapping alone, but the lens problem affects anyone who has unique knowledge of anything: the boss who understands a proposal inside out and is trying to convey the ideas to new clients, the inventor who knows precisely why her invention is so important speaking to impatient venture capitalists, or the coworker who is "just teasing" a new hire who knows nothing of the teaser's friendly intentions.[35] The expert's problem is assuming that what's so clear in his or her own mind is more obvious to others than it actually is.

Each of us has unique areas of expertise, but we are all experts on one issue very near and dear to us: ourselves. We live, work, and sleep with ourselves every day. We know what we looked like in the morning, how we felt yesterday, what we were doing five years ago. We know that our butt looks better in *these* pants than in *those* pants, that we are more attractive than most of our friends, but that we are not as fit as we would hope to be. Nobody in the world knows as much about you as you do. This fact helps explain why you may have such surprising difficulty understanding what others think of you.[36]

Think back to the finding I described in chapter 1, in which we asked our research volunteers to predict how attractive they would be rated by a member of the opposite sex who looked at a photograph of them. Accuracy in such situations is abysmal, partly because the expertise you have about yourself leads you to evaluate yourself through a much more microscopic lens than others do. You know that your hair is slightly out of place just above your left eye and that your complexion looks worse than normal, or that your smile is slightly out of whack. Indeed, when we asked our volunteers to write down how the evaluator would describe their picture, they included small details and subtle features that only a detailed examination would pick up on. These included "wearing no makeup," "mouth looks a little large (at least my lips do)," "my smile isn't as wide as normal," and "sexy hands." Of course, nobody knows how wide your smile normally is, and I don't even know what it means to have "sexy hands." You can sense our volunteers dialing in the microscope on themselves.

Others, of course, know much less about you and therefore cannot notice all of your fine-grained details. They look at you with the broader lens of a novice, evaluating you in general and in comparison to other people. When we asked our evaluators in this experiment to write a description of the picture they were looking at, they noted more general, stable, and holistic features rather than small details: "*very* thin," "white girl," "average height-weight," "somewhat friendly," "metrosexual," "weirdo."

It's not impossible to know what others think of you, but it does require using the same lens to evaluate yourself that others use. Other people generally know less about you than you know about yourself, and to understand what others think of you requires stepping back from the microscopic lens through which you view yourself. You have to think about how this person would evaluate you compared to others in general and overall, not how this person would evaluate you compared to your past or based on your fine-grained features. In this experiment, we also asked one group of people to think about themselves in these general terms by instructing them to consider how they would be judged by someone looking at their photograph way off in the future, three months from the day of the experiment. From abysmal accuracy rates that were no better than chance, these participants became quite accurate (the accuracy correlation was .55). Our volunteers did not become perfectly accurate, but they became about as accurate as any mind reader could reasonably expect to be. Knowing how you are seen through the eyes of others requires looking at yourself though the same lens that others do.

BLANKISH SLATES, E-MAIL, AND GOD

The problem of expertise is one of many examples of mistakes that come from projecting our own minds onto others: assuming that others know, think, believe, or feel as we do ourselves. Of course, we do not project ourselves onto others completely. We do so in some situations more than in others, and we project more onto some minds than others. The less we know about the mind of another, the more we use our own to fill in the blanks. Conservatives and liberals don't know what the "average" person thinks, or how people who didn't vote *would have* voted, and so they rely more on what they think themselves. Ask conservatives and liberals what their neighbor thinks, what their parent thinks, or what their spouse thinks and you are likely to see much less egocentrism. The lens problem therefore becomes larger as other minds become more unknown.[37] Understanding this allows you to explain, simultaneously, the problem with e-mail and the problem with God.

Let's tackle the big one first: e-mail. Much of what we communicate to others depends not only on what we say but on how we say it. The same comment about one's *"nice* hair," *"great* question," or *"brilliant* idea" can be taken as a compliment or an insult, depending on the tone of your voice or the smirk on your face. None of this subtlety makes it into your in-box. Although it's not as bad as tapping out a novel in Morse code, text-based mediums like e-mail and Twitter nevertheless communicate the content of what is said but little of the subtle context of *how* it is said, making them considerably more ambiguous and open to egocentric influences than face-to-face communication.

Consider an experiment that highlights the lens problem in such ambiguous communication. My collaborators and I asked one group of volunteers to write two different sentences about ten topics, one intended to be serious and one intended to be sarcastic.[38] The topics were whatever came to Justin Kruger (my collaborator) and me while brainstorming in Justin's office—things like food, cars, California, dating, and movies. We then asked each of our volunteers to convey these messages to another person in the experiment. In one condition, they sent the message via e-mail; in the other, they spoke it over the telephone. What we found was perfectly consistent with the lens problem. As you can see from the figure on the next page, our senders predicted that they could communicate just as well via e-mail as they could over the phone (roughly 80 percent accuracy in both cases). Those actually receiving the messages, however, could understand the speaker's intention only when the communication was clear (that is, when the speaker was on the phone). With e-mail, they were no more accurate than you'd expect from a coin flip.

The problem for our volunteers was that they knew whether their message was meant to be sincere or sarcastic. So when they said, *"Blues Brothers 2000*—now, there's a sequel," they could hear the sarcasm dripping from their voice regardless of whether they were actually using their voice or typing with their fingers. Those receiving the message, of course, could hear the sarcasm only through the speaker's voice and heard nothing from the speaker's fingers.

Not only was the ambiguity in the text unclear to the senders, it was unclear to the receivers as well. At the end of the experiment, we asked the receivers to guess how many of the items they had interpreted correctly. They thought they had done a superb job, interpreting nine out of ten of the sentences correctly, regardless of whether the communication had been over the phone or by e-mail. Here you can see why ambiguous mediums like e-mail and texting and Twitter are such fertile ground for misunderstanding. People using ambiguous mediums think they are communicating clearly because they know what they *mean* to say, receivers are unable to get this meaning accurately but are certain that they have *interpreted* the message accurately, and both are amazed that the other side can be so stupid.

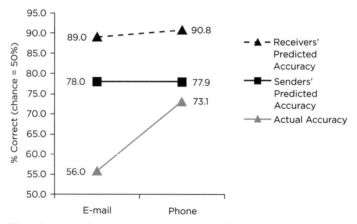

Senders delivered sincere and sarcastic messages to receivers either by e-mail or by phone. Receivers were able to distinguish sarcasm from sincerity better over the phone than with e-mail, but senders predicted that they communicated equally well over both mediums. Receivers, likewise, thought that they interpreted the messages equally well over both mediums. With the ambiguous medium of e-mail in particular, both senders and receivers thought they understood each other far better than they actually did.

As the context in which you're trying to understand another mind becomes more ambiguous, the influence of your own perspective increases. If you really want to understand your coworker or competitor or children, don't rely on modern mediums of communication that give you only a modern Rorschach test about the mind of another person. Twitter does not allow others to understand your deep thoughts and broad perspective. It only allows others to confirm how stupid they already think you are.

Now to the other problem: God. Just as the medium through which you communicate can be more or less ambiguous, so, too, can the target you're reasoning about. You do not need to rely on your own beliefs to know that Barack Obama is liberal and George W. Bush is conservative. Both express their beliefs loud and clear, they are identified with liberal and conservative parties, and other people can tell you that they are, respectively, liberal and conservative. Their beliefs are relatively obvious. So, too, with your spouse, your friends, your kids, and your neighbors, who can respond to questions you ask them. Even the general public can answer opinion polls. But the less willing or able others are to give you a piece of their minds, the more their minds become a blank slate onto which you project your own.

Enter God. Believers consult few figures more often than God when it comes to weighty measures, from moral issues such as gay marriage, abortion, and martyrdom to personal issues such as career planning or dating choices. The problem is that God doesn't answer opinion polls, and the books that supposedly report God's beliefs are notoriously open to interpretation. Many of the world's wars are still fought over what God apparently does or does not want, fueled by the sense of having God on one's own side. "Both read the same Bible and pray to the same God," Lincoln noted during his second inaugural address, at the height of the Civil War, "and each invokes his aid against the other. It may seem strange that any men should dare to ask a just God's assistance in wringing their bread from the sweat of other men's faces, but let us judge not, lest we be not judged." Sadly, few people have Lincoln's gift of self-reflection. Does Jesus believe that small government or big government would more effectively help the poor?[39] Does religion condemn gay marriage or condone it?[40] Did God want you to get that mortgage? Does God want you to be rich?[41] Lloyd Blankfein, the CEO of Goldman Sachs, once told a reporter that he was just a banker "doing God's work."[42] I believe that this assessment is open to debate.

Like any belief, these beliefs about God surely come from multiple sources. On some issues, the religious position is clear and one's own beliefs are unlikely to play any role. Religion creates beliefs, after all. But where there is wiggle room, God may become another example of the lens problem, created in one's own image. Many have suggested this hypothesis. Xenophanes, a sixth-century B.C. Greek philosopher, was the first person to describe anthropomorphism; he noted how Greek gods invariably had flowing hair and fair skin, whereas African gods had curly hair and dark skin.[43] As Darwin put it, humans interpreting religious experiences "would naturally attribute to spirits the same passions, the same love of vengeance, or simplest form of justice, and the same affections which they themselves feel." Bob Dylan even put the sentiment to music, in the song "With God on Our Side." But understanding the lens problem suggests an even more specific prediction than these generalities. If religious agents are more ambiguous than other people, then believers might be *even more* egocentric when reasoning about God's beliefs than when reasoning about other people's beliefs. Other people agree with me, but God is *really* on my side.

Several pieces of evidence support this possibility, at least within monotheistic conceptions of God.[44] In surveys, my collaborators and I have consistently found a stronger correlation between people's own beliefs and their predictions of God's beliefs than with their predictions about people's beliefs. From attitudes on abortion to support for same-sex marriage or the death penalty, Judeo-Christian believers' own attitudes match what they think God believes much more closely than what they think other people believe. These are consistent results, but they're nothing more than correlations. The opposite causal direction is also completely plausible: people come to believe what they think their God believes.

More compelling evidence comes from a neuroimaging experiment. We asked volunteers to report their own beliefs, God's beliefs, and the average American's beliefs on a wide variety of social issues while they were lying on their backs in an fMRI scanner. We found some clear distinctions. Major differences in neural activity emerged when people reasoned about their own beliefs and the average American's beliefs. We found the very same pattern of differences when people reasoned about God's beliefs versus the average American's beliefs. But the most amazing result of all was that we could not tell the difference in overall neural activity between people reasoning about their own beliefs versus God's beliefs. In the scanner, reasoning about God's beliefs looked the same as reasoning about one's own beliefs.

The most compelling evidence, however, comes from experiments in which we manipulated people's own beliefs and measured how it affected what people think God and others believe. In one, we showed volunteers persuasive arguments either in favor of or opposed to affirmative action. The arguments worked: those who read the pro–affirmative action information became more in favor, whereas those who read the anti–affirmative action arguments became more opposed. More important, our manipulation moved our volunteers' estimates of God's beliefs in lockstep with their own, whereas estimates of other people's beliefs were unaffected by the arguments the volunteers read. Creating God in one's own image, indeed.

If God is a moral compass, then the compass seems prone to pointing believers in whatever direction they are already facing.[45] There's nothing magical about God in this regard, just something ambiguous. When legislators speak of the founding fathers' intentions while interpreting the Constitution or politicians talk about what "the people" want, you are likely witnessing an act of divination that tells you more about the speaker's own beliefs than their target's beliefs. The injunction here is not for more cynicism when listening to others but, rather, for more humility when it seems that other people, gods, founding fathers, or legal teams are, in fact, on your side. When others' minds are unknown, the mind you imagine is based heavily on your own.

THROUGH THE EYES OF OTHERS

Oliver Sacks once told a story about someone who became blind later in life and in so doing provided a textbook example of adult egocentrism. Sacks describes research showing two extreme outcomes of adult-onset blindness, one in which people lose their mental imagery altogether and another in which they do precisely the opposite and hone their mental imagery so acutely that you might not even know they were blind. Those in this latter group can often do things you would never imagine possible, including one blind man whose mental imagery was so acute that he replaced all of the roof gutters on his multi-gabled house singlehandedly. Of course, his neighbors were startled to see this. More telling for egocentrism, he reported that his neighbors were *doubly startled* when they saw him working in the dark of night!

That doubled startle reflects an immediate moment of egocentrism—imagining *oneself* on the roof at night—that is only undone after you remember that darkness is no problem for the blind.

In some cases, the need for overcoming an egocentric default is not obvious until it's too late. In 1628, the most impressive warship of its day, the Swedish vessel *Vasa,* sank only twenty minutes into its maiden voyage, killing thirty men and embarrassing the nation. One major problem was that the ship had been built by at least two carpentry crews using different rulers, one Swedish and one Dutch. The Swedish measurement system had twelve inches to a foot whereas the Dutch system had only eleven. These crews, working with their own rulers from the very same blueprints had built a warship with considerably more wood on one side than on the other, causing it to roll over as soon as the wind caught its sails on the lighter side. Presumably it had never occurred to anyone that "a foot" could mean something different on opposite sides of the boat.[46]

In other cases the need to correct one's own viewpoint is obvious but the ability to do so depends on the source of the problem. I have described two different versions of egocentric biases, one produced by differences in attention (the neck problem) and the other produced by differences in interpretation (the lens problem). Of these two, I believe the existing evidence suggests that the neck problem is easier to overcome than the lens problem.

Think back to the earlier studies that showed "overclaiming." In these versions of the neck problem, you might claim more responsibility for group activity simply because you are more aware of your own contributions than you are of others' contributions. This kind of problem is relatively easy to solve. All you need to do is shift your attention to other people—in this case, to think about what others in your group contributed. Recall the Harvard MBA study groups whose members claimed more responsibility as the size of the group increased. We had another condition in that experiment, one in which the MBAs wrote down what each other member of the group contributed to the overall effort before they wrote down how much they personally contributed. This brought evaluations much closer to a realistic baseline. Ashley Todd wouldn't have drawn the *B* on her cheek backward if she had paused for a moment and considered an onlooker's visual perspective. The *Vasa* wouldn't have sunk if the carpenters had paused to look at each other's rulers. And you can reduce the anxiety that comes from believing that you are in the center of the social spotlight if you just pause for a moment and consider everything others are likely to be thinking about in their lives (almost none of it having anything to do with you).[47]

The lens problem, in which two people view the very same event differently, appears much harder to overcome. You've probably heard the old saying that you can't judge another person until you've walked a mile in their shoes. You hear this because it's true, but you hear it so often because the advice is so routinely ignored—by the rich who judge the poor as lazy and incompetent, the sober who judge the addicted to be weak and immoral, and the happy who can't understand why the depressed don't just "snap out of it." When senseless gun violence breaks out in a school or a movie theater, gun rights activists imagine that if only *they* had been there packing heat, they would not have panicked (as soldiers often do in war) but instead would have calmly drawn their weapon—as one might imagine doing while reading the news in the living room recliner—and shot the one bad guy without a hitch. Mark Wahlberg, an actor whose tough guy reputation matched the professional boxer he played in *The Fighter,* was supposed to have been on one of the hijacked planes that brought down the World Trade towers on September 11, 2001; when interviewed in the cool of the moment years later, he imagined that he would have made a difference. "If I was on that plane with my kids, it wouldn't have went down like it did. There would have been a lot of blood in that first-class cabin and then me saying, 'OK, we're going to land somewhere safely, don't worry.'"[48] Judging people without ever walking in their shoes seems to be a popular pastime.

You cannot simply try harder to view the world through the eyes of another and hope to do so more accurately, because the lens that biases your perceptions is often invisible to you. The food scientists at Clorox were trying very hard to put themselves in the consumer's shoes, but they simply couldn't appreciate how knowing the taste of the original recipe was influencing their assessment of the alternatives. For one modest test of this claim, recall the experiment in which we took photographs of volunteers and asked them to predict how attractive others would rate them. We included another condition in one of those experiments in which we asked volunteers to put themselves in the observer's shoes, with the admonition that the observer might view their own image differently. This deliberate perspective taking did not solve the lens problem; it did nothing to improve accuracy whatsoever.

It's easy, however, to think that it's simpler to overcome the lens problem than it actually is. For instance, the legal standard for torture endorsed by most developed nations is "any act by which severe pain or suffering, whether physical or mental, is intentionally inflicted on a person." This assumes that those charged with defining torture will be able to evaluate experiences they've never had. Most intuitively think they are up to the task. Despite never having been waterboarded herself, for instance, U.S. congressional representative Michele Bachmann felt informed enough to say, "I don't see it as torture." She's not alone. If you've never experienced it before, it's likely that the thought of lying on your back and having water poured over your nose doesn't sound *so* bad. You get in the shower every day, after all.

Before actually experiencing it live on his radio show, Chicago shock jock Erich "Mancow" Muller was also convinced that waterboarding wasn't that bad and shouldn't be considered torture. "The average person can take this for fifteen seconds," said marine Sergeant Clay South just before subjecting Mancow to the procedure. "He's going to wiggle, he's going to scream, he's going to wish he never did this." In fact, the sergeant was wrong. Mancow lasted only seven seconds. "It was way worse than I thought it would be, and that's no joke," he said. "It is such an odd feeling to have water poured down your nose with your head back. . . . It was instantaneous . . . and I don't want to say this: absolutely torture."[49]

No amount of trying to overcome this lens problem, of imagining yourself being waterboarded or sleep deprived or poor or left in solitary confinement for years on end, can allow you to understand what it is like to be in a situation radically different from your own. We can all lecture *other* people about the danger of judging others until you've walked a mile in their shoes, but we easily overlook it when we're doing the same thing ourselves. You don't overcome the lens problem by trying harder to imagine another person's perspective. You overcome it by actually being in that perspective, or hearing directly from some who has been in it. Judges may need to take the radical step of experiencing a practice they're considering before they can evaluate it clearly.

■ ■ ■

Other minds can be blank slates onto which we project our own, but other minds come into sharper focus as we learn more about them. Other people are professors or priests or politicians. They are liberal or conservative, rich or poor, black or white, men or women. These visible identities tell you something about a person's invisible mind. Their identities may match your own, suggesting that they have a mind like your own. But others may have an identity that differs from your own, suggesting a mind that also differs from your own. As you know more about another person, the tools you use to understand them changes. Liberals might use their own beliefs to understand what other liberals think, but they will use what they know about conservatives to predict what a conservative would think. Atheists might use their own beliefs to understand what other atheists think, but they will use what they know about Islam to predict what a Muslim thinks. In the 1950s, four thousand workers and supervisors at a large manufacturing plant were asked to rank how much they cared about different sources of motivation in their jobs. The supervisors were also asked to read their workers' minds: to predict their workers' rankings.[50] Supervisors and

their workers ranked their most fundamental motivations very similarly (they were correlated very highly with each other: .76, to be exact).
But when supervisors predicted what was important to their workers,
they treated them almost like members of another species. There was
almost no correlation between what they personally valued and what
they believed their workers valued (the correlation was .05, not significantly higher than would be expected by chance alone).

This is a consistent result.[51] Once *they* become a group, *I* am no longer as relevant. Learn that someone is a member of a different group
than you, the existing evidence suggests, and you will drop egocentrism and pick up a stereotype to reason about that person's mind
instead.

This tool switching might be perfectly rational. Just as a carpenter
looking at a metal spike might instinctively reach for a hammer but
put it down for a screwdriver once a screw comes into view, so, too,
would you rely on the knowledge you have about a group when making judgments about members of that group. In modern life, however,
stereotypes are discussed in the same tone of voice as cancer or choles-
terol: as mental tools used by only the bigoted or ignorant that should
be discarded and avoided. When put to the scientific test, however,
this unqualified condemnation is too extreme. Stereotypes typically
provide some useful insight into the minds of others, giving you a
more accurate understanding than you might otherwise have. But like
egocentrism, viewing others though a lens of stereotypes also creates
predictable mistakes. In fact, as I'll show you in the next chapter, it
creates at least three predictable mistakes.

6

The Uses and Abuses of Stereotypes

Stereotypes: Each of us lives and works on a small part of
the earth's surface, moves in a small circle, and of these
acquaintances knows only a few intimately. . . . Inevitably,
our opinions cover bigger space, a longer reach of time, a
greater number of things, than we can directly observe. They
have, therefore, to be pieced together out of what others have
reported and what we can imagine.

—Walter Lippmann (1922), first using "stereotypes" to describe
social thought rather than a duplicating plate in a printing press

We live, we are told, in a world divided. A world divided by
politics and religion, by race and gender, by social class and
education, by borders and nations. You may never have talked to a
homeless person or eaten across the dinner table from a radical Muslim. You almost certainly have never spent a week sampling the opinions of a thousand people across the political spectrum to learn their
actual beliefs. Yet having little or no direct contact rarely leaves anyone
dumbfounded. Your opinions about the minds of others cover a much
"bigger space" than your direct observations, pieced together in your
imagination from things you've read and heard from others. How do
you imagine the minds of these distant and relatively unknown others,
and how accurately do you imagine them?

Let's start with an example of two presumably enormous divides:

wealth and politics. Around the globe, wealth inequality is generally rising, with the world's richest getting richer and the poor stagnating. This divide over money creates a divide inside minds, between those who favor equality versus those who favor meritocracy. The world over, liberal politicians deplore the widening gap between rich and poor and suggest increasing taxes on the wealthiest to redress the balance, whereas conservative politicians deplore the unfairness of taxing success and suggest that free markets with lower taxes will improve conditions for all. Sound bites from entrenched partisans make for great television and dysfunctional government. Do they give accurate insight into the actual beliefs of liberals and conservatives?

To find out, two psychologists measured the attitudinal divide by asking one thousand randomly selected Americans to report their preferences on wealth inequality.[1] First, they presented respondents with three pie charts depicting hypothetical nations with different degrees of wealth inequality: complete equality, shown in chart A; severe inequality, shown in C; and intermediate inequality, shown in B. Respondents considered the nations one pair at a time, and for each possible pair reported which nation they would prefer to join if they were randomly assigned to one of the wealth quintiles (top 20 percent, next 20 percent, and so on, to the bottom 20 percent). Nobody actually lives in the perfectly equal Country A, so let's consider the two realistic nations, B and C. Take a look at the figure on the next page. Which country would you prefer to live in if you were randomly placed in one of the quintiles?

Now, how about *other* people? What percentage of those who voted for a relatively liberal politician in the last presidential election (the Democrat) would prefer the more equitable distribution B? How about those who voted for a relatively conservative politician in the last U.S. election (the Republican)? What percentage of those conservative voters would favor B?

If you preferred more equitable Country B to less equitable Country C, then you have the same preference as 92 percent of these survey responders. Almost nobody wants extreme inequality.[2] And if you thought a larger percentage of Democratic voters preferred B than did Republican voters, then you were absolutely right. Give your stereotypes about liberals and conservatives a hand. In this respect, they're right.

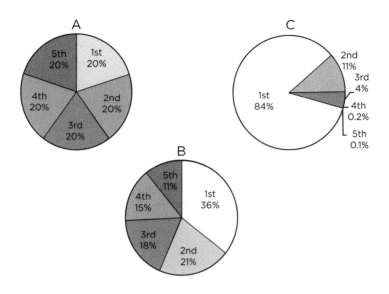

Each pie chart represents a country, showing how much wealth is controlled by each quintile (20 percent) of the population, from the wealthiest (top 20 percent) to the poorest (bottom 20 percent). Country A is hypothetical, but Country B and Country C represent the actual wealth distribution of real countries.

Your stereotypes are likely to be right in other ways as well. In this survey, the relatively poor (those making less than $50,000 per year) preferred a more equitable distribution than did the relatively rich (those making more than $150,000 per year). Women also preferred a more equitable distribution than men did.[3] None of these results are surprising. Everyone is motivated at least somewhat by their own self-interest, and so the poor prefer more equitable distributions than the rich. Women are considered the fairer sex for apparently good reason. Again, your stereotypes get these differences right.

But what your stereotypes about groups may get right when you're predicting the direction of these differences, they may get very wrong when you're predicting the size of those differences. Liberals favor a more equitable distribution than do conservatives, but by how much? If you thought the difference was anything more than trivial, then you were dead wrong. The difference between Democratic and Republican presidential voters was only 3.5 percent. If you thought the political gap was much larger, then you're not alone. When I surveyed a group of 481 Americans using an online questionnaire, they predicted a 35 percent difference between Democratic and Republican voters on this exact measure. My survey responders understood the direction of this difference but misunderstood its magnitude by a factor of ten.[4] I found exactly the same thing with predicted preferences of the relatively rich and poor. My survey responders again understood the direction of the difference but completely misunderstood its magnitude, expecting a 40 percent gap between poor and rich when the actual gap was only 3 percent. My respondents were somewhat closer with the gender gap, but they still estimated a gender gap of 12 percent when the actual gender gap was only 2 percent.

Neither you nor my survey respondents had to run out and talk to a conservative or a liberal, a rich or a poor person, a man or a woman to guess their beliefs. You already had a sense of their beliefs. That sense is a stereotype—"a set of beliefs about the personal character-istics of a group."[5] These beliefs do not emerge from thin air. They reflect your brain's general attempt to extract average tendencies from a complicated world, using both your own and others' observations to make inferences about the minds of others. Your sense of liber-als and conservatives, of rich and poor, and of men and women all contain some element of truth—in this case, getting the direction of differences correct. Your sense also contains some predictable error—in this case, getting the magnitude of those differences wildly wrong.

Common stereotypes often reflect this mixed picture, bringing us closer to the mind of another person by identifying group averages at above-chance levels but creating predictable mistakes as well. To help you understand the rather complicated nature of this accuracy and error, I first have to show you how impressive your brain on stereotypes *could* be, if people were circles.

CIRCLEOLOGY

First, look at the set of circles on the left on the next page. Next, look at the test circle on the right.

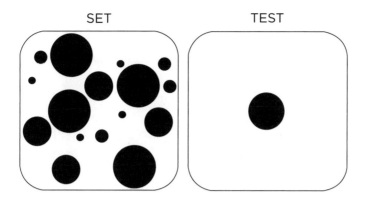

In an experiment ostensibly testing one's vision, volunteers were shown pictures like these although their task was harder. Instead of seeing the images side by side, they saw each image one at a time: first a set of circles like those on the left, then a single test circle like the one on the right.[6] They were then asked whether or not the single test circle was included in the preceding set of circles. After the researchers repeated this many (many, many) times,[7] varying the number and size of the circles, two consistent findings emerged. One finding was rather dull, but the other was, quite frankly, stunning.

First, the dull finding: this test is *really* hard. The volunteers were completely unable to tell whether or not a single target circle was one they had seen in the larger set. When you've just seen a large group, it's nearly impossible to remember the individuals. Anyone who's ever spoken in front of a large audience or walked down a crowded city sidewalk can confirm this. Individuals within large groups are almost invisible. What's true of people is shown clearly here with circles.[8]

Now the stunning finding: mistakes on this test are almost perfectly predictable, and they reflect your brain's brilliance. In the figure above, the test circle on the right is not actually in the set on the left. Nevertheless, almost all of the people shown the test circle in this experiment mistakenly reported that it *was* in the set. People make this mistake so consistently because the test circle on the right is the *average* size of the circles in the set on the left. What your brain extracts automatically from a group is an overall assessment, not its distinct individuals. While you were busy looking at the larger set of circles, your brain was busy calculating the average diameter of the group and posting this image to your memory in less than half a second. No training in statistics required, no math book to reference, no Google search needed. Your memory may be mistaken, but it's not stupid.[9]

Other people's minds are more complicated than circles, but these findings tell us something critical about how your brain thinks of groups of anything. Instead of remembering exact details, you extract the "gist" of the information. The "gist" of a group is not its individual members but, rather, its average. This includes groups of people. If you look at a crowd expressing different emotions, research suggests that you're likely to have a very difficult time remembering any of the individuals but will be left with a fairly decent sense of the crowd's general mood.[10] This is surely a very adaptive skill. An organism unable to learn that tigers are generally dangerous but that tiger lilies are not would rarely succeed in a dangerous world. A person unable to get a general sense of what others do, think, believe, feel, or want—the social norms of the broader society—would rarely succeed in our highly social world.

REALITY BITES

The circles test gives us an impressive benchmark for what your brain can do with groups under ideal circumstances. It also gives us a starting point for thinking about how the real world falls short of an ideal circumstance. In the circles test, every member of the group is visible, shown clearly before your eyes. There are no circles you have to remember seeing yesterday or hear about from other people or read about in the news. There are no missing circles out for a smoke break, and no really attractive circles that capture your attention and keep you from spotting the unattractive ones. Every circle is also completely honest. None of them distort their appearance to impress you, perhaps sucking in their waist to keep from looking so fat in their shorts. Nor are you asked to judge invisible features of the circles, like the circle's feelings or intentions or beliefs or attitudes. When reality sits clearly before your eyes, your brain's statistician is brilliant.

The real world falls far short of these ideal circumstances on every dimension, but it does not fall completely flat. Many researchers have measured the accuracy of stereotypes by asking groups of people to make judgments about verifiable characteristics of other groups of people and then comparing those judgments to some measure of reality. Results consistently show evidence of both accuracy and error in varying degrees, just as a brilliant baseball player batting against tough pitchers will hit sometimes and miss other times, in varying degrees across different pitchers.

One telling example comes from a stereotype that never tires the imagination: differences between men and women. Here, a large group of university students—139 men and 162 women—predicted men's and women's attitudes on questions from the General Social Survey (a poll administered to several thousand randomly selected people every year since 1972, to "measure the pulse of America").[11] These included attitudes like whether employers should offer paid time off to new parents, the degree of support for government regulation of business, support for public housing for the poor, and the extent to which a person agrees that it is better for "everyone involved if the man is the achiever outside the home and the woman takes care of home and family." For each statement, volunteers predicted the percentages of men and women who would give each possible response.

If your stereotypes about the minds of men and women were perfect, then your predicted percentages would be perfectly in line with the actual percentages, yielding a correlation of 1. If your stereotypes were completely inaccurate, then there would be no relationship between your predicted percentages and the actual percentages, yielding a correlation of 0. In fact, the accuracy correlations showed considerably good sense—a correlation of .50 for predictions of men's attitudes and .58 for predictions of women's attitudes. Men and women tended to respond in ways consistent with their gender roles, with men expressing relatively more competitive and meritocratic attitudes and women expressing relatively more cooperative and egalitarian attitudes. Amid this accuracy, however, was also systematic error. In particular, women tended to think men would be more sexist than they actually were, exaggerating the differences between men and women on the issues most often presumed to divide the sexes.

This mixed picture is a fairly typical result. Stereotypes are rarely completely accurate or inaccurate. They come in endless shades of gray, varying between a solid sense of group averages and nonsense. The interesting question is not why many stereotypes about group differences contain a fair amount of accuracy. The circles test gives an obvious explanation: some genuine differences exist in the world between groups of all kinds, you can observe some of those differences directly, and your memory generates a reasonably accurate average of those genuine differences. No, the more interesting question is, What keeps stereotypes about groups of people from being as accurate as they could be, given the accuracy we see in the circles test? The three-pound meat loaf between your ears can calculate the average qualities of geometric shapes in half a second without even breaking a sweat. What leads our brain's brilliant statistician astray when thinking about other people?

The short answer is that we live in what decision scientist Robin Hogarth calls a "wicked environment,"[12] one that gives imperfect data to your brilliant statistician. For understanding where our stereotypes go wrong, three wicked ways matter most: getting too little information, defining groups by their differences, and being unable to observe the true causes of group differences directly.

TOO MUCH FROM TOO LITTLE

Brilliant statisticians can look stupid when they conduct analyses on incomplete data. Four days before the 1936 U.S. presidential election, having polled 2.4 million Americans, the *Literary Digest* predicted a landslide victory for Republican Alfred Landon over Democrat Franklin D. Roosevelt. It was indeed a landslide, one of the largest in U.S. history, but in precisely the opposite direction. Landon won only two states, earning the fewest electoral votes in a presidential election since the 1850s. The *Digest*'s mistake came from sampling almost exclusively from the two states Landon actually won (Vermont and Maine), using respondents from its own magazine (predominantly conservative), and then interviewing people over the phone (a luxury generally owned by wealthy households at the time). Analyze only part of the data and you're bound to look stupid.

The implication is obvious. Our stereotypes about people are imperfect assessments of group averages because we poll like the *Literary*

Digest. Each of us views only a small slice of the world's people, hears only haphazard bits of highly selected evidence from news outlets or other sources, and talks to only a narrow group of generally like-minded friends. Worse yet, some of our beliefs about others (perhaps many of them) are not observed directly but, rather, are learned secondhand through stories told among family members, friends, and neighbors. Our brain's statistician then runs analyses on the data we've seen, imagined, or heard, a data set that has to be less accurate than what we see in the circles test.

In general, stereotypes are more accurate when you've had direct experience with a group (such as one you belong to), know a lot about the group in question (because it's in the majority), and are asked about clearly visible facts (such as about visible behavior rather than about invisible mental states, like attitudes, beliefs, or intentions).[13] University students, for instance, have a pretty impressive sense of the behavior and attitudes of other students at the same university.[14] Watching, talking, and living with one another gives them reasonably good data to work with. Stereotypes about majority groups also look to be more accurate than stereotypes about minority groups, simply because larger groups provide more observational evidence than smaller groups.[15] And communicating with people via mediums that offer only the thinnest amounts of information, like Twitter or text messages or e-mail, is precisely the wicked environment where mistaken stereotypes are likely to persist most strongly.[16] The less we know, the more our stereotypes mislead.

This seems obvious enough in theory, but it's hard to recognize in practice because you can't know what evidence your brain's statistician is missing. Consider the common stereotype that women are more emotional than men. You can see the evidence for this almost everywhere you look. Women smile more often, cry more often, and laugh more often than men. Women just seem to *feel* more than men do—boys don't cry, after all. But what we all lack is direct access to the actual minds of the average man or average woman, to see whether these differences reflect the emotions people feel or just the emotions they show to others. Fortunately, emotional experiences leave physiological traces that can be captured with expensive laboratory equipment. When people are hooked up to this equipment, research confirms that men and women watching the same emotionally evocative scenes show the same emotional reactions, on average, of the same intensity. Where men and women differ is in the outward expressions of their emotions, with women being more expressive than men.[17] But when people watch these men and women, they infer that women are feeling more emotion than men because they are *showing* more emotion than men. Stereotypes mislead here because they are based on expressions we can see rather than on experiences that remain invisible.

When behavior is an honest reflection of a person's mind, our stereotypes can be pretty impressive. When behavior is deceptive, however, our stereotypes are less impressive. Using observed behavior to make inferences about minds we cannot see will, at times, befuddle even the best statistician. When politicians grandstand for their constituents, lawyers argue to the jury, unions strike for their members, and advocates fight for their cause, it is critical to remember that there is more to the world than meets your eyes.

DIFFERENT, BY DEFINITION

Simply being exposed to more evidence would calibrate our stereotypes if we paid equal attention to all of the evidence before us. Only we don't. Some pieces of evidence are easier to ignore than others. When you go on a trip, much of your experience involves doing the same thing for long stretches of time—flying, driving, sleeping, standing, waiting, walking—but the story you tell your friends afterward is all about the *different* things you experienced along the way—going here and there, doing this and that. The same goes for how you think about yourself. You define yourself not by the attributes that make you the same as everyone else—has two arms, two legs, breathes air—but, rather, by the attributes that make you *different* from everyone else— spent time in the Peace Corps, works as a physicist, loves to go fishing, and so on.[18] A man who claims to be searching for himself is not looking for a map; he is looking for a sense of distinction.

Similarity is boring, but differences are exciting. This hypersensitivity to difference is built into our being, all the way down to our retinas. You and I can see the visible world because our eyes wobble back and forth ever so slightly and uncontrollably, jerking this way and that in what are known as "saccades." These eye wobbles allow your retina to detect differences, changes in texture and contour and lighting, and it is this ability to detect changes in visual input that enables sight. Paralyze your eyes with anesthetic to keep them from wobbling, and everything goes dark. Place a contact lens with an image tattooed on it on your retina, and the design will slowly become invisible as the lens begins to wobble in sync with your eye.[19]

Groups emerge just as objects do: when you detect differences between them. Men and women, black and white, old and young, rich and poor are all groups defined by their "wobbles"—by what makes them *different* from other groups. A group defined by its similarity to others is, by definition, no group at all. Your social senses, just like your eyes, are difference detectors.

Noticing the differences between groups is not inherently problematic for stereotypes, but defining groups by their differences can be. Consider a simple experiment in which volunteers were asked to estimate the length of eight different lines.[20] For some volunteers, the lines were divided into two groups, A and B, as you can see below on the left. All of the short lines are in group A and the taller ones in B. Height is their defining difference. For the other volunteers, the lines had no labels—and therefore no groups—at all. Volunteers saw each line one at a time, in a random order, and estimated its length.

Defining groups of lines by their height does not affect how tall they actually *are*, but it can affect how tall they *look*. In particular, the most ambiguous lines, those right at the category boundary—the longest in the A group and the shortest in the B group—were misperceived by research volunteers as being more consistent with their group's defining quality than they actually were. And so a short line in a tall group was thought to be taller, and a long line in a short group was thought to be shorter. Calling someone a basketball player won't make a short person grow taller, but it might make you remember a short baller as being taller. When groups are defined by their differences, borderline cases can be squished to fit the definitions, exaggerating differences between the groups when reality is unclear.

Defining groups by their differences is not as big a problem for our vision as it is for our imagination. People on opposite sides of a negotiation are well aware that they are opposed to each other, but they are often left to imagine the precise ways in which they are opposed. Members of different political parties can see that they vote for different candidates, but they are left to imagine what members of those parties actually believe. And men and women can see that they differ from each other in their outward appearance and behavior, but they are left to infer what members of the opposite sex *really* want.

Let's stick with this last example again, about gender differences. The biggest gender differences are biological: men have penises and women have vaginas, and, yes, research confirms that most men throw a baseball faster and farther than most women.[21] The gender differences that most strongly capture our imagination and define our genders, however, are psychological: women are communal, emotional, relational, and think mainly about others, whereas men are independent, logical, spatial, and think mainly about sex.

Scientists also love to talk about psychological gender differences, in part because the scientific method—just like our senses—uses methods that detect differences between groups rather than similarities. Consider the largest single study of gender preferences ever conducted in psychology, a survey of 10,047 men and women (ages twenty to twenty-five) from 37 cultures. These men and women were asked to rate the importance of thirteen attributes in a romantic partner (from 0, meaning it's unimportant, to 3, meaning it's indispensable). The *differences* in the preferences of men and women attracted, by far, the most attention (and had motivated the study in the first place). In all cultures, men consistently rated "good looks" as more important than women did, and women rated "good earning potential" as being more important than men did.[22] Hence the article's title, "Sex *Differences* in Human Mate Preferences" (italics added).

But buried at the end of the paper, under "Qualifications and Limitations," is this result about gender *similarity:* "neither earning potential nor physical appearance emerged as the highest rated or ranked characteristic for either sex. . . . *Both* sexes ranked the characteristics 'kind—understanding' and 'intelligent' higher than earning power and attractiveness in all samples, suggesting that species-typical mate preferences may be more potent than sex-linked preferences." Nonacademic translation: there are real differences in what men and women want but even larger similarities because men and women are both human beings. Both men *and* women want someone who is kind and smart. "Feminism," as a favorite definition goes, "is the radical notion that women are people." I'll add that men are people, too.

Those who write about gender are perfectly human, and are therefore more attentive to differences than to similarities, just like the rest of us. Janet Hyde is the only psychologist to ever propose a theory of gender *similarities,* where she notes that large-scale studies of gender differences typically identify overwhelming similarities but that secondhand reports nevertheless focus on the small number of differences that define our stereotypes.[23] Popular writers and news accounts often pay lip service to these similarities, just before executing an about-face to make wildly exaggerated claims about observed differences. Among the recent inductees into the Gender Exaggeration Hall of Fame is Louann Brizendine, author of *The Female Brain* and *The Male Brain.*[24] In one article for CNN describing what she calls "the male brain," Brizendine's second paragraph begins with good sense about gender similarities: "Our brains are mostly alike. We are the same species, after all." The about-face to exaggeration comes immediately, like a movie cut. After another four paragraphs, all good sense is long gone: "This [testosterone in fifteen-year-old boys] fuels their sexual engine and makes it impossible for them to stop thinking about female body parts and sex." Really? *Impossible?* I was once a testosterone-fueled boy of fifteen who thought plenty about sex but also had enough time to play football and basketball, get decent grades, play the tuba, go fishing, and spend time with my parents, finding it quite possible to think about things other than sex most of the time.

Again, our stereotypes about the minds of men and women are not completely wrong. Research confirms the obvious fact that men think about sex more than women do. In one study that tracked the thoughts of men and women throughout the day over a week, researchers found that college-aged men thought of sex, on average, 34 times per day, and women thought of sex, on average, 19 times per day.[25] That looks like a big gender difference (the effect is actually considered small in statistical terms, because the variability among men and women is very large), but it's nothing like Brizendine's "male brain" that finds it "impossible to think about anything but sex." That's *almost* accurate in the same way that a paper airplane is *almost* a 747. Nor is this result anywhere near the cliché that men think of sex every seven seconds. At least for these male college students, it was about once every thirty waking minutes.

More interesting is that even this surprisingly modest gender difference doesn't look to be about sex at all. The researchers also tracked how much men and women thought about food and sleep. Equally large gender differences emerged here as well. Gender stereotypes define groups by their central differences—sex—and thus run the risk of exaggerating those differences dramatically and missing other differences. It's not that men thought more about sex than women in this study, it's that they thought more about *all* of their urges than women did.[26]

The most central claims of the gender difference crowd are so perfectly consistent with our stereotypes about men and women that their conclusions hardly seem surprising. In *The Essential Difference,* neuroscientist Simon Baron-Cohen argues that the most important gender difference is that women tend to have better social senses—are better able to empathize with others, to recognize others' emotions, and to read the minds of others—than men do. Baron-Cohen, in contrast to other writers on this topic, makes a point of highlighting the large degree of similarity between men and women even on this apparently essential difference, advising us to be "careful not to overstate what can be concluded." Unfortunately, his book's title, which almost necessarily simplifies complicated matters, does that caveat a disservice.

Just how big is this *essential* difference? You've guessed it: not as big as your stereotype suggests. As with thoughts about sex, your stereotypes can get the direction of differences right but their magnitude wrong. The typical way to calculate the magnitude of an observed difference in a survey or experiment is to transform the average difference into a correlation where a score of 0 would indicate no difference (men and women perform identically, with perfect overlap in the distributions) and a score of 1 would indicate the largest possible difference (all women, say, perform better than all men, with no overlap in the distributions). The typical effect sizes on these tests of empathy and mind reading are around .2, which means that the differences *among* men and women are far larger than the differences *between* men and women.[27] However, when Tal Eyal and I asked groups of men and women to predict the size of these differences on these same measures, they estimated effect sizes around .7, more than three times larger than the actual gender differences.[28] Other researchers find similar results.[29] And yet a best-selling book by John Gray tells you that men are from Mars and women are from Venus. So say our stereotypes, but the truth is more like men are from Iowa and women are from Illinois.

Men and women differ from each other in ways that can lead to exaggerated differences in the presumed minds of the opposite sex, but they are not inherently *opposed* to each other. Sure, we love to talk about the "battle of the sexes," but the truth is that the vast majority of adults have fallen in love with at least one member of the other sex (and often with many more). Men and women get along well enough. Not so in cases of true conflict or in politics, where the dangers of defining groups by their differences is even more apparent.

Consider politics. Surveys of the American electorate over the last thirty-five years have shown surprisingly stable differences of opinion between Republicans and Democrats on attitudes such as government-run health care, military defense spending, school choice, and funding for government welfare programs. The American electorate has also exaggerated the magnitude of these differences, particularly in recent years, as elected officials have become more polarized in their own behavior.[30] Graphical depictions that highlight the differences between "red states" and "blue states" only make matters worse, according to research, increasing the perceived differences between groups rather than merely reflecting them.[31] And on specific issues ranging from affirmative action to welfare policies, people on opposing sides of each issue consistently assume that the other side is more extreme than it actually is.[32] The sad fact is that real partisanship increases partly because of imagined partisanship on the other side.

Disputes about abortion rights, for instance, focus both on the rights of the mother and on the rights of the unborn. Partisans in the midst of this disagreement, research demonstrates, tend to assume that the other side is opposed on the very issue that their own side holds the most dear—that is, on the defining feature of the dispute itself. Pro-choice advocates value the rights of the mother and therefore assume that pro-life advocates value the rights of the mother very little. Pro-life advocates, in contrast, value the rights of the unborn and therefore assume that pro-choice advocates value the rights of the unborn very little. These beliefs on both sides actually exaggerate the real differences between the two groups in a way that inflames the conflict most intensely.[33] The exaggerated differences about wealth inequality that I opened this chapter with are no anomaly.

Every student in a negotiation class learns that the secret to solving disputes is recognizing that the other side may not have completely opposing interests, and may have more overlap in interests than you would guess. Solving disputes therefore requires openly discussing each others' actual interests, identifying similarities, and then identifying integrative solutions that maximize the benefits for both sides. This ideal played out almost perfectly when Israel and Egypt were disputing ownership of the Sinai Peninsula in 1976. Israel had occupied the territory since the Six-Day War, in 1967, and Egypt wanted the land back. Instead of fighting a zero-sum battle, with each side imagining (and therefore exaggerating) the other side's interests, the two sides came together at Camp David and figured out each other's actual interests. Israel wanted security, and Egypt wanted sovereignty. The Israelis didn't want the Sinai Peninsula; they just didn't want to be attacked from it. The solution reached at Camp David was to give the land back to Egypt but to create a demilitarized band along the border. Israel got its safety, and Egypt got its land.

Sadly, negotiations over our differences rarely end so sensibly. When groups are defined by their differences, conflict is fought over the differences we imagine, suppose, or expect from others rather than over the genuine, multifaceted, and often more moderate differences that actually exist.[34] When groups are defined by their differences, people think they have less in common with people of other races or faiths or genders than they actually do and, as a result, avoid even talking with them.[35] When groups are defined by their differences, the minds we imagine in others may be more extreme than the minds that actually encounter.

WHY THEM?

Describing how stereotypes can exaggerate group differences runs the risk of implying that no meaningful differences exist at all. That is patently false. Ignoring real group differences is every bit as mistaken as exaggerating them.

But even if your brain's statistician worked as well with people as it did with circles, identifying the magnitude of real group differences accurately, it would still be left with the fundamental problem that plagues all statistics: explanation. Your brain's statistician can calculate averages and detect differences in a matter of milliseconds, but the world gives wicked evidence to explain why those differences actually exist. One of my sons brought this to our attention very clearly one day when he asked my wife, "Mom, why do only dads get gray hair?" His brain's statistician was brilliant enough to notice a very large gender difference in his world, where none of the older women have gray hair but nearly all of the older men do, but his statistician missed on the explanation. When a statistician moves beyond the data, problems ensue.

Stereotypes routinely stray beyond observation and into explanation. When groups differ, the easy answer is that the differences are due to something essential, internal, or stable about the group members, rather than to something external and therefore unstable, such as social norms and hair dye. Blacks achieve less because of poor genetic endowment. Men are unfeeling because they have a "male brain" with too much testosterone. Or women are bad at math because they lack logical reasoning skills—perhaps from too much estrogen and oxytocin? But the real world is more wicked than these simple explanations suggest. Even if you recognize a difference between groups perfectly, you may still misunderstand its cause completely.

To see how, let's start with a difference that you and I will hopefully experience very personally: differences between the minds of the young and the old. In many ways, growing old is no fun. Over the years, our bodies slowly fail. Not only that, but our minds slowly fail as well. Tests of cognitive performance consistently show a steady decrease in performance across the life span on almost every test of cognitive functioning you can imagine. On the following page is the most depressing figure for anyone looking to the life ahead.

Every year, when I ask my MBA students to explain these differences in class, I get two kinds of explanations. One kind is "you just get old and stuff stops working": cells die and nerves fray and strokes happen. The other kind is "use it or lose it": older people get stuck in their ways, stop learning new things, no longer take classes, and therefore have brains that work less effectively than they once did. Both theories describe a widely held assumption that "aging" and "decline" are synonyms. "When biological gerontologists and laypersons use the term *aging*," writes gerontologist Edward Masoro, "they are most often referring to . . . the progressive deterioration during the adult period of life."[36] Aging and decline go hand in hand. Just accept it. Your life is all downhill from here.

Notice, however, one other important feature of this aging process: the cognitive and physical declines are no surprise to you. Your stereotypes tell you that memory declines with age, along with your knees and your back and everything else. It's a part of the cultural ether in many parts of the world. Might knowing these stereotypes be self-

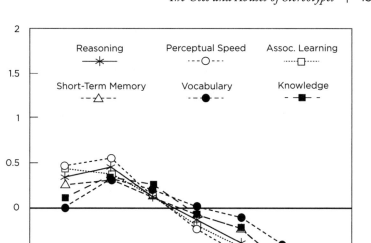

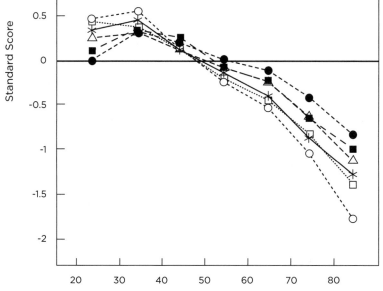

This figure shows performance on six different tests of cognitive functioning across the life span. All decline precipitously with age.[37]

fulfilling in some way? If you believe you can't jump, how hard would you try to dunk a basketball? If you spent your entire life believing that your mind declines with age, how hard would you try to think when taking a test? Might elderly people perform worse at least partly because of their own *stereotypes* about the elderly, rather than because of something about *being* elderly? Maybe, according to several research findings.

First, the cognitive declines observed across age vary around the world. Cultures that revere the elderly as wise, sage, and learned—such as in parts of China—do not show the same degree of decline observed in cultures with more negative views of the elderly—such as in most of the United States.[38] These stereotypes about aging not only seem to affect mental functioning, they seem to affect a person's physical functioning as well. One representative study measured the aging stereotypes of 229 volunteers who were eighteen to thirty-nine years old and then tracked their health histories for thirty-eight years.[39] At the end of the study, 56 percent of those with negative stereotypes about the elderly (remember, measured thirty-eight years before) had suffered a major cardiovascular event (mainly a heart attack or stroke), compared to only 18 percent of those who had positive elderly stereotypes. Given this, it's not surprising that young people who have positive stereotypes about aging tend to live longer as well. In one study, middle-aged adults with relatively positive stereotypes about aging lived, on average, 7.5 years longer than those with relatively negative stereotypes about aging.[40]

Second, even if the prevailing stereotypes about aging are negative within a culture, glimmers of positive stereotypes exist as well. If beliefs about aging affect mental functioning, then older adults should function better when they're thinking about the positive stereotypes associated with aging. In one experiment, elderly volunteers looking at a computer screen were briefly shown words consistent with either a positive stereotype about the elderly ("wise," "sage," "learned," and so on) or a negative stereotype about the elderly (for example, "senile," "demented," "confused"), in order to trigger either positive or negative stereotypes.[41] The psychologists measured the volunteers' cognitive functioning on six different tests, both before and after they saw the flashed words, testing for changes in performance. These measures are presumed to index relatively stable cognitive abilities that are known to decline precipitously with age, but the results of this experiment suggest otherwise. Those flashed positive stereotypes about the elderly did significantly better on these tests after seeing the words than they had done before, whereas those flashed negative stereotypes did significantly worse. When we observe age-related declines in cognitive functioning, are we learning something about inevitable biological decline, or are we learning something about how stereotypes could be self-fulfilling?

Stereotypes about aging are not unique. Consider another: beliefs about intellectual performance by race and ethnicity, as measured by standardized tests. Think for a moment about Asians, Caucasians, and African Americans. Which group scores the best on standardized tests of verbal and math performance, which group scores the worst, and which is in the middle? It's just you and me here at the moment, so you're well away from the eyes of political correctness and can think honestly. I'm confident that your honest stereotypes capture the observed differences well. On math, Asians consistently do better than Caucasians, who, in turn, do better than African Americans. On verbal exams, Caucasians do a little better than Asians, who, in turn, do better than African Americans. These differences are no surprise. The differences between Asians and Caucasians are relatively small, whereas the achievement gap for African Americans is very large, and these differences have been observed now for decades. The question is, Why?

There are certainly many reasons, but one seems to involve knowing the stereotypes associated with your own group's expected performance. In one experiment that sparked a cottage industry of subsequent research, black and white Stanford University students took a short version of the verbal SAT exam.[42] All students completed a cover sheet before taking the test, requiring them to fill in some demographic information (such as age, year in school, and college major). Then came one small twist. For some students, the last item on the cover page asked them to indicate their race. For the other students, this last item was simply omitted. This slight manipulation had a profound effect: the African American students did significantly worse when they listed their race on the first page than when they did not. This effect has now been replicated so many times and in so many different ways that a large number of psychologists study little else.[43] It is also leading to effective interventions that improve minority student performance by reducing the threat posed by negative stereotypes.[44] When we observe race-related differences in intellectual performance, are we learning something about fundamental differences between blacks and whites or are we learning something about how stereotypes can be self-fulfilling?

Finally, consider again the reportedly *essential* gender difference in social skills—that women are more empathic than men and are better able to understand others' thoughts and feelings. When men and women were paid to do well on a test of mind reading, making everyone try as hard as they could, even this typically modest gender difference was eliminated.[45] Men who took a test of their ability to decode nonverbal cues did worse when they were told that the test measured social sensitivity than when they were told that it measured information processing.[46] The major difference between men and women in their social senses seems to be as much about how hard they try as about some stable difference in how good they are. Again, when we observe differences in empathy between men and women, are we learning something about fundamental differences or something about how stereotypes about gender roles can be self-fulfilling?

The point of these findings is that our stereotypes about group differences could be precisely right but our explanations of those differences could be profoundly wrong. The elderly can behave differently than the young, blacks differently than whites, and women differently than men *because* of stereotypes about these groups rather than because of any inherent differences between these groups that our brain's statistician observes. The tragic history of intergroup violence, prejudice, and discrimination does not then come so much from mistaken awareness of differences between groups as it does from mistaken explanations for those differences. The late Harvard biologist Stephen Jay Gould expressed this sentiment best when describing the shameful history of explanations for race differences in science:

> We pass through this world but once. Few tragedies can be more extensive than the stunting of life, few injustices deeper than the denial of an opportunity to strive or even to hope, by a limit imposed from without, but falsely identified as lying within. . . . We inhabit a world of human differences and predilections, but the extrapolation of these facts to theories of rigid limits is ideology.

■ ■ ■

Our impressions about the minds of others seem to reflect the world we observe. Stereotypes, in this way, seem like mirrors. But our stereotypes about other people can also affect the world we observe, and in this way can also act like magnets. Our belief that groups are opposed to each other may push those groups even further apart in our minds than they are in reality, leading to stereotypes that exaggerate genuine differences between groups. Our belief that groups differ can also push the targets of these stereotypes to behave in ways that are consistent with them. The historian Jan Morris, for instance, felt these forces acutely after changing her gender from male to female. "The more I was treated as a woman, the more woman I became," she wrote. But most of the time, the subtle magnetic distortion of the data observed by our brain's statistician are every bit as invisible as any other magnetic force. Failing to appreciate its influence on both our beliefs about the minds of distant others and on reality itself is a primary source of error for your brain's otherwise brilliant statistician.

If there's anything surprising left to learn about stereotypes, however, it's how quickly we drop them as soon as we go from reasoning about the mind of a group to the mind of an individual whose behavior we observe directly. Almost everybody, for example, hates politicians. "Bloodsucking," "lying," "cheating," and "philandering" are just a few of the adjectives that come quickly to mind. And yet, for all of this hatred, incumbents have an enormous advantage in elections. Since 1964, 93 percent of incumbents in the U.S. House of Representatives have been reelected.[47] At the point when disapproval of "Congress" as a whole was at a historic low in the United States, with less than 20 percent of citizens approving of its performance, a majority nevertheless said their *own* representative deserved to be reelected. "Politicians" are terrible, but *yours* may not be thought of as a typical politician.

The speed with which you can drop a stereotype when evaluating an individual can be startling (or perhaps encouraging). In one experiment, volunteers who watched a fifteen-*second* interview of either a black or a white student describing campus life showed clear evidence of thinking about these students in terms of their ethnic stereotypes. After 12 *minutes,* however, no trace of stereotypical thinking could be found.[48] When you know very little about someone, the gaps in your knowledge are filled in by information about who a person *is.* But when you know more, that stereotypical knowledge seems to be quickly supplanted by what a person *does*. The final way we come to know the minds of others is by watching how someone acts and then working backward one step to the presumed thoughts and beliefs and attitudes that caused this behavior.

This is a great strategy, but, like many great strategies, it can lead to unexpected failures. The problem with this mind-reading strategy is that behavior provides a window into another's mind that operates like a magician's mirror, sometimes twisting and misleading and at other times operating as a clear pane of glass. The magician's trick is to make you think you're looking at a clear pane that reflects what lies behind it when you're actually looking at a curved mirror that distorts your vision. Believing that you're looking at a clear pane instead of a curved mirror is exactly the same mistake you can make when thinking about the minds of other people. These mind-reading mistakes, as I'll try to show next, may be some of the most unfortunate of all.

7

How Actions Can Mislead

There is no such thing as an accident; it is fate misnamed.

—Napoleon Bonaparte

Walter Vance was a wonderful person who had a heart attack at the worst possible time—in the aisle of a crowded Target store on the busiest shopping day of the year, Black Friday. Amid the throngs of deal-crazed shoppers, Vance's fatal struggle was almost completely ignored. Witnesses later reported seeing nearby shoppers going about their normal business as Vance lay collapsed in an aisle; one person after another passed without stopping to help.[1]

Having a heart attack is horrible but not entirely surprising. In America alone, roughly two thousand people die each day from heart disease.[2] What's surprising is having a heart attack in the middle of a crowded store on the busiest day of the year and being almost completely ignored. What on earth could these bystanders have been thinking?

The explanation was obvious to one of Vance's friends. "Where is the Good Samaritan side of people?" she asked. "I just don't understand if people didn't help what their reason was, other than greed because of a sale." The obvious reason is that these shoppers were indifferent bargain hunters who cared more about reaching up to grab a cheap coffeepot than about reaching down to help a dying man. Callous actions are caused by callous minds.

This explanation is obvious because it reflects a common sense that a person's mind corresponds directly to that person's actions, a systematic sense that psychologists refer to as the *correspondence bias*.[3] People show how they feel, choose what they want, and do as they please. You can therefore, according to this common sense, infer a person's emotions, motivations, and preferences from their expressions, choices, and actions. Like Napoleon, our sixth sense about the minds of others suggests that there are no accidents. When a shopper fails to help a dying man, his callous mind is clear.

This common sense is good sense as long as expressions are honest, choices are deliberate, motives are simple, and everyone is indeed free to do whatever they desire without being influenced by the context around them. But life is riddled with exceptions to all of these general rules that lead to predictable mistakes when trying to understand the minds of others. In fact, believing that shoppers deliberately failed to help Walter Vance simply because of their callous greed is one of those mistakes. To show you how, I first need to describe what our common sense about others' actions can miss.

OUT OF SIGHT, OUT OF MIND

In ancient human history, most people believed that the world was flat because that's exactly how it looked. No amount of squinting or jumping or moving this way and that made it look any different. No person ever said it looked curvy if you stand *right here,* or exactly like a ball if you were way up *there.* Our distant ancestors therefore tended to believe their eyes. The world is flat.

It's impossible to fault our forebears. They were smart people who came by this mistake honestly, believing what they could see and being unaware of what they couldn't. Recognizing roundness requires a broader perspective than what your eyes at ground level can see.[4]

Judging a mind based only on a person's behavior can resemble flat-earth thinking because understanding the mind of any person requires a broader perspective than our experience routinely provides. It requires considering not only what a person does in plain sight but also the less obvious context within which that behavior occurs. When a man looks into the camera and renounces his citizenship, you have every reason to assume that he means what he says. When that camera zooms out to show a jihadist holding a gun to the man's head in one hand and a script in the other, you know his words are misleading. Considering the broader context allows you to understand the hostage's mind more accurately.

The problem is that life is viewed routinely through the zoom lens, narrowly focused on persons rather than on the broader contexts that influence a person's actions. When an Olympic gold medalist sprints across the finish line, we see the triumph of an individual's talent, skill, desire, and will to win. Invisible are the thousands of hours spent in practice, the time and money shelled out by parents and sponsors for support, the luck of finding just the right coach at just the right time, and the tremendous fortune that comes from living in a peaceful country where a person can devote a life to sports rather than survival. The recipe for winning a gold medal involves many ingredients that are completely hidden from view while you're watching the final race. Similarly, when a company performs well, the CEO's decisions and strategies are on full display. Harder to notice is the health of the broader economy, the quality of the company's existing employees, the organizational structure responsible for all day-to-day activities, and the luck of having the right company at the right time that also contributed to the CEO's success.

When the broader perspective is out of view, it's hard to fault sportscasters who explain gold medals as the product of will and desire ("She just wanted it more today") without considering the broader context that also enables success, or market analysts who explain a company's performance by describing the CEO's wisdom and brilliance while neglecting dominant market forces and existing organizational structures. They come by their inferences honestly.[5]

To see how such inferences can lead to obvious mistakes when thinking about others, imagine yourself in the studio audience of a classic psychology experiment. The experiment runs like a game show—we'll call it the Quiz Bowl.[6] Taking center stage in front of you is the Quiz Bowl's host (the experimenter) and two research volunteers, one who is randomly chosen to be the "contestant" and the other to be the "questioner." The questioner is told to head backstage and come up with ten questions—on his or her own, without any other assistance—designed to stump the contestant. This is actually pretty easy to do. Think for a moment about bits of trivia or facts you happen to know from your experiences, hobbies, job and it won't take you long to come up ten questions that could stump almost anyone.

After taking some time to think, the questioner returns and begins posing the questions he or she generated to the contestant. As requested, the questions are extremely difficult: "How many islands are in the Philippines?" "What are the real names of Axl Rose and Slash from Guns n' Roses?" "How long does it take the moon Phobos to circle Mars?"[7] The contestant is indeed stumped. In the original experiment, contestants were able to answer, on average, only four out of ten of the questioner's items correctly.

Now the critical question: How knowledgeable is the questioner, and how knowledgeable is the contestant? The answer seems obvious. The questioner looks bright, and the contestant looks dim. Indeed, in the original experiment, audience members rated the questioners as exceptionally knowledgeable (in the eighty-second percentile compared to their peers) but the contestants as merely average (forty-ninth percentile). Even the contestants took their performance to heart, rating the questioners as considerably more knowledgeable than themselves.

This demonstration illustrates what may be the most profound insight about how we understand the minds of others, one that reflects a bit of flat-earth thinking. The two players in this experiment were on center stage, and audience members' evaluations of their performance had everything to do with the minds of the players and seemingly little to do with the context those minds were in. The questioner asked difficult questions and, therefore, looked bright. The contestant answered incorrectly and, therefore, looked dim. This is the correspondence bias, inferring a mind that corresponds with observed actions.

In fact, you don't learn anything about the intellect of these two players, any more than you learn about the beliefs of a hostage renouncing his citizenship at gunpoint or learn that the Earth is flat by opening your eyes and looking at it from ground level. In this context, the questioner is given an enormous role-conferred advantage over the contestant, one ensuring that every questioner will be able to stump every contestant. Like the boss grilling employees or professors quizzing their students, the questioner was able to generate questions from any area of expertise whatsoever and overlook all areas of his or her own ignorance. The contestant, in contrast, had no such luck and simply had to answer whatever questions came along. But because the benefit of the questioner's role is less obvious than a hostage's gun, common sense infers that the players are of unequal intellect rather than on an unequal playing field. As is sometimes said of the questionable accolades given to those born into success, we conclude that a person who started on third base actually hit a triple.

Only a fool would infer that a person who slips on an icy sidewalk *wanted* to fall, but the contextual forces that contribute to our successes and stumbles are routinely less obvious than ice on a sidewalk. This makes it easy to be misled by a person's actions. When Hurricane Katrina hit New Orleans, for instance, Americans were befuddled by the thousands who stayed rather than evacuating. As ABC News put it, "It's hard to understand the mind-set of those who ignored evacuation orders." This befuddlement comes straight from the correspondence bias: the commonsense assumption that those who stayed *chose* to stay and deliberately *ignored* evacuation orders. You can hear hints of this assumption in the words of Homeland Security chief Michael Chertoff: "Officials called for a mandatory evacuation. Some people chose not to obey that order. That was a mistake on their part."[8] Michael Brown, the infamous director of FEMA, also stated that the death toll is "going to be attributable to a lot of people who did not heed the advance warnings. I don't make judgments about why people chose not to leave but, you know, there was a mandatory evacuation of New Orleans."[9]

Brown may say he doesn't make judgments, but others miles away and worlds apart from the reality of those who stayed are more than happy to. "There's a certain amount of denial involved," asserts psychiatrist John Stutesman of Northwestern University. "They allow themselves to believe they can handle the storm."[10] A survey of randomly selected Americans and university students found similar sentiments.[11] When asked to list three adjectives to describe those who left, words related to "smart," "responsible," and "independent" were most common. For those who stayed? Words related to "stupid," "passive," and "inflexible" topped the list. Only a mindless idiot, after all, would choose to withstand a category 5 hurricane. Stupid is as stupid does.

This explanation resonates with a commonsense belief that behavior reveals a person's mind, but it does not resonate as well with the actual experience of most who left and stayed, because the broader context is not quite as easy to see. Compared to those who left, those who stayed were disproportionately poor, had a geographically narrower social network, had larger families (both children and extended members), had less access to reliable news, and were considerably less likely to own a car.[12] If you had money to pay for an extended hotel stay, a relatively small family to move, a car to get all of you there, or had far-away friends to stay with, you could *choose* to leave. If you had no money for an extended hotel stay, no car to get you out, a large family to move, and no long-distance friends to stay with, what choice did you have? Little (or none) of this broader context is captured when news cameras zoom in on people standing on rooftops or wading through floodwater. Believing that those who stayed *chose* to do so is therefore like believing the Earth is flat or that the questioner is brilliant. Only if you look with a broader perspective will you see that many stranded on their rooftops were waving the contestant card.

The point of these findings is not that people are simply victims of their circumstances or that people's actions never reveal their preferences. Certainly some people did choose to stay and deliberately ignored the hurricane warnings, and some questioners are definitely more knowledgeable than some contestants in the Quiz Bowl. The point is that the difficulty of observing broader circumstances makes it easy to assume that actions reveal much more about a person's inner mind than they actually do.

SPOCK AND A POINTY ROCK

It's hard to take the broad perspective when evaluating the minds of others because the contextual forces that guide our actions are routinely lost in the background rather than waved clearly before our eyes.

It is therefore those who know the most about the broader context who are least likely to assume a simple correspondence between minds and actions. In the Quiz Bowl experiment, for instance, contestants and audience members came to believe that the questioners were geniuses, but the questioners themselves, who knew the most about their random good fortune, did not make this mistake. They understood the difficulty of generating ten challenging questions and were well aware of all of the questions they couldn't ask because they didn't know the answers themselves. As a result, the questioners did not think they were any more knowledgeable than the contestants were. Only the questioners, aware of the broader perspective, understood the minds involved.

This makes it clear that committing the correspondence bias is far from inevitable, but avoiding it requires a broader view of someone's actions. Shortly after beating a cancer diagnosis and winning his first Tour de France, in 1999, for instance, Lance Armstrong held a press conference in which he was asked a question that allowed him to reveal his broader perspective.[13] Speaking straight from common sense and a limited perspective, a reporter asked Armstrong whether his Tour victory proved that with enough will and determination you could overcome anything. Certainly a narrow focus on Armstrong's success suggested as much, but Armstrong knew the broader context of his recovery, which had nothing to do with his mind. His response? "No," he reportedly said, describing how, while undergoing chemotherapy, he had seen plenty of people who'd wanted to live even more than he did, who'd fought just as hard, but who had still died. Beating cancer, he said, was about much more than grit. It was about science, money, and luck.

Armstrong was more attentive to the broader situation he was in than the reporter was. Around the globe, people in cultures that are more attentive to the situations people are in are also less likely to infer another person's mind simply from their actions. Those living in collectivist cultures and those generally more concerned with social norms and interpersonal harmony (such as in Southeast Asia) are, broadly speaking, more likely to recognize when people's actions reflect the dictates of their roles and environments rather than their corresponding states of mind, compared to people in cultures that place an emphasis on individual freedom and choice—namely, individualistic cultures (such as the United States and Western Europe).[14] Those of lower socioeconomic status who frequently experience contextual constraints on their choices are also somewhat more sensitive to context when explaining others' actions, compared to those of higher socioeconomic status with fewer constraints.[15] Even religions that place more emphasis on ritual, practice, and tradition (such as Judaism) than on belief itself (such as Protestant Christianity) preach a more complicated relationship between minds and actions and have followers who may be more sensitive to context.[16]

Like many habits, the tendency to make inferences about a person's state of mind simply from their observed actions can be weakened intentionally; you can learn to overcome it. But just as with the egocentric biases we discussed in chapter 5, mental habits are hard to eliminate completely. Even when it is transparently obvious that a person's mind does not match his actions—that the CEO benefited from great fortune rather than great wisdom or that a person is going along just to get along—it can still be hard to disbelieve your eyes entirely. Just ask Spock.

Or, more precisely, ask Leonard Nimoy, the actor who played Spock on *Star Trek*. As you may recall, Mr. Spock is a fictional character from a fictional planet, part human and part alien. The alien part made Spock completely rational and entirely unemotional, the economists' notion of a purely rational actor brought to life. Every viewer knew that Nimoy was only acting, with every line scripted, but Nimoy nevertheless found people treating him like Spock in his everyday life. Nimoy wrote two books of poetry, for instance, and his readers' most common reaction was one of surprise because the "writing was so sensitive" and "not what you'd expect . . . from a cool, rational, pragmatic, logical person." Passengers would flash him the Vulcan salute on airplanes, women were attracted to his presumed rationality, and one even asked him to heal her friend by "extending his powers." When actors are typecast by the roles they play, movie fans are merely doing what seems to come naturally even when they know that actors are only pretending. It's like assuming that the hostage believes, just a little bit, what he's being told to say at the end of a loaded gun. This treatment eventually got to be too much for Nimoy, who felt it necessary to publish an autobiography pushing hard against the correspondence bias to describe what he was *really* like as a person. The title was *I Am Not Spock.*

Star Trek fans are notoriously unusual, but they're perfectly normal in this respect. Most of us are fooled by competent acting. This is why we enjoy fictional movies in the first place. But it is also why psychologists find that most people trust what others tell them even when they might be lying,[17] why a coerced but competently delivered apology creates just as much forgiveness as an honest apology,[18] and why insincere flattery works nearly as well as sincere flattery.[19] These mistakes come not from mindlessly believing what you know is false but, rather, from the difficulty of disbelieving behavior that we naturally take at face value.

These mental habits appear to go way back into childhood. At a very early age, you and I learned to understand other people's actions in terms of their corresponding intentions, because doing so generally makes such darned good sense. When your mother reaches for a cup, she's not just grabbing something randomly but is showing what she *wants*. What you can see—a reaching hand—is showing you something you cannot see—your mother's motives and intentions. By age one, human infants have become experts at associating people's actions with their underlying intentions. By age three, kids have become so accustomed to this association that they apply it almost everywhere. Ask children in an experiment to tell you why a rock is pointy and they are more likely to offer an explanation that implies a mindful designer—"so that animals could scratch on them when they got itchy"—than one that implies an unintended accident—"because bits of stuff piled up over time."[20]

Psychologists find that this strong form of the correspondence bias declines in American and British children around the age of nine or ten, and that it does so because children learn to overcome their first instinct with more careful thought rather than dropping their first instinct altogether. Distract adults by making them solve math problems while explaining the existence of pointy rocks,[21] or impair their ability to think hard by splitting their attention,[22] and the correspondence bias shows itself again loud and clear. Even if careful thought suggests otherwise, the first instinct is still to assume that actions are produced by corresponding intentions.

This persistent first instinct helps explain some mistakes we might make in thinking about the minds of others. When juries are asked to disregard impermissible evidence they once believed was relevant, they do their best to undo its influence but still render verdicts biased in the direction of its implications.[23] When people learn that a criminal confession was coerced under duress, they do their best to disregard it but nevertheless conclude that the confessor is guilty.[24] And when people are given flattering feedback by a judge in an experiment, they like a judge who says nice things more than a judge who says mean things even when they know that the judge is reading the comments verbatim from a script.[25] Now you know why insincere flattery will get you everywhere.

It may now be a little less surprising that movie stars so routinely fall in love with their costars after pretending to be in love in a scripted romance. Think of Pitt and Jolie, Bogart and Bacall, Burton and Taylor, Ryan and Crowe, or Warren Beatty and nearly every woman he pretended to love (Natalie Wood, Julie Christie, Diane Keaton, and Madonna). The list of scripted-to-serious romances is long,[26] but perhaps no longer surprisingly long. Even though you know that Leonard Nimoy was only pretending to be rational, you might still be inclined to hire him if your company needed a decision analyst.

THE OFFSPRING OF ERROR

Failing to calibrate our sixth sense to recognize the power of the broader context can create considerable misunderstanding, from assuming that accidents were intentional to crediting people for successes beyond their control. Those who carry out immoral instructions are often punished more harshly than those who give the instructions in the first place,[27] and those who benefit from chance are viewed as talented. The earnings of active mutual fund managers, for instance, are no better than one would expect by random chance alone,[28] and yet they are paid and promoted as if their performance reflects some personal intellect or talent.

More important, misunderstanding the power of context can lead us to design ineffective solutions to important problems. If our intuitions tell us that people do what they want, then one path to changing their behavior is obvious: you need to make people *want* the right things. You can hear this thinking rolling right out of Michael Brown's mouth when explaining how to avoid repeating the disaster following Hurricane Katrina: "We've got to figure out some way to convince people that whenever warnings go out, it's for their own good." The main problem in Brown's mind was that people didn't *want* to leave, and so the solution is to persuade people more effectively the next time. This solution may create a great warning system that leaves just as many people stranded the next time. Many who stayed wanted desperately to leave but couldn't. They didn't need *convincing*, they needed a *bus*.

You can see the offspring of this error in many well-meaning interventions. People littering too much? Fund a campaign to change people's minds about littering. Students doing poorly in class? Pay them for good performance so that they *want* to do better and therefore work harder. The poor making unwise financial choices? Roll out a financial literacy program to make their minds smarter. Americans getting too fat? Try to raise awareness about the dangers of obesity so that they'll be more motivated to lose weight. Common sense suggests targeting people's minds to change their actions, but many of these solutions are useless because they misunderstand the cause of the problems. As my colleagues Richard Thaler and Cass Sunstein point out in their book *Nudge,* much more effective for changing behavior is targeting the broader context rather than individual minds, making it easier for people to do the things they already want to do.[29] Consider four examples:

- ENCOURAGING ENVIRONMENTALISM. Convincing people not to litter is hard, and most already know that they're not supposed to simply toss their garbage on the ground. The bigger problem is that human beings are social animals and tend to do what others around them are doing. If you want to keep people from littering in your county park, a good start would be to add additional trash cans to make it easier to do the right thing, and then to pick up existing trash that otherwise makes it look like everyone else is littering. Human beings, like any animal, are more likely to do things that are easy rather than hard. They don't have some deep desire to litter; they're just more likely to do whatever is going on around them.

- IMPROVING SCHOOL PERFORMANCE. Free-market economists believe the same thing our common sense does: that people do what they're incentivized to do (that is, want to do). So according to this analysis, poor-performing students should do better if you reward them with something everyone wants: money. However, recent mega-experiments involving tens of thousands of students and teachers, costing roughly $80 million in all, found that paying students and teachers for improved performance was completely ineffective. Writes Roland Fryer, the Harvard economist who directed the research, "I find no evidence that teacher incentives increase student performance, attendance, or graduation, nor do I find any evidence that the incentives change student or teacher behavior. If anything, teacher incentives may decrease student achievement, especially in larger schools." If you want to improve students' performance, manipulating their own will, or the teacher's will, to do better doesn't seem to be the way. Most students and teachers want to succeed, and so more effective is identifying barriers in their environment that keep them from doing better. The biggest barrier? Arguably not spending enough time actually learning in school. Longer school days, shorter summer breaks, and fewer vacations improve student achievement. If you want students to do better in school, a good place to start is to have them spend more time in it.

- REDUCING POVERTY. Poverty is one of society's most persistent problems, and the poor don't seem to be helping themselves as much as they should. They disproportionately take out payday loans with obscenely high interest rates, getting themselves caught in endless debt traps that require taking on more debt to pay off past debt. One common theory about poverty explains it in the language of mental deficiencies: the poor are simply not as smart as the rest of us, and they do stupid things with their money that keep them poor. What's the fix? A common strategy is to roll out financial literacy classes to teach the poor to be smarter. The problem? Those classes seem to help the poor very little.[30] The reason may be that the poor turn out to be smarter and more informed about money than these policies imply. In one set of experiments, psychologists found that poor people make fewer mistakes on financial problems that routinely trip up the wealthy.[31] One of the bigger problems is the lack of trust in financial institutions that is rampant in poor communities, which is compounded by the lack of access to simple banking services like savings accounts. The poor take out payday loans in part because they don't have other banking services they can rely on. One effective way to help break the chronic debt trap is to give the poor access to banking services. Poverty will not yield to simple solutions like this alone, of course, but it's unlikely to yield at all using assumptions that poverty is largely the product of stupidity.

• REDUCING OBESITY. Americans are in the midst of a growing obesity epidemic. The solution is obvious—eat less and exercise more—but the problem persists. Common sense again suggests that people who eat too much either don't know any better or don't *want* to lose weight, and so public service campaigns tend to target one or the other. For instance, the "Take Five to Live Light" national awareness campaign sponsored partly by the Obesity Action Coalition "aims to educate the more than 93 million Americans affected by the disease of obesity." The implication is that people are overweight because they don't know any better. This is a very well-intentioned campaign, but it misses potentially more effective solutions because it misdiagnoses the problem. These solutions would not try to educate us about the importance of eating less but would instead make it easier to do what we all already know we should be doing. Most of us, for instance, have a strong tendency to eat whatever amount of food is placed before us. Serve movie popcorn in larger buckets and people eat more in direct proportion to the size of their bucket, even if the popcorn is old and stale.[32] Allow people to scoop M&M's with a larger spoon and they will eat more in direct proportion to the size of the spoon.[33] Over the last one hundred years, dinner plates in the United States have gotten 40 percent larger, and when you give people larger plates, they take more food from the buffet.[34] If you'd like to eat less, a good place to start is to stop overestimating your own willpower, toss out the junk food in your house so that you can't eat it, and move your modern megasized plates into a distant cupboard and eat off your smaller salad plates instead. Brian Wansink, the researcher responsible for most of these results, has even created a movement for you to join: the Small Plate Movement. Don't worry, only your waistline will notice the difference. Diners report feeling just as full when they eat everything off of a modestly sized plate as they do when they eat considerably more off an enormous plate.

A sixth sense that assumes that a person's mind corresponds directly to his or her actions misses the importance of context in shaping behavior, misunderstands the causes of behavior, and is unable to change anyone's behavior for the better, including one's own.

UNHELPFULLY GOOD SAMARITANS

With all of this chapter behind us, let's go back to Walter Vance and take a second look at the callous bystanders who failed to help him to see if we can understand them more clearly. The bystanders may have been callous and greedy, as their actions imply, but there's little reason to think they were markedly greedier than the rest of us. Their problem was being in the very kind of context that could keep people who would otherwise be Good Samaritans from helping.

Every bit of our common sense tells us that some people are helpful and others are not. If you're suffering in an emergency, it therefore makes sense that the more people around you, the more likely you are to find one of these Good Samaritans who will help you. But research confirms over and over that as the number of bystanders increases, the likelihood that any one of them will help you actually decreases.[35] If you find yourself in an emergency situation in public, you want only a few people around instead of a huge crowd. The ideal number might be two: one to help you and the other to call an ambulance.

Understanding why more bystanders actually reduces helping requires a broad lens rather than a zoom lens. If someone has a heart attack in a store as you're going about your holiday shopping, two things have to happen before you can intervene. First, you need to notice that some event has occurred. This seems easy in hindsight, but it is surprisingly difficult in real sight because attention is limited.[36] You're focused on either this *or* that but rarely on both this *and* that. As the number of shoppers going about their business increases, the likelihood that you'll miss one of them in need increases as well. Second, to intervene you have to recognize the situation as an emergency. This is where an increasing number of other bystanders gets really problematic. What is so clearly a heart attack when you're reading about it in the newspaper may look considerably less obvious when it's happening right before your eyes. At midnight on the busiest shopping day of the year, might someone be lying down to take a rest? Or maybe drunk? On drugs? You're concerned, but this is an odd situation. And so you do what social animals do when they're unsure: you look to other people for information about how to behave, to see if others seem as concerned as you feel. But everyone's playing it cool just like you, not wanting to be the first person to jump in and help someone who doesn't need it. Because everyone else looks unconcerned, you conclude that it must not be an emergency, and so does everyone else. The irony is that every bystander may be deeply concerned but conclude that every other bystander is not, making it inappropriate to intervene in what does not appear to be an emergency.[37] Failing to recognize an emergency makes someone human, not necessarily a callous jerk.

Calibrating common sense to recognize this broader context helps explain not only why good people may fail to help in an emergency but also why many bystanders *do* intervene. According to Vance's wife, six women eventually came to his aid, all nurses. Notice that unlike most other shoppers that night, nurses know exactly what an emergency looks like and what to do when they see one. They are also likely to be more attentive to such emergencies because they spend their work lives attending to them. Does this make these six women heroes? Of course it does, because they acted to save a dying man's life. But we can now understand their actions in a way that appreciates heroism more accurately, as something less foreign and more readily achievable for any of us. Just as evil can be banal, so, too, can heroism.[38] It need not require unwavering self-control or inherently altruistic tendencies, acts performed by angels that bear little resemblance to the rest of us. The truth of the human condition is that the capacity to be a Good Samaritan can reside in all of us, if we're put in the right circumstances at the right time. That does not in any way diminish the acts of those who intervene to save lives in need, often at tremendous personal risk. Instead, it should lead to a recognition that under the right circumstances, you could do it, too.[39]

■ ■ ■

Others' minds are not open books, but this doesn't deter us from trying to read them anyway. The tools at our intuitive disposal—our own mind, stereotypes about the minds of others, and others' observed actions—are simplifying heuristics that give imperfect insight into the minds of others. The mistakes they lead to do not render them useless: each provides some accurate insight. But these mistakes are also not accidental: each creates predictable errors that keep us from perfect understanding. Egocentrism exaggerates the extent to which others' minds match one's own. Stereotypes can highlight differences at the expense of similarity. And others' actions can prompt oversimplified assumptions about the minds behind them. These heuristics provide simple shortcuts for understanding the minds of others, but they come at the cost of oversimplifying them. Others' minds are more complicated than your sixth sense often suggests.

Wisdom comes partly from knowing our limits and, therefore, being able to correct for them. But wisdom also comes from recognizing our strengths and trying to improve on them. If you really wanted to increase your understanding of others, what would you do? I think the answer, based on the evidence I'll describe next, is clear.

PART 4

THROUGH THE EYES
OF OTHERS

How can you be wiser about the minds of others?

8

How, and How Not, to Be a Better Mind Reader

> I am just as deaf as I am blind. The problems of deafness are
> deeper and more complex, if not more important than those of
> blindness. Deafness is a much worse misfortune. For it means
> the loss of the most vital stimulus—the sound of the voice
> that brings language, sets thoughts astir, and keeps us in the
> intellectual company of man.
>
> —Helen Keller

In religion, science fiction, and psychic nonsense, those who read minds do so with extrasensory powers. Gods are supernatural. The wizards in the Harry Potter books master Legilimency. Psychics claim clairvoyance.

None of these are available to you. I've just spent many pages detailing how our perfectly natural brains enable us to read, and sometimes misread, the minds of others, using no supernatural powers whatsoever. If you want to improve on that, what's a mere mortal to do?

One of two things, I'm told. While writing this book I've had the same conversation over and over again. After I mention that I'm working on a book about mind reading, my conversational partner assumes I'm writing about either body language (learning to read facial cues or physical gestures) or perspective taking (learning to imagine yourself in another person's situation). Both approaches have intuitive appeal.

If you're unsure whether someone really likes you or not or is telling you the truth or not, you need to read the subtle cues their body presumably gives away. And self-centeredness keeps us from considering others' perspectives, making the injunction to "put yourself in another person's shoes" the go-to remedy for social misunderstanding. President Barack Obama, for instance, told the United Nations that "the deadlock [between the Israelis and Palestinians] will only be broken when each side learns to stand in each other's shoes."[1] Perspective taking is often described as a panacea for almost any kind of social conflict, whether it's between little kids on the playground or big kids on the battlefield, because imagining your reactions from a different perspective is presumably a good way to know another person's mind.

Both approaches suggest that you can hone the intuitive tools we've already described, the first by improving your perception and the second by improving your imagination. Which approach does the scientific evidence support?

Neither. Instead, I think the evidence suggests a third approach. Let me explain.

BODIES SPEAK, IN WHISPERS

Every liar supposedly has a tell. This is patently true among children, whose first attempts at lying are laughable, but the belief that a person's true intentions and emotions leak out in subtle cues is presumed to apply to adults as well. In *The Expression of the Emotions in Man and Animals,* Darwin even told us exactly where to look. "A man when moderately angry," he wrote, "or even enraged may command the movements of his body, but . . . those muscles of the face which are least obedient to the will, will sometimes alone betray a slight and passing emotion." The Supreme Court of Canada agrees, at least in principle: it now requires juries to view a witness in person in order to "adequately evaluate body language, facial expressions and other indicators of credibility."[2] Cable news channels employ "nonverbal analysts" to decode the true meaning of political posturing, some of whom write books that promise to make you a "veritable lie detector" by honing your body reading to perfection.[3] Sometimes this attention is comically overblown. As a sarcastic headline from the *Onion* jokes: "Nation demands more pre-debate news stories about body language."

How much of our minds do our bodies *really* show? Of course, nobody expects to communicate complicated thoughts with one's body, as if you could describe your life history, or articulate how it feels to be in love, or explain the Bill of Rights through pantomime alone. Bodies presumably reveal emotions rather than thoughts, but how much of our *emotions* do our bodies show compared to other channels of communication, such as our voices?

One way to find out is to make someone momentarily deaf or momentarily blind and test how accurately they can evaluate others. Thankfully, this doesn't require any actual eardrum piercing or eyeball popping. All that's required is to have a research participant watch a person on videotape describing an emotional experience with either the sound or the screen off. Researchers then compare the participant's beliefs about the speaker's emotions with the speaker's actual reported emotions. In one such experiment, volunteers listened to someone describing either a very positive or a very negative emotional experience. Storytellers reported how positive or negative they were feeling as they were telling the story by moving a slider along a scale in front of them. Volunteers used the same type of slider to predict how the storyteller was feeling at each moment. The more a volunteer accurately understood what a storyteller was feeling, the more closely their scale movements would align.

When the researchers calculated the volunteers' accuracy, they found that those who could only *see* the storyteller were significantly less accurate than those who could only *hear* the storyteller. That is, emotions were carried primarily on the speaker's voice.[4] Those who could only see the storytellers were still more accurate than they would have been simply by random guessing, but not by all that much. Body language speaks, but only in whispers.

Jen and I learned to keep the importance of body language in perspective after bringing our adopted children home from Ethiopia. At the ages of five and three, they spoke barely a word of English beyond "mommy" and "daddy." We knew only enough Amharic to understand whether they wanted to go to the refrigerator or to the bathroom. Our life shrank instantly when using only body language. We could discuss nothing with our new children beyond what we could point at or touch in the immediate here and now. Anything that had happened in the past or might happen in the future was out of bounds. Time and space were lost. Where I went when I left for the office in the morning or when I'd come back, what I did while I was away, what we might have for dinner, what they might do this afternoon, and how we would now be their parents for as long as we live—all of that was off-limits. We started exaggerating our facial expressions and body gestures to almost comedic proportions in the hopes that they would understand what little our bodies could show more clearly. We looked silly but got along fine, as any new parents do with preverbal children, but we had only the shallowest understanding of our new son and daughter.

Over time, all parents learn to decode their children's bodily cues more effectively, going from almost no understanding to some understanding. You can see these gains from training in scientific research as well. Training to read body language and facial expressions through practice and feedback reliably increases one's ability to recognize those same cues in the near future. The gains are modest and fleeting but reliable.[5] However, even these modest gains tend to benefit only those who know the least or who are least motivated to do well to begin with. Those with autism, for instance, can benefit significantly from training in emotion recognition.[6] In studies with nonautistic adults, men benefit most because they perform slightly worse initially.[7] But if you're already moderately accurate to begin with or are already socially adept, then the benefits are likely to be minimal, at best. You're probably doing about as well as you can do.

Darwin's hypothesis, however, was more sophisticated. He argued that nonverbal facial cues ran deep in our evolutionary heritage and were therefore guided by the reflexive neural machinery we share with other animals. One's true emotions, such as fear and happiness, would then leak out in a quick expression and only be masked subsequently. You get your PhD in mind reading, according to Darwin, by learning to compare what a person shows quickly with what they say slowly.

The modern legacy of Darwin's *inhibition hypothesis* is what psychologists refer to as "microexpressions," very brief flashes of emotion lasting less than one-fifth of a second and shown either on the entire face or in just a small part of it. When a man shows a microexpression of a frown while saying he's happy, the idea goes, you learn that he's lying. This seems intuitively plausible. When you tell a blatant lie, you're aware of both what you know to be true and the inconsistent story you're relating. It's hard not to feel that the truth is leaking out, whether in microexpressions or other expressions that you can't control completely. The intuitive appeal of this idea has lent it considerable credence outside the scientific community. For three seasons, the television show *Lie to Me,* for instance, dramatized how the ability to read microexpressions can be used to identify criminals. Although *Lie to Me* is clearly fictional, the Transportation Security Administration was deadly serious when it based a massive training program on the presumed validity of microexpressions.[8] The program, called Screening of Passengers by Observation Techniques (SPOT), trains TSA agents to spot microexpressions and other purportedly subtle cues to deception. These "behavioral analysts" question passengers standing in the security line about seemingly innocuous topics. As of 2010, there were roughly three thousand trained analysts conducting these chat-downs at a reported 161 airports.[9]

Despite this popular appeal, the scientific credibility of claims about microexpressions is currently weak, at best. First, our intuitive sense that our emotions leak out and are clearly visible to others looks to be more of an egocentric illusion than objective reality. In experiments, when people are asked to lie or to conceal strong emotions, they tend to think the truth will be detected by others significantly more often than it actually is.[10] Most of us, for better or worse, are better liars than we think we are. Second, when researchers actively look for microexpressions that imply deceit, these clues not only seem to be exceptionally rare but also seem just as likely to be shown when people are telling the truth as when they are lying. In one experiment, researchers asked volunteers to look at a series of emotionally arousing photographs and to either express their true emotion or conceal it.[11] Out of the 697 facial expressions shown in this study, not one revealed a full microexpression (shown on both the top half and bottom half of the face), and only 14 (2 percent of the total) contained a partial microexpression (appearing only on either the top or bottom half of the face). And of those 14 partial microexpressions, half came when the person was trying to conceal their true emotion and the other half when the person was trying to reveal their true emotion. These exceptionally rare microexpressions seem just as likely to mislead you about the mind of another as they are to reveal it to you. Of course, this does not mean that all emotions can be concealed. What's surprising, though, is just how little our true emotions leak out, how often misleading expressions show up on our faces, and how hard any of these subtle cues are to detect accurately.[12]

Even high-stakes lies do not seem to produce dramatically more distinguishing cues than tiny white lies. One group of researchers summarized its findings this way: "Although high-stakes lies [may] be harder for liars to tell, their behavioral manifestations are neither obvious nor necessarily simply magnified versions of those of lower stakes lies."[13] Just because you can experience your own thoughts and emotions so clearly does not mean that they leak out anywhere near as clearly to others.

The SPOT program has been widely criticized as being built upon a weak scientific foundation. It's hard to fault the TSA for trying anything that might detect dangerous terrorists or criminals more effectively, but SPOT does not appear to be such a program. In the Government Accountability Office's report to Congress, of the approximately 2 billion passengers who traveled through SPOT airports between 2004 and 2008, roughly 152,000 were detained for additional questioning. Of those, 14,000 were detained further to be interrogated by law enforcement officers, eventually resulting in 1,083 arrests. This means that less than 1 percent of those identified by SPOT officers were actually arrested for a criminal offense, and 99 percent were needlessly detained. Ignoring the 151,000 people who were needlessly detained, were those arrested actually concealing guns, drugs, bombs, or terrorist information, as the program was originally designed to catch? Almost never (and not a single terrorist). The most common violation, accounting for 40 percent of these arrests, was categorized as "illegal alien." The SPOT program looks like an expensive way of enabling racial profiling.[14]

Bodies and faces can reveal thoughts and emotions, but the amount they communicate seems surprisingly limited, and the gain from learning to read others better seems minimal, at best.[15] Learning to read others' actions better does not seem to be a promising approach for understanding others better. Let's evaluate the evidence for another method.

PERSPECTIVE TAKING

In *How to Win Friends and Influence People,* one of the best-selling books of all time, Dale Carnegie lists a series of principles for how to do what his title promises. Principle 8, he writes, is a "formula that will work wonders for you." The formula? "Try honestly to see things from the other person's point of view."

To interact effectively with other people, according to Carnegie's formula, you have to know their minds. One way to do that is through perspective taking: imagining, honestly, the other person's psychological point of view. You do not literally *see* the world through the eyes of another, but you imagine how you would understand the world if you were in the other person's circumstances.

This imagination can be a wonderful thing. When my twelve-year-old son asks me for help with his school essay, I don't return it with the same frank criticism I'd give to another college professor. Kids learning to write need more encouragement than consternation. Just like every teacher, you tailor your feedback to meet your students' needs. Being able to imagine another person's reactions before actually observing them is one of the greatest achievements of the human mind.

But even great achievements have their limits. Trying honestly to put yourself in another person's shoes combines your intuitive tools of egocentrism and stereotyping in the hopes of maximizing the benefits of both. You take what you already know about others and then use your own brain to simulate the results if you were someone else. Would I like this action movie if I were a woman? If I were my wife, what would I want for my birthday? How would I feel if I were living in poverty? Would I understand this presentation if I were one of our clients? Would this harsh interrogation technique feel like torture to me?

The benefit of perspective taking is obvious. You maximize your use of what you already know about another person, information that you might otherwise mistakenly overlook. Following the worst oil spill in the planet's history, British Petroleum's CEO, Tony Hayward, earned the title of World's Dumbest CEO by offering a let-them-eat-cake apology that failed to consider any perspective other than his own.[16] "There's no one who wants this over more than I do," he said. "I would like my life back." Surely you hope Hayward would have spoken differently if he had actually considered the perspective of Gulf Coast residents who lost their livelihoods.

The weakness of perspective taking is also obvious: it relies on your ability to imagine, or take, the other person's perspective accurately. If you don't really know what it's like to be poor, in pain, suicidally depressed, at the bottom of your corporate ladder, on the receiving end of waterboarding, in the throes of solitary confinement, or to have your source of income soaked in oil, then the mental gymnastics of putting yourself in someone else's shoes isn't going to make you any more accurate. In fact, it might even decrease your accuracy. In a series of experiments that my collaborators and I conducted, we asked our volunteers to take several commonly used mind-reading tests. These included trying to detect what emotion someone was feeling by looking at a picture of their face and trying to tell what someone was thinking by looking only at their eyes. Never have we found any evidence that perspective taking—putting yourself in another person's shoes and imagining the world through his or her eyes—increased accuracy in these judgments. In fact, in both cases perspective taking consistently *decreased* accuracy. Overthinking someone's emotional expression or inner intentions when there is little else to go on might introduce more error than insight.

What's more problematic is that if your belief about the other side's perspective is mistaken, then carefully considering that person's perspective will only magnify the mistake's consequences. This is particularly likely in conflict, where members of opposing sides tend to have inaccurate views about each other. Ironically, conflict is also the time when perspective taking is most often endorsed as a solution. If an Israeli imagines himself as a Palestinian, what kind of derogatory stereotypes is he likely to access in order to imagine a Palestinian's mind? If a union leader tries to adopt the management's perspective, what beliefs about the other side's circumstances will she bring to bear? If a woman imagines that she is a man, what will her stereotypes lead her to picture? If the image you have about the other side's circumstance is mistaken, then considering yourself in those circumstances could *increase* misunderstanding.[17]

To see this possibility, consider a negotiation experiment in which my colleagues and I simulated a real-world conflict about overfishing cod stocks in the North Atlantic.[18] The conflict represented a classic commons dilemma. Any one fisherman would do better catching as many fish as possible, but the entire resource would collapse if every fisherman caught as much as possible, thereby making everyone worse off. The solution is getting each individual to commit to catching the most they can while leaving enough to maintain the resource. The problem is that fishermen mistakenly believe that *other* fishermen are more selfish than they actually are. If each fisherman assumes that he can't trust any of the others, then it's every man for himself and the ecosystem collapses.

We simulated this dilemma in our experiment by asking four people in each negotiation session to represent different fishing groups. Each group member saw the total amount of fish needed to maintain the stocks, how many fish each group was capable of catching on its own, as well as the other fishing options they might have if the fishing stock collapsed. Each group spent twenty-five minutes in a "simulated conference," talking about how to solve this dilemma fairly. Afterward, each group member reported how many fish they would harvest the next year. In our control condition, each person simply determined the number of fish their group could catch the following year. In our perspective-taking condition, each group member first considered how much each of the other people, with their own differing interests and concerns, would think was fair to harvest before then reporting their own projected harvest.

Our results were clear. Perspective taking exaggerated the perceived differences between the groups, thereby increasing distrust and enhancing selfishness. Those in the perspective-taking groups looked carefully and honestly into the minds of others and did not like what they saw. Perspective taking collapsed the ecosystem the fastest. In real life, cod fishermen facing this exact dilemma did the same. They distrusted one another, overfished the stocks, and collapsed the fishery; many fishermen subsequently lost their livelihood when regulators slashed (or eliminated) the quotas. Stereotypes exaggerate the differences between groups that are defined by their differences, a mistake *enhanced* by considering the other side's perspective.[19]

Not all perspectives are so deeply divided, but even here we've found that gains in accuracy from perspective taking are elusive. In one experiment, we invited 104 couples (most of them married) and asked each person to predict how their partner would respond to twenty questions about their attitudes. These included some relatively unimportant attitudes, such as "I like to pay cash whenever possible," and also relatively major concerns, such as "If I had my life to live over, I would sure do things differently" and "Our family is too heavily in debt today." In our control condition, one partner simply predicted how the other would answer each question. In our perspective-taking condition, one partner was asked to carefully adopt the other partner's perspective by writing about a typical day in his or her life, and then to carefully put themselves in their partner's shoes while answering the questions. Couples in the control condition were reasonably accurate. The correlation between predicted and actual preferences was .5, reflecting considerable accuracy, and predictions were off by 1.5 points on a scale ranging from 0 to 10. Those who carefully tried to put themselves in their partners' shoes did not do any better. In fact, they actually did a little worse. The correlation shrank (to .39) and the average error grew (to 1.7). Whatever our couples saw when they put themselves in their spouse's shoes did not more closely resemble their actual spouse.

We've now looked many times for evidence that perspective taking—actively trying to imagine being in another person's circumstances—systematically increases mind reading and have yet to find any supportive evidence. Trying to predict which activities your spouse will like most? Perspective taking doesn't help. Trying to predict how attractive you'll be rated by someone else on the basis of a photograph, as in the experiment I described in chapter 1? Again, perspective taking does not increase accuracy.[20] In interracial interactions, other researchers find that perspective taking harms the interaction because it leads people to focus too much on how they are being viewed by the other side and too little on the interaction itself.[21] Dale Carnegie's Principle Number 8 may work many wonders, such as simply getting you to recognize that another person may have a perspective that differs from your own, but providing insight into that perspective does not seem to be one of them.

The main issue is that carefully considering another's perspective is no guarantee that you'll be able to do it accurately. I am reminded of this problem every year at Christmas, where the gifts I give after carefully, honestly, and deliberately putting myself in my family members' perspectives seem to miss the mark as often as they hit it. One miss is particularly memorable. Several years ago, I got what I believed was the best gift ever for my wife: spending a day as an animal handler at Chicago's Shedd Aquarium. My wife has always adored dolphins, and she loves the aquarium. If I had those two preferences, I reasoned while putting myself in her shoes, then this was the best possible gift in the entire city I could get.

I could not have been more mistaken. My wife was kind, as always, but she returned my gift. What I'd missed was how her current circumstances had changed what I believed were her long-term preferences, a common mistake among gift givers, according to research.[22] She had just given birth to our second son two months before and was in no mood to squeeze into a wet suit and hold stinky fish while exhausted from a lack of sleep. This perspective is obvious in hindsight, and yet gift givers tend to overlook details of such new circumstances in foresight. I'd tried hard to take her perspective but ended up badly mistaking it.

What's the best way to get someone a gift? The science is clear. You don't try to adopt another person's perspective and guess better. Instead, you adopt a different approach. You have to actually *get* the other person's perspective, and perhaps the only way to do that is to ask what they want, or listen carefully while they drop hints, and then give it to them.[23] That turns out to be widely applicable wisdom.

PERSPECTIVE GETTING

Recognizing the limits of your sixth sense suggests a different approach to understanding the minds of others: trying harder to *get* another person's perspective instead of trying to *take* it. As the old reminder to doctors trying to understand their patients goes, "The patient is trying to tell you what's wrong with him. You have to shut up and listen."

Consider an example of how perspective getting might work. In 1993, the U.S. government signed the "don't ask, don't tell" policy into law, banning gays and lesbians from serving openly in the military. By 2010, the Obama administration was considering the consequences of repealing the law. Moral implications aside, knowing how current soldiers felt about this repeal was essential for assessing its practical consequences. This is a textbook mind-reading problem, with at least two approaches to solving it.

One is exemplified by the 1,167 retired military officers who used their perspective-taking ability to imagine the consequences for current soldiers of repealing the law. In an open letter to President Obama and members of Congress, they expressed their strong opposition. "Our past experience as military leaders," they wrote, "leads us to be greatly concerned about the impact of repeal on morale, discipline, unit cohesion, and overall military readiness. We believe that imposing this burden on our men and women in uniform would . . . eventually break the All-Volunteer Force." Elaine Donnelly, president of the Center for Military Readiness, argued that this opposition must be taken very seriously. "They have a lot of military experience," she said, "and they know what they're talking about."

The Pentagon took a second approach to this mind-reading problem. Its officials *asked* the soldiers their opinions directly by surveying 115,052 soldiers and 44,266 of their spouses in one of the largest studies in military history. The soldiers themselves expressed relatively few concerns. In fact, 70 percent believed that the repeal would have no effect or a positive effect on the military. More telling, roughly the same number (69 percent) said that they had worked with a gay service member already. Among those, 92 percent said it had no effect or a positive effect on the unit's ability to work together. From these responses, Defense Secretary Robert Gates concluded that the repeal "would not be the wrenching dramatic change that many have feared and predicted." Gates pushed for its repeal.

Who was right? In 2012, one year after the actual repeal of "don't ask, don't tell," the military released a study of its consequences. The answer was clear: soldiers could speak their minds when asked directly, but the retired officers who'd imagined the soldiers' reactions were wrong. The title of the press release says it best: "First Study of Openly Gay Military Service Finds 'Non-Event' at One-Year Mark." Getting the soldiers' perspective by asking them for it enabled understanding.

We communicate the contents of our minds primarily through language. As Daniel Gilbert writes in *Stumbling on Happiness,* "If you were to write down every thing you know and then go back through the list and make a check mark next to the things you know only because someone told you, you'd develop a repetitive-motion disorder because nearly everything you know is secondhand."[24] This is why William Ickes, an expert on empathic accuracy, finds that "the best predictor [so far] of empathic accuracy appears to be verbal intelligence."[25] Knowing others' minds requires asking and listening, not just reading and guessing.

The gains that come from getting perspective directly instead of guessing about someone's perspective can be big. A few pages ago, I described an experiment in which romantic partners predicted each other's attitudes. In that study, encouraging perspective taking increased error and reduced accuracy, compared to a simple control condition. That study also included a variation I didn't tell you about, a "perspective-getting" condition in which one member was given the chance to actually *ask* the other person the survey questions before predicting their responses. The couples in that group were given the questionnaire, and one partner essentially interviewed the other by asking him or her all of the questions—which is a bit like being able to ask the teacher for the answers to the test just before taking it. To make the task just a little more challenging, the partner being interviewed did not give a numeric response to each question, as was required on the actual survey; instead, the couple just talked through the ques-

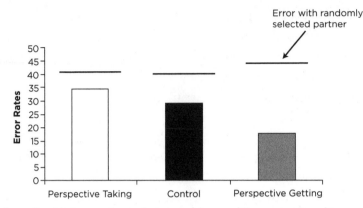

Couples predicted their partner's attitudes in one of three conditions: perspective taking, control, or perspective getting. This graph shows the total amount of errors summed across the twenty items in the survey. The lines above each of these bars represents the total error rate married couples would have achieved if they had predicted the answers for any randomly selected other partner in the experiment. The bars show the error rates couples actually achieved in each of our three conditions. Getting your partner's perspective by asking them directly works much better than taking your partner's perspective by using your imagination.

tions, and nobody was allowed to write down any of their partner's responses. They would have to rely on their memory alone.

Getting perspective was far more effective than taking perspective. You can see the results in the figure above. Those who first *asked* for their partner's thoughts cut their overall error rate nearly in half compared to those in our control condition, and they did even better than that compared to those in the perspective-taking condition. It may seem like cheating to ask your spouse what he or she thinks instead of guessing at the answer, but remember that life is not an in-class exam with an honor code. If you want to know, ask rather than guess.

Interestingly, the only people who might be surprised by these results are the couples who actually participated in our experiment. When we asked them, "How confident are you that your predictions were correct?," we found no significant differences across our conditions despite enormous differences in accuracy. When we asked a more precise question—"How many out of the twenty items did you predict correctly?"—we found only a relatively small amount of insight into their performance.[26] As you can see in the following figure, despite more than doubling their accuracy, those who got their partner's atti-

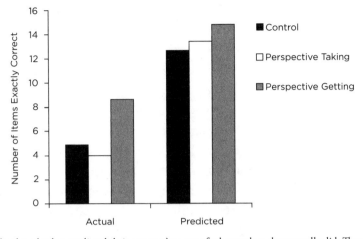

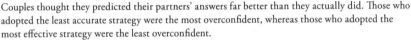

Couples thought they predicted their partners' answers far better than they actually did. Those who adopted the least accurate strategy were the most overconfident, whereas those who adopted the most effective strategy were the least overconfident.

---

tudes right from their mouths thought they were only slightly more accurate than those who imagined their partner's perspective. Our couples were all again wildly overconfident, but those who adopted the least effective strategy (perspective taking) were the most overconfident, whereas those who adopted the most effective strategy (perspective getting) were the least overconfident.

This rampant overconfidence in our sixth sense helps to explain why people may avoid asking others for their perspective in the first place. One military survey from 2007 tried to assess why junior officers were leaving their posts to go back to civilian life in such high numbers. Of those surveyed, 75 percent said this was the first time anyone had asked them why they'd left. The senior officers believed they already knew the answer. The previous year, Harvard University had conducted a survey about the faculty's well-being. All organizations want happy and satisfied employees with good morale, but this was the first time in its 370-year history that Harvard had gotten around to asking. Getting perspective first requires knowing that you need it.

After class one day, the spouse of one of my MBA students gave me a particularly interesting example of the benefits that can come from getting someone's perspective rather than guessing it. He was a military officer stationed in Afghanistan whose unit was promoting the Guardians of Peace program, which, in his words, "tried to get the Afghan civilians to see themselves as the keepers of the peace by reporting bad guys and thus preventing violence." The main idea was to give Afghan civilians a phone number to call whenever they saw Taliban fighters in the area. His unit handed out thousands of leaflets, played advertising messages over loudspeakers as they rode through town, and, in his estimate, spent $2 million on billboards and banners. And yet, few people wound up calling. The American officers imagined that the Afghan civilians weren't calling because they didn't *know* the number or didn't *want* to turn in the bad guys, a textbook example of the correspondence bias I described in chapter 7.

Eventually, military officials took a different approach. Instead of guessing why the civilians weren't calling, they talked to the civilians directly. The problem was clear almost immediately. The Afghans knew about the program and wanted to call. Indeed, many had apparently tried. The problem was that the Taliban came into town at night but shut down the cell phone towers before doing so. "So here we had people willing to call when they saw bad guys," he wrote to me, "but when the bad guys came they couldn't call because the phones were down!" The solution was not handing out more flyers to increase awareness; it was installing secure cell phone towers.[27] The relatively slow work of *getting* a person's perspective is the way you understand them accurately, and the way you solve their problems most effectively.

GETTING PERSPECTIVE

Although getting people to tell you their minds is the best overall solution for understanding them, implementing that solution may still be problematic. Every organization I know utilizes a policy designed explicitly to enable bosses and managers to understand their employees' perspectives, and vice versa. That policy is the performance appraisal, the time when bosses and their employees get together and are supposed to give each other direct performance feedback.

Every year in class I have my MBA students simulate a performance appraisal between an executive and a manager. Both the executive and the manager receive background information describing their own perspective on the situation. It's a fairly typical scenario. The executive learns that the manager has been doing quite well but also has some serious problems that need to be addressed. The manager learns that he has been doing quite well but knows little or nothing about the executive's concerns. For instance, the executive is concerned that the manager works at home and is not spending enough time directly developing his staff, whereas the manager thinks that working from home makes him more productive and believes his staff is getting along just fine. These perspective differences are all fairly typical: the manager is evaluating his own performance more favorably than is the executive. At the end of the simulation I ask each student to predict the other side's impressions and then calculate their accuracy. The results are always the same. Despite having talked for thirty minutes, without the heightened emotions and mixed incentives that could lead to miscommunication in real work environments, my students end up with little to no accurate insight into their partner's true impressions, particularly on concrete measures such as the likelihood that the person will be promoted to a better job within two years.

I think my students' failures are informative. First, the main barrier to getting perspective is that others won't tell you what you'd like to know. They lie, mislead, misdirect, avoid, or simply refuse to divulge the truth. It's important, however, to keep the magnitude of this barrier in perspective. Anonymous surveys suggest that the average person reports telling between one and two lies each day. That's more than zero, of course, and it almost certainly underestimates the true number, but even an underestimate leaves far more truth being told than lies. These surveys also indicate that the vast majority of these lies are told by a small number of chronic liars. In one random sample of one thousand Americans, 60 percent reported—under conditions that enabled accurate responding—not telling any intentional lies in the study's twenty-four-hour period. Of the reported lies, nearly half were told by only 5 percent of the responders. In *Why Leaders Lie,* political scientist John Mearsheimer describes how even politicians are not quite the chronic liars we assume they are.[28] I am not encouraging naïveté but, rather, advising you to keep your cynicism in check. Many people will tell you the truth, or at least something closer to the truth, if you ask a direct question in a context where they feel at liberty to give an honest answer and you are open to hearing it.[29]

Direct questioning cannot, however, prevent more subtle forms of deception. In conversation, bad news often gets sugarcoated, and unpleasant conversations are avoided. The main reason people lie is to avoid being punished, and so enabling people to give you their perspective requires putting them in a context that diminishes the fear of punishment. Here we can take a lesson from professional interrogators, who are in the business of getting the truth out of people who have no interest in giving it. In *How to Break a Terrorist,* military interrogator Matthew Alexander describes how he enabled detainees to provide the truth that led U.S. forces to Abu Musab al Zarqawi, the leader of Al Qaeda in Iraq. Instead of pressuring suspects until they crack from intimidation, fear, and pain, the new and more effective interrogation approach is one that establishes rapport and reduces fears of punishment. Detainees tell you the truth when they are more willing to do so. Interrogators enable this by establishing a human connection with detainees, offering reduced punishment for telling the truth, offering to protect their families, and making detainees feel more comfortable than terrorized. This shift in tactics, according to Alexander's account, marks a sea change in the intelligence community. You can hear the same story from George Piro, the FBI interrogator who gently coaxed valuable information out of Saddam Hussein after his capture in 2003.[30]

You're (hopefully) not a criminal interrogator in your relationships at home or at work, but many of the same lessons apply. Not long ago, for instance, my wife and I were having trouble with our five-year-old son. Every time he'd do something wrong, he'd reflexively lie. Typically this was laughable. "I didn't do it," he'd say while still in the midst of doing the very thing he was denying. Interrogators often learn that they, as the interrogator, are the main barrier to truth telling. This was true in my son's case: I was part of the problem. Every time he'd do something wrong, I'd get angry and he'd be in trouble. To avoid that, he turned to lying. Getting him to stop lying required reducing the barriers to telling the truth. For my son, this first required controlling my own temper and reducing his fear. We did this with a quick five-minute cooling-off session. A very clever experiment by one group of researchers showed that people were *more* willing to admit to having done something immoral when confronted a few minutes after the event—when their fear had subsided a bit—than when questioned immediately after the incident.[31] Knowing this, I would send my son to his room, and I would take a few minutes to chill out. We then developed a household policy of complete immunity as long as you tell the truth. This combination of delay and immunity has worked wonders for us. My son is now considerably more willing to admit to doing almost anything. He doesn't get punished, I don't get mad, and then we have a constructive opportunity to talk about what actually happened and how to avoid it in the future.

Performance appraisals at work face some of these same problems. When the employee fears retribution and the boss isn't open to hearing the truth, nobody speaks their mind and the event becomes pointless. This is one of the reasons why people are unable to tell who likes them within a group and who does not: nobody gives honest feedback about their true feelings.[32] I tried to combat this when I asked my graduate students to give me feedback on a draft of this book: I told them that the only thing I wanted to hear was advice about how I could make the book better and that what I really wanted was the most critical feedback they could give me. That did not mean that I was able to fix all of the problems they told me about, but I did my best to let them tell me about these issues openly and honestly. Getting someone's perspective requires that you be open to hearing it and that you enable others to give it to you.

The second problem with getting perspective is that others don't really know themselves honestly. Recall the limits of self-knowledge I described back in chapter 2. Here I think we can take insights from another kind of interrogator—namely, professional pollsters. Major elections used to be a surprise, but they aren't anymore. Pollsters do not guess what citizens are thinking, they go straight to the source and ask directly. More important, they don't just ask any question; they ask questions that voters are able to answer reasonably accurately. Recall from chapter 2 the challenges many of us have accurately reporting on certain aspects of our minds, particularly those questions that start with "why." It makes no more sense for a pollster to ask you *why* you're voting for someone than it does for a doctor to ask you *why* you're feeling sick. And so pollsters instead ask about *what* people think rather than *why* they think that way. Pollsters also understand that people know their feelings right now more accurately than they can project what they'll be feeling months from now, and so pollsters generally focus their questions on the present rather than the future. They usually ask who you would vote for if the election were held *today,* not who you *will* vote for once the election arrives. When you're trying to understand another person, getting perspective fails if your direct questions turn speculative. Good pollsters, like good interrogators, prefer questions that their targets are better able to answer. Attempts to get perspective should focus on "what" more than "why."

A final challenge to getting perspective is that others' words are unclear, leaving room for misinterpretation. The egocentric biases we discussed in chapter 5 make you believe you are communicating your thoughts, beliefs, attitudes, and instructions more clearly than you actually are. To really enable someone to understand what's on your mind, you not only need to be clear, you need to be *painfully clear.* If you're getting someone's perspective, you not only need to listen, you need to verify that your understanding is correct. Native Americans reportedly had a method for doing this very thing, called the "talking stick." When different tribes had a dispute, they would gather to discuss their differences. During these conversations, only the person holding the talking stick was allowed to speak. When that person finished, they would hand the stick to another elder, who would first have to reiterate the last speaker's position to that person's satisfaction. Only when the first person felt understood could the next person make a new point. The brilliance of this method comes not from its ability to enable speaking but, rather, from how it fosters listening. If you have to reiterate someone else's point to their satisfaction, then you'll find out if you've understood correctly or incorrectly.

Although the talking stick is commonly recommended on the public-speaking circuit, I have yet to see it used regularly in any modern household or organization. Perhaps the implementation is just too tricky. When we tried it at our own house, the benefits were short-lived because the talking stick soon became a weapon rather than a tool. My kids wanted every object in the house to serve as the talking stick. "Be quiet, everybody," we heard one night at dinner, "I have the talking *spoon!*"

The point here is to practice the general lesson rather than adopt this particular method. In performance appraisals, asking someone to reiterate your feedback in order to increase your understanding— something often called "parroting"—implements the lesson without resorting to gimmicks. In organizations more generally, those who are better listeners are also more effective leaders and persuaders.[33] In marriages, psychologist Howard Markman advises couples to use the "speaker-listener technique," a less formalized version of the talking stick, to resolve their disagreements; a coin flip determines who speaks first, and each partner then reiterates the other's point before making his or her own.[34] In schools, educators try to make such careful listening and understanding habitual by using activities that require the psychological equivalent of the talking stick.[35] Understanding other people requires getting their perspective and then verifying that you've understood it correctly.

IN DEFENSE OF TRANSPARENCY

Nobody would want a world in which every half-baked or self-indulgent thought was put on public display. TMI, indeed. But pulling back the curtain and opening up a bit more often, when your own perspective matters and when that perspective is wanted, benefits both those who give their perspective as well as those who are willing to use it.

Sometimes these benefits are personal in nature. One study tracking 278 incoming college freshmen found that more emotionally expressive students had higher levels of social support, felt closer to their friends, and were more satisfied with their college experience than those who were more guarded with their emotions.[36] In another, those who were more open about themselves to others were not only better understood but also happier and more satisfied with their lives in general than those who kept their minds more hidden.[37] In fact, one common laboratory technique for creating fast friends is to have two strangers disclose private thoughts or memories to each other.[38] This is why shyness is one of social life's biggest curses. Not only are shy people commonly misinterpreted as arrogant rather than anxious, but their anxiety also keeps them disconnected from the very relationships that could increase their happiness.

At other times, the benefits of opening up are more public. Months before an explosion on the Deepwater Horizon oil rig caused the largest spill in history, a confidential survey of rig workers uncovered serious safety concerns but strong fears of reprisals for reporting those concerns. According to a report in the *New York Times,* "only about half of the workers interviewed said they felt they could report actions leading to a potentially 'risky' situation without reprisal."[39] One worker surveyed said, "The company is always using fear tactics. All these games and your mind gets tired." To hold on to their jobs and avoid punishment, workers routinely kept quiet about obvious risks, even faking data in the company's safety system to make the rig appear more stable than they knew it was. Under these conditions, the rig passed an internal safety inspection just one month before the disaster. Would this disaster have been averted if the company's executives had been willing to hear what their employees knew? I'd bet on it.

Doctors have even discovered that opening up their minds and admitting their mistakes can actually *reduce* one of their biggest fears: litigation. In 2001, the University of Michigan Hospitals began a medical-error-disclosure program in which doctors openly admit their medical mistakes in meetings with patients, explain what led to the mistake, and then offer fair compensation. Compared to the no-disclosure policy practice in the six preceding years, this open-apology system cut malpractice lawsuits in half (from 39 per year to 17 per year) and reduced the time to resolution by roughly 30 percent (from 1.36 years to .95 years).[40] According to the lead doctor reporting these results, "Everybody worries that disclosure will lead to liability going through the roof, but here's one institution that set up their disclosure program privately and independently, helped their patients avoid using the courts and tort system, and did not sustain the skyrocketing claims and costs that others might have predicted."[41] In fact, this program actually reduced overall liability costs by roughly 60 percent. The bigger problem had been requiring patients to *imagine* what their doctors were thinking, or having to sue to find out, rather than just allowing doctors to explain how a mistake happened.

Reducing litigation is good, but what the disclosure program really does, according to the medical center's chief risk officer, Richard Boothman, "is give permission to doctors and other caregivers to do what's important and what they want to do—take care of the patients and make sure the same error doesn't ever happen again in the future. . . . When you break that paradigm of litigation and give patients the chance to understand the human element of the other side—of the doctor and what they are struggling with—you find that people are far more forgiving and understanding than has been typically assumed." Now, that's something your sixth sense might never have imagined.

If being transparent strengthens the social ties that make life worth living, shares knowledge that could help us live our lives better, and enables others to forgive our shortcomings, then why not do it more often?

■ ■ ■

Others' minds will never be an open book. The secret to understanding each other better seems to come not through an increased ability to read body language or improved perspective taking but, rather, through the hard relational work of putting people in a position where they can tell you their minds openly and honestly. Companies truly understand their customers better when they get their perspective directly through conversation, surveys, or face-to-face interaction, not when executives guess about them in the boardroom. Managers know what their employees think when they are open to the answers and employees feel safe from retaliation, not when managers use their intuition. Spouses understand each other when they are willing to share their thoughts openly and verify that they've heard correctly, not when they walk past each other in silence thinking that they already understand their spouse perfectly. And parents get insight into what their children are going through only when the lines of communication are fully open, when they listen as well as speak, not when the main lines of communication run through inferences and assumptions. If we want to understand what's on the mind of another, the best our mortal senses can do may be to rely on our ears more than our inferences.

I knew all of this when meeting our children's biological father in Ethiopia, as we sat in the van just before being introduced to him. As the gate to the orphanage opened with our children's father somewhere behind it, my mind raced, making presumptions about what he was thinking and feeling, extrapolating from the shreds of information we had, trying to guess what I'd feel if I were him. I resisted these as best I could, knowing full well the errors and overconfidence they would likely produce. Sadly, we lacked the real tool we would need to understand each other, as we did not have the team of linguists needed to translate a tribal dialect into English. That conversation will have to come some other time, if ever. The closest I could get was an embrace, some tears, and a handful of universally recognized facial expressions, which, I am aware, reveal less than our sense imagines.

I learned a lot in that embrace but am careful not to overestimate how much. Lacking the ability to speak directly, to use the most effective channel of understanding available, the best I could do was accept the superficial insight that came through our embrace without presuming that I understood anything more. Knowing the limits of our brain's social sense does not always mean that we can overcome them to understand others better. Sometimes a sense of humility is the best our wise minds can offer, recognizing that there's more to the mind of another person than we may ever imagine.

AFTERWORD

Being Mindwise

The stellar universe is not so difficult of comprehension as the
real actions of other people.

—MARCEL PROUST

The world as we know it nearly came to an end because of a misunderstanding of minds. For a tense period in October 1962, the
United States and the Soviet Union stood on the brink of a nuclear
World War III. The two nations got to this point after years of apparent provocations and perceived threats, the most recent of which was
a botched invasion of Cuba in the Bay of Pigs by CIA-trained opera-
tives. Seeking to defend his Cuban ally and deter any broader acts of
aggression, Russian premier Nikita Khrushchev reached an agreement
with Fidel Castro to install nuclear weapons on Cuba. The United
States interpreted this as an act of aggression rather than an act of
self-defense and considered invading Cuba a second time. Luckily,
John F. Kennedy had learned valuable lessons from the Bay of Pigs
fiasco. He decided against invasion and instead set up a navy blockade to stop oncoming Soviet ships. What Kennedy did not know was
that the Soviets were anticipating an invasion and already had their
nuclear weapons lying in wait behind the blockade. Had Kennedy
invaded Cuba, the Soviet generals were already authorized to start a
nuclear war.[1]

The only official channels of communication between Khrushchev and Kennedy went through intermediaries. This indirect communication was filled with all the distortions, misinformation, and posturing that anyone who has ever played the telephone game knows well. Each side was therefore fighting a battle against an imagined enemy rather than the real one.

The two sides averted a nuclear holocaust mainly because of a private, undisclosed, and direct line of communication between Khrushchev and Kennedy themselves. The letters came painfully slowly, by telegram, at the height of the crisis, but this channel offered each man an opportunity to express his mind directly to the other, unfiltered by public posturing. On October 26, Khrushchev sent a letter explicitly encouraging Kennedy to consider his perspective; he then explained that perspective in detail and pointed toward a possible resolution.[2] After three days of direct and mostly honest exchanges, the sides reached a peaceful resolution.

Asked later what could trigger two countries to start a nuclear war, one of the Soviet intermediaries in the negotiation knew precisely: "mutual fear, misinformation, and mistrust can do it."[3] Misreading each other's minds was such an obvious cause of this near Armageddon that the two leaders signed an official agreement establishing a direct phone line between the two nations to be used whenever needed. The channel came to be known as the "red phone." The lesson we have learned from social science is the same as this lesson from war: we could all use a red phone. Our ability to reason about the minds of others is one of our brain's greatest powers. At its best, this ability allows us a clear understanding of what others want, need, believe, and know in the present, an understanding that also gives us a preview of what others are likely to do in the future. It is the very ability that enables a seamless coordination between completely disconnected brains, enabling social life on the grand scale as we know it today.

But even our greatest abilities are far from perfect, and our sixth sense's mistakes also cause some of our life's greatest pains. Broken relationships, failed organizations, stalled careers, and needless conflicts are common casualties.

I believe a more accurate understanding of our social failings is the key to making our brain's greatest sense even better. You, I, and nearly all other human beings have a rich conscious experience, through which we all get a clearer understanding about what it's like to be someone else. Our window into others, however, is limited. Like moving from an old black-and-white television to modern high-definition, the image we get of others' minds is grainy and limited in comparison to the detailed and rich experience of our own. The mistakes we make when reasoning about the minds of others all have the same central outcome: underestimating their complexity, depth, detail, and richness. When we're indifferent to others, it's easy to overlook their minds altogether, treating such people more as relatively mindless animals or objects than as fully mindful persons. Once we're trying to understand another person, our intuitions can provide several revealing, but also oversimplifying, mechanisms of understanding. We may begin by assuming that others think or feel as we do, then rely on stereotypes as we gather more information, and finally utilize the actions we observe as a direct guide to the mind behind them. Each technique provides some understanding but also reduces the apparent complexity of the other person's mind. Instead of seeing others in their full and varied detail, we may see others as like us, like others in the group they're part of, or like what they do.

Knowing the shortcomings of your own social sense should push you to be more open in sharing what's in your own mind with others, but also more open to listening to others. Modern technology enables everyone to express themselves, in outlets from blogs to Twitter to online comment sections, but when everyone is speaking, it's hard to tell that anyone is listening. And when the main modes of expression are superficial texts and tweets and snarky one-liners, we're only getting ambiguous snapshots that stoke our mistakes more often than they correct them. When Kennedy got Khrushchev's perspective on the crisis directly, it was not through 140 characters; it was through thousands of carefully crafted words in a back-and-forth exchange. In these words Kennedy found a surprisingly similar adversary. "One of the ironic things," he later told a journalist, "is that Mr. Khrushchev and I occupy approximately the same political positions inside our governments. He would like to prevent a nuclear war but is under severe pressure from his hard-line crowd, which interprets every move in that direction as appeasement. I've got similar problems. . . . The hard-liners in the Soviet Union and the United States feed on one another."[4]

A former field producer for *The Daily Show,* Michael Rubens, discovered the very same thing when he set up fake interviews to mock people with what he describes as "blecchy" views. To his surprise, when he met these presumed crackpots in person, they turned out to be remarkably human. "I like to loathe people," he wrote. "It just feels so good. . . . So imagine how irksome it was to discover that those persons, in person, generally weren't loathsome persons after all. In fact, to my great consternation and disappointment, I often liked them." Stanley Fish, professor of law and humanities and a frequent contributor to *The New York Times,* suggests that the same risk lurks if you meet your enemies directly rather than imagining them at a distance. He therefore avoids meeting one particular archenemy, whom he prefers to think of as detestable. "Why? Because were I ever to meet him, the odds are that I would like him. . . . Indeed, this has happened to me several times. I got to know long-time personal piñatas and found that they were—can you believe it?—human beings, often perfectly nice human beings with perfectly nice families. Even worse, the first words out of their mouths were sometimes, 'I admire your work.'"[5] If maintaining a misunderstood population of hostile enemies is important to you, then it's probably best not to meet them. If understanding is your goal, then you know how to do much better.

Only by recognizing the limits of our brain's greatest sense will we have the humility to understand others as they actually are instead of as we imagine them to be.

ACKNOWLEDGMENTS

If my debt of gratitude for all of the great minds who helped me write this book was converted into dollars, then I'd have to declare bankruptcy.

First are the students, collaborators, and mentors who helped conduct the research I describe in this book. Tom Gilovich, my PhD advisor, put a big red X across the entire first page of the first paper we wrote together and has been showing me how to do almost everything better ever since. Leaf Van Boven, Kenneth Savitsky, and Justin Kruger made research in graduate school so much fun that I figured I could continue doing it for the rest of my life. So far that continued research has been improved by many wonderful people whose talents I do not deserve: Scott Akalis, Max Bazerman, John Cacioppo, Eugene Caruso, John Chambers, Benjamin Converse, Alexa Delbosc, David Dunning, Tal Eyal, Kurt Gray, Chuck Huff, Boaz Keysar, Nadav Klein, Carey Morewedge, Erin Rapien, Jesse Preston, Juliana Schroeder, Adam Waytz, and Yan Zhang.

Several colleagues have proven invaluable, even if their names never appeared on the papers. For the last decade, Dan Gilbert has provided inspiration, guidance, and a vote that helped secure my first job. I can't possibly thank him enough for all he's done. Dan Wegner, one of psychology's most creative minds and its biggest goofball, pushed me to write this book and then told me how to do it. Sadly, he died before I was able to finish it. I hope he would have been proud of what he made me do. And Dick Thaler has nudged, and sometimes shoved, me to make the right decision every time I've asked him (which is probably not often enough). Few people know that the Father of Behavioral Economics is also the fairy godmother.

I developed the idea for this book while on sabbatical at the Center for Advanced Studies in the Behavioral Sciences at Stanford University, where my family and I truly spent the best year of our lives. The University of Chicago Booth School of Business funded that sabbatical. Chicago Booth has also funded much of my research, as have grants from the National Science Foundation and the Templeton Foundation. I am very grateful to these institutions for making my work possible.

While at the Center for Advanced Studies, I met my wonderful agent, Max Brockman, who took my gibberish and helped develop it into a narrative that sounded suspiciously like a book. From there, Martin Asher gambled that I could actually write it, and Jeff Alexander provided the brilliant editorial work necessary to make me finish it. Bonnie Thompson then showed why Random House considers her to be one of their best copy editors. Kathleen Fridella, Maggie Hinders, Jocelyn Miller, and Lisa Montebello did the last nipping and tucking to finalize the book-writing process that at some points seemed like it would never end. And Peter Mendelsund created the best possible cover image for a book about interpersonal illusions. I didn't choose this entire book production team, but I will demand them if I ever do this again.

The most encouraging aspect of writing this book was learning how helpful people are willing to be if you just ask them. Many people answered questions, improved my ideas, read chapters, or in some way made this book better. These include: Kaushal Addanki, Travis Carter, Farr Curlin, Dave DeSteno, Tom Gilovich, Reid Hastie, Lee Jussim, Nadav Klein, Sarah Molouki, Elizabeth Majka, Ann McGill, Liz Necka, Ara Norenzayan, Harold Pollack, Stephen Porter, Emily Pronin, Dennis Regan, Kenneth Savitsky, Juliana Schroeder, Anuj Shah, Emily Shaw, James VanderMeer, Adam Waytz, Natalie Wheeler, Kaitlin Wooley, Mike Yeomans, and Haotian Zhou. A few went far and beyond the call of friendship (or even kinship) and commented on the entire book, including Ben Converse, Rachel Epley, Dan Gilbert, Sendhil Mullainathan, and Dick Thaler. And from the very start of this book project until the very end, Jasmine Kwong came through on every conceivable request, over and over again, from proofreading to chasing down references to even taking the picture of the smiling VW Bug in the notes of chapter 4. Thank you, thank you, thank you.

Finally, I thank Jen, and our children Ben, Habtamu, Nathan, and Tsion, for showing me every day why being connected, deeply and honestly, to the minds of others really matters. I love you.

NOTES

PREFACE

1. On p. 205 of A. Bourdain (2000). *Kitchen confidential: Adventures in the culinary underbelly.* New York: Bloomsbury.
2. Dunbar, R. I. M. (1998). The social brain hypothesis. *Evolutionary Anthropology* 6: 178–90; Dunbar, R. I. M., and S. Shultz (2007). Evolution in the social brain. *Science* 317: 1344–47.
3. Sallet, J., et al. (2011). Social network size affects neural circuits in Macaques. *Science* 334, 697–700.
4. And, just for good measure, this experiment also included thirty-six orangutans. These orangutans performed like the chimps. Herrmann, E., et al. (2007). Humans have evolved specialized skills of social cognition: The cultural intelligence hypothesis. *Science* 317: 1360–66.
5. This poll asked each respondent which of the following superpowers he or she would most like to have. Here are the results:

ABILITY	% PREFERRED
Mind Reading	28
Time Travel	28
Fly	16
Teleport	11
Invisibility	10

You can learn more about this poll here: http://maristpoll.marist.edu/28-holy-super-powers-batman-mind-reading-and-time-travel-top-list/.

CHAPTER 1: AN OVERCONFIDENT SENSE

1. Wyatt, C. (June 16, 2001). Bush and Putin: Best of friends. BBC News. Retrieved from http://news.bbc.co.uk/2/hi/1392791.stm.
2. Todorov, A., M. Pakrashi, and N. N. Oosterhof (2009). Evaluating faces on trustworthiness after minimal time exposure. *Social Cognition* 27: 813–33.

3. Todorov, A., et al. (2005). Inferences of competence from faces predict election outcomes. *Science* 308: 1623–26.

4. Kenny, D. A., and B. M. DePaulo (1993). Do people know how others view them? An empirical and theoretical account. *Psychological Bulletin* 114: 145–61.

5. On p. 159 of D. A. Kenny (1994). *Interpersonal perception: A social relations analysis.* New York: Guilford Press.

6. In one experiment we found a slightly positive correlation between predicted and actual accuracy of .23, but we found an equally negative correlation in another experiment (−.24). Combining these experiments, the overall correlation we observe is roughly zero. Eyal, T., and N. Epley (2010). How to seem telepathic: Enabling mind reading by matching self-construal. *Psychological Science* 21: 700–705.

7. Bond Jr., C. F., and B. M. DePaulo (2006). Accuracy of deception judgments. *Personality and Social Psychology Review* 10: 214–34.

8. Mearsheimer, J. J. (2011). *Why leaders lie: The truth about lying in international politics.* New York: Oxford University Press.

9. Rollings, K. H., et al. (2011). Empathic accuracy and inaccuracy. In S. Strack (ed.), *Handbook of interpersonal psychology: Theory, research, assessment, and therapeutic interventions* (pp. 143–56). Hoboken, NJ: John Wiley & Sons.

10. Savitsky, K., et al. (2011). The closeness-communication bias: Increased egocentrism among friends versus strangers. *Journal of Experimental Social Psychology* 47: 269–73.

11. The actual experiment I'm describing is reported in W. B. J. Swann and M. J. Gill (1997). Confidence and accuracy in person perception: Do we know what we think we know about our relationship partners? *Journal of Personality and Social Psychology* 73: 747–57. The quote is on p. 755.

12. My collaborators and I found a similar result in one set of experiments where we asked married couples to communicate an ambiguous message, such as a sarcastic statement, to either their spouse or a stranger. The married couples thought they communicated the ambiguous messages more accurately to each other than to a stranger; in fact, there was no difference in actual understanding. Being close to your partner again seems to create an illusion of understanding that can outstrip actual understanding, an effect we described as the "closeness communication bias." Savitsky, K., et al. (2011). The closeness-communication bias: Increased egocentrism among friends versus strangers. *Journal of Experimental Social Psychology* 47: 269–73.

13. Swann, W. B., D. H. Silvera, and C. U. Proske (1995). On "knowing your partner": Dangerous illusions in the age of AIDS? *Personal Relationships* 2: 173–86.

14. If you're still not completely convinced, here's one more example. In this experiment, research volunteers looked at photos of people expressing one of seven different emotions—anger, contempt, disgust, fear, happiness, sadness, or surprise—and selected which of these emotions was being shown in the photo. This task is easy— mind reading for preschoolers—because these emotions are the very ones that are universally recognized. These volunteers also reported their beliefs about how well they could read the minds of others by assessing the extent to which they agreed with statements like "I can determine someone's personality traits at first sight," "I can understand others' feelings even if they try to hide them," and "Usually, I know beforehand what my conversation partner is going to say." If people know how good

they are at intuiting the minds of others, then their estimates of their ability should be correlated with their actual ability. It is not. On this particular test, the correlation between people's beliefs about their ability to read the minds of others and their actual ability to identify the emotion conveyed in the photograph was precisely zero (yes, the correlation was .000). Correlations can get no smaller. Other mind-reading tests, such as being able to guess another person's impressions after an interview or to detect emotions conveyed by a person's voice, showed the same profound lack of self-insight. Interestingly, the only personality variable that predicted people's actual mind-reading ability was IQ—a basic measure of intelligence. The only personality variable that predicted people's *beliefs* about their mind-reading ability, however, was extroversion. Smart people are good mind readers, but outgoing people *think* they are good mind readers. As anyone who has ever watched politics knows, intelligence and extroversion do not necessarily go hand in hand. This study is reported in A. Realo et al. (2003). Mind-reading ability: Beliefs and performance. *Journal of Research in Personality* 37: 420–45.

15. On p. 341 of E. B. Titchener (1896). *An outline of psychology.* Madison, WI: Macmillan.

CHAPTER 2: WHAT YOU CAN AND CANNOT KNOW ABOUT YOUR OWN MIND

1. LaPiere, R. T. (1934). Attitudes vs. actions. *Social Forces* 13: 230–37.

2. Kawakami, K., et al. (2009). Mispredicting affective and behavioral responses to racism. *Science* 323: 276–78.

3. LaFrance, M., and J. Woodzicka (2001). Real versus imagined reactions to sexual harassment. *Journal of Social Issues* 57: 15–30.

4. Milgram, S. (1963). Behavioral study of obedience. *Journal of Abnormal and Social Psychology* 67: 371–78. A recent replication of this experiment found nearly identical obedience rates: Burger, J. M. (2009). Replicating Milgram: Would people still obey today? *American Psychologist* 64: 1–11.

5. Buehler, R., D. Griffin, and M. Ross (1994). Exploring the "Planning Fallacy": Why people underestimate their task completion times. *Journal of Personality and Social Psychology* 67: 366–81.

6. Buehler, R., D. Griffin, and M. Ross (1995). It's about time: Optimistic predictions in work and love. *European Review of Social Psychology* 6: 1–32.

7. Hall, G. S. (1898). Some aspects of the early sense of self. *American Journal of Psychology* 9: 351–95.

8. Geller, U. (1996). *Uri Geller's mindpower kit.* New York: Penguin Studio.

9. Ramachandran, V. S., and S. Blakeslee (1998). *Phantoms in the brain: Probing the mysteries of the human mind.* New York: William Morrow.

10. Murphy, S. T., and R. B. Zajonc (1993). Affect, cognition, and awareness: Affective priming with optimal and suboptimal stimulus exposures. *Journal of Personality and Social Psychology* 64: 723–39.

11. Slater, A., et al. (1998). Newborn infants prefer attractive faces. *Infant Behavior and Development* 21: 345–54.

12. Perrett, D. I., et al. (1999). Symmetry and human facial attractiveness. *Evolution and*

Human Behavior 20: 295–307; Rhodes, G., F. Proffitt, J. M. Grady, and A. Sumich (1998). Facial symmetry and the perception of beauty. *Psychonomic Bulletin and Review* 5: 659–69; Rhodes, G., et al. (2001). Attractiveness of facial averageness and symmetry in non-Western cultures: In search of biologically based standards of beauty. *Perception* 30: 611–25.

13. Betts, E. F. (1909). *The complete Mother Goose.* New York: A. Stokes.

14. Langer, E. J., A. Blank, and B. Chanowitz (1978). The mindlessness of ostensibly thoughtful action: The role of "placebic" information in interpersonal interaction. *Journal of Personality and Social Psychology* 36: 635–42.

15. Epley, N., and E. Whitchurch (2008). Mirror, mirror on the wall: Enhancement in self-recognition. *Personality and Social Psychology Bulletin* 349: 1159–70.

16. Jung, C. G. (1953). *Collected Works: Civilization in Transition* (vol. 10). New York: Pantheon Books.

17. Wilson, T. (2004). *Strangers to ourselves: Discovering the adaptive unconscious.* Cambridge, MA: Harvard University Press.

18. Nisbett, R. E., and T. D. Wilson (1977). Telling more than we can know: Verbal reports on mental processes. *Psychological Review* 84: 231–59. For another example, see R. E. Nisbett and T. D. Wilson (1977). The halo effect: Evidence for unconscious alteration of judgments. *Journal of Personality and Social Psychology* 35: 250–56.

19. Johansson, P., et al. (2005). Failure to detect mismatches between intention and outcome in a simple decision task. *Science* 310: 116–19.

20. Strack, F., L. L. Martin, and S. Stepper (1988). Inhibiting and facilitating conditions of the human smile: A nonobtrusive test of the facial feedback hypothesis. *Journal of Personality and Social Psychology* 54: 768–77.

21. Stepper, S., and F. Strack (1993). Proprioceptive determinants of emotional and nonemotional feelings. *Journal of Personality and Social Psychology* 64: 211–20; Brinol, P., R. E. Petty, and B. Wagner (2009). Body posture effects on self-evaluation: A self-validation approach. *European Journal of Social Psychology* 39: 1053–64.

22. Ross, L., and A. Ward (1996). Naive realism: Implications for social conflict and misunderstanding. In T. Brown, E. Reed, and E. Turiel (eds.), *Values and knowledge* (pp. 103–35). Hillsdale, NJ: Lawrence Erlbaum Associates.

23. Kennedy, K. A., and E. Pronin (2008). When disagreement gets ugly: Perceptions of bias and the escalation of conflict. *Personality and Social Psychology Bulletin* 34: 833–48.

24. For a brilliant description of naïve realism, see Gilbert, D. T. (April 16, 2006). I'm okay, you're biased. *New York Times.*

CHAPTER 3: HOW WE DEHUMANIZE

1. My report of the Standing Bear trial comes largely from Stephen Dando-Collins's book *Standing Bear Is a Person.* I have described the trial only in general terms; the actual details are even more remarkable. Dando-Collins, S. (2004). *Standing Bear is a person: The true story of a Native American's quest for justice.* Cambridge, MA: Da Capo Press.

2. Jahoda, G. (1999). *Images of savages: Ancient roots of modern prejudice in Western culture.* London: Routledge.

3. The earliest recorded example of this comes from the ancient Greek historian Herodotus, who divided the world into two categories, those that speak Greek and the rest of the world, which does not. Predictably, those distant others speaking a foreign language were described as unsophisticated, uncultured, incompetent, and animalistic, something less than fully human. Herodotus named them "barbarians." See N. Asherson (1996). *Black Sea.* New York: Hill & Wang.

4. Wynter, S. (1992). "No humans involved": An open letter to my colleagues. *Voices of the African Diaspora: The CAAS Research Review* 8: 1–17, cited in P. A. Goff et al. (2008). Not yet human: Implicit knowledge, historical dehumanization, and contemporary consequences. *Journal of Personality and Social Psychology* 94: 292–306.

5. Anand, K. J. S., B. J. Stevens, and P. J. McGrath, eds. (2000). *Pain in neonates.* Amsterdam: Elsevier.

6. Niedenthal, P. (2007). Embodying emotions. *Science* 316: 1002–1005.

7. Stepper, S., and F. Strack (1993). Proprioceptive determinants of emotional and nonemotional feelings. *Journal of Personality and Social Psychology* 64: 211–20.

8. Strack, F., L. L. Martin, and S. Stepper (1988). Inhibiting and facilitating conditions of the human smile: A nonobtrusive test of the facial feedback hypothesis. *Journal of Personality and Social Psychology* 54: 768–77.

9. Alter, A., et al. (2007). Overcoming intuition: Metacognitive difficulty activates analytical thought. *Journal of Experimental Psychology: General* 136: 569–76; Stepper, S., and F. Strack (1993). Proprioceptive determinants of emotional and nonemotional feelings. *Journal of Personality and Social Psychology* 64: 211–20.

10. Niedenthal, P. M., et al. (2001). When did her smile drop? Facial mimicry and the influences of emotional state on the detection of change in emotional expression. *Cognition and Emotion* 15: 853–64; Neal, D. T., and T. L. Chartrand (2011). Embodied emotion perception: Amplifying and dampening facial feedback modulates emotion perception accuracy. *Social Psychological and Personality Science* 2: 673–78.

11. Havas, D. A., et al. (2010). Cosmetic use of botulinum toxin-A affects processing of emotional language. *Psychological Science* 21: 895–900.

12. Other research highlights the importance of sensory engagement even more clearly. In one experiment, a person who had just crushed his finger as part of a staged accident either looked directly at a research volunteer, showing his facial grimace and pain clearly, or did not make direct eye contact with the volunteer. Video recording showed that volunteers who were looked at directly by the person in pain imitated the person's pained facial expression more and showed significantly more concern about the accident than those who were not looked at directly. If a tree falls in the forest and nobody is around to hear it, does it still make a sound? Of course it does. If a person falls in the forest but she doesn't show you her grimace, is she still in pain? Of course she is, but you might not feel it.

In another experiment, research volunteers were somewhat distracted from considering another person's mind by the person's body. In this experiment, volunteers saw pictures of other people and reported their impressions of each person. These volunteers rated the scantily clad as being less mindful—less able to remember, to think, or to exert self-control—than the fully clad. These results are not an anomaly. Men looking at women in bikinis while having their brains scanned in an fMRI machine show neural activity in the part of the brain responsible for thinking about objects and tools, but the part responsible for thinking about the minds of others was relatively unresponsive. When your eyes are drawn to a person's body, that person seems to lose some of his or her mind.

For more on these experiments, see: Bavelas, J. B., et al. (1986). "I *show* how you feel": Motor mimicry as a communicative act. *Journal of Personality and Social Psychology* 50: 322–29; Gray, K., et al. (2011). More than a body: Mind perception and the nature of objectification. *Journal of Personality and Social Psychology* 101: 1207–20; Cikara, M., J. L. Eberhardt, and S. T. Fiske (2011). From agents to objects: Sexist attitudes and neural responses to sexualized targets. *Journal of Cognitive Neuroscience* 23: 540–51.

13. My evidence regarding soldiers in this paragraph comes from Lieutenant Colonel Dave Grossman's book *On Killing*, which describes not only the difficulty soldiers have killing enemy men but also what modern military forces now do to overcome it. Grossman, D. (1996). *On killing: The psychological cost of learning to kill in war and society.* New York: Back Bay Books.

14. Interestingly, medical students are trained in a way that creates some distance from patients, so that they can do what needs to be done. The desensitization process begins in school. Medical students do not start by slicing into live human beings; they begin by dissecting cadavers. Even with cadavers, care is taken to ease the natural aversion to cutting into another human being. Can you guess where students begin their dissections? Start right off cutting into the cadaver's face, or maybe pulling out an eye? Definitely not. The most standard method, I'm told by physicians who oversee it, is to start with the most intimately human parts out of view. With the patient lying facedown, students first cut along the back. They then move down the legs, and only much later do they flip the patient over. Only after having worked on this body for months, growing accustomed to cutting into a human body, do they move to the more sensitive parts. Students *end* their dissection at the face.

15. Increased activity among the physicians compared to controls was also found in the parahippocampal gyrus, the superior frontal gyrus, and the right temporoparietal junction (RTPJ). The RTPJ is also typically found to be associated with reasoning about the minds of others. Cheng, Y., et al. (2007). Expertise modulates the perception of pain in others. *Current Biology* 17: 1708–13.

16. Amodio, D. M., and C. D. Frith (2006). Meeting of minds: The medial frontal cortex and social cognition. *Nature Reviews Neuroscience* 7: 268–77.

17. One interesting neuroimaging experiment examined how voters thought of their favored U.S. presidential candidate in the months leading up to the 2008 election (Obama versus McCain). Results indicated that people utilized their MPFC more when thinking about their favored candidate than when thinking about the opposing candidate, and that this difference increased as the election neared. As the importance of the election increased, these voters reasoned about their own candidate using

regions that are active when thinking about close friends, and they reasoned about the opposing candidate using regions active when thinking about mindless objects. Falk, E. B., R. P. Spunt, and M. D. Lieberman (2012). Ascribing beliefs to ingroup and outgroup political candidates: Neural correlates of perspective taking, issue importance, and days until the election. *Philosophical Transactions of the Royal Society* 367: 731–43.

18. Harris, L. T., and S. T. Fiske (2006). Dehumanizing the lowest of the low: Neuroimaging responses to extreme out-groups. *Psychological Science* 17: 847–53.

19. Harris, L. T., and S. T. Fiske (2011). Dehumanized perception: A psychological means to facilitate atrocities, torture, and genocide? *Zeitschrift für Psychologie* 219: 175–81.

20. Pronin, E., and M. B. Kugler (2010). People believe they have more free will than others. *Proceedings of the National Academy of Sciences* 107: 22469–474.

21. Haslam, N., et al. (2005). More human than you: Attributing humanness to self and others. *Journal of Personality and Social Psychology* 89: 937–50.

22. Leyens, J.-P., et al. (2000). The emotional side of prejudice: The attribution of secondary emotions to ingroups and outgroups. *Personality and Social Psychology Review* 4: 186–97; Vaes, J., et al. (2003). On the behavioral consequences of infrahumanization: The implicit role of uniquely human emotions in intergroup relations. *Journal of Personality and Social Psychology* 85: 1016–34; Cuddy, A., M. Rock, and M. Norton (2007). Aid in the aftermath of Hurricane Katrina: Inferences of secondary emotions and intergroup helping. *Group Processes and Intergroup Relations* 10: 107–18.

23. Wohl, M. J. A., M. J. Hornsey, and S. H. Bennett. (2012). Why group apologies succeed and fail: Intergroup forgiveness and the role of primary and secondary emotions. *Journal of Personality and Social Psychology* 102: 306–22.

24. On p. 305 of P. W. Singer (2009). *Wired for war.* New York: Penguin Books.

25. The full quote is on page x in the preface to the 2004 edition: "It's beyond my skill as a writer to capture that day, and the days that would follow—the planes, like specters, vanishing into steel and glass; the slow-motion cascade of the towers crumbling into themselves; the ash-covered figures wandering the streets; the anguish and fear. Nor do I pretend to understand the stark nihilism that drove the terrorists that day and that drives their brethren still. My powers of empathy, my ability to reach into another's heart, cannot penetrate the blank stares of those who would murder innocents with abstract, serene satisfaction." Obama, B. (2004). *Dreams from my father: A story of race and inheritance.* New York: Three Rivers Press.

26. Krueger, A. B., and J. Maleckova (2003). Education, poverty, and terrorism: Is there a causal connection? *Journal of Economic Perspectives* 17: 119–44.

27. Scott Atran makes the most impressive scientific case for parochial altruism in his book *Talking to the Enemy.* Atran, who describes himself as an anthropologist who acts like a psychologist, interviewed Muslim jihadists and subjected them to a battery of questionnaires to uncover their underlying motivations. Atran found that their motivations to benefit a cause they hold dear are hardly nihilistic. Their motivations are recognizably human. Atran, S. (2010). *Talking to the enemy: Faith, brotherhood, and the (un)making of terrorists.* New York: HarperCollins.

28. This was not the first time Americans seem to have made this mistake. On p. 305 of

Wired for War, Singer explains, "In World War II, General Curtis LeMay ordered American bombers to use firebombs on Japanese cities, with the intent to terrorize the Japanese public into a realization that continuing the war was futile. The raids killed hundreds of thousands, but many in Japan instead interpreted the 'message' as that it was dangerous to surrender unconditionally to an enemy willing to drop flaming napalm on civilians living in wooden houses."

29. You can obtain the report from the website of the magazine *Foreign Policy:* http://www .foreignpolicy.com/files/fp_uploaded_documents/Falk-Rogers%20PAE%2003-11 %20vF.pdf.

30. Heath, C. (1999). On the social psychology of agency relationships: Lay theories of motivation overemphasize extrinsic incentives. *Organizational Behavior and Human Decision Processes* 78: 25–62.

31. In one of my favorite experiments demonstrating the power of intrinsic incentives, researchers asked volunteers to do mindlessly menial work—circle pairs of consecutive letters on a sheet of paper. Everyone was paid for each sheet they completed, up to twelve sheets. In the acknowledged condition, the experimenter looked at you and acknowledged each page you completed, saying, "Thank you." This was the intrinsic motivation condition: you got a trivial amount of recognition for your work. In the ignored condition, the experimenter simply took each sheet you completed without looking at it, or at you, and stacked it on top of a huge pile of papers. In the final condition—the shredded condition—the experimenter took each sheet you handed over and dropped it right into a shredder, not even acknowledging or checking your work whatsoever. Who worked the most? Those with just the tiniest bit of intrinsic motivation—those acknowledged with a "thank you." Intrinsic motivators matter every bit as much for other people as you know they do for yourself. This experiment is reported in Ariely, D., E. Kamenica, and D. Prelec (2008). Man's search for meaning: The case of Legos. *Journal of Economic Behavior and Organization* 67: 671–77.

32. Keller, M. (1989). *Rude awakening: The rise, fall, and struggle for recovery of General Motors.* New York: William Morrow.

33. Diener, E., and M. E. P. Seligman (2002). Very happy people. *Psychological Science* 13: 80–83.

34. Epley, N., et al. (2008). Creating social connection through inferential reproduction: Loneliness and perceived agency in gadgets, gods, and greyhounds. *Psychological Science* 19: 114–20.

CHAPTER 4: HOW WE ANTHROPOMORPHIZE

1. Morris, M. W., et al. (2007). Metaphor and markets: Agent and object schemas in stock market interpretations. *Organizational Behavior and Human Decision Processes* 102, 174–92.

2. There is a very interesting story behind this image. It was taken on September 11 by Mark D. Phillips, a photojournalist who picked up his camera while at home during

the attack and starting taking pictures. This image was one of many he took that day, and it was one of the first to be submitted to the Associated Press. Interestingly, Mark told me in an e-mail that he did not notice the "face" in the image himself until he saw it the next day on the cover of the *Delaware Journal,* where it was blown up to fill the entire front page. You can read more about the story surrounding this image at Mark Phillips's website (http://www.markdphillips.com/) or in his e-book, *Satan in the Smoke? A Photojournalist's 9/11 Story.*

3. Landwehr, J. R., A. L. McGill, and A. Herrmann (2011). It's got the look: The effect of friendly and aggressive "facial" expressions on product liking and sales. *Journal of Marketing 75*: 132–46. Here's a smiling VW Bug:

4. Welsh, J. (March 10, 2006). Why cars got angry. *Wall Street Journal,* pp. W1, W10.
5. In this experiment, dog owners put their pets through an obedience test in the laboratory. Each dog owner told his or her dog not to eat a special treat and then left the room. While the owner was away, an experimenter in the room then either took the treat (which was out of the dog's reach) or allowed the dog to eat it. After a minute, the owner was instructed to go back into the room and was told by the experimenter whether the dog ate the treat. Owners knew they were then either to scold the dog for eating the treat or to praise the dog for obeying the command. What the owners did not know was that the experimenter had either taken away the treat (ensuring the dog did not eat it) or given it to the dog (ensuring that the dog would eat it). The experimenter's report was then randomly determined, ensuring that some owners were told truthfully what their dogs had done whereas others were misled.

    All of this was videotaped, and the dogs were judged on how much they showed different aspects of the "guilty look." If dogs *knew* they had disobeyed and felt guilty as a result, then they would look guiltier when they had actually eaten the treat than when they had not. In fact, dogs showed nothing like this. Instead, the videos showed dogs that looked guilty only when their owner *believed* they had eaten the treat and were scolded by their owner, not when they had *actually* disobeyed and eaten the forbidden treat. A dog's guilty look is produced by what the owner believes, not by what the dog "knows." This experiment is reported in Horowitz, A. (2009). Disambiguating the "guilty look": Salient prompts to a familiar dog behavior. *Behavioral Processes 81*: 447–52. She reports more experiments like this one in her book *Inside of a Dog* (Scribner, 2009).

6. Research on chimpanzees, however, makes it clear that they have many of the same

higher-order cognitive capacities humans do; these research findings are now being used to grant them limited human rights.

7. Nagel, T. (1974). What is it like to be a bat? *Philosophical Review* 83: 435–50.

8. Kass, J. (December 15, 2011). The worst Christmas story ever: Wisconsin vs. Charlotte the deer. *Chicago Tribune*. Retrieved from http://articles.chicagotribune.com/2011–12 –15/news/ct–met–kass–1215–20111215_1_charlotte–deer–population–horses.

9. Yoon, C. K. (March 14, 2011). No face, but plants like life too. *New York Times*. Retrieved from http://www.nytimes.com/2011/03/15/science/15food.html?pagewant ed=all.

10. Audi, T., J. Scheck, and C. Lawton (November 5, 2008). California votes for Prop 8. *Wall Street Journal*. Retrieved from http://online.wsj.com; Glover, K. (November 6, 2008). California's Prop 2 restricts farm animal confinement. CBS News. Retrieved from http://www.cbsnews.com.

11. Rota, J., and D. L. Wagner (2006). Predator mimicry: Metalmark moths mimic their jumping spider predators. *PloS ONE* 1: e45.

12. On p. 97 of T. Eisner and E. O. Wilson, (2003). *For love of insects*. Cambridge: Belknap Press.

13. "Eye spots deter animals: spicebush swallowtail," the Biomimicry Institute, accessed July 26, 2013; http://www.asknature.org/strategy/52764d8222258823367873d6ca7 67d3b.

14. Many social scientists make this argument, such as Stewart Guthrie in *Faces in the clouds* (1995, Oxford University Press), Pascal Boyer in *Religion explained* (2001, Basic Books), and Justin Barrett in *Born believers* (2012, Free Press).

15. Burnham, T. C., and B. Hare (2007). Engineering human cooperation: Does involuntary neural activation increase public goods contribution? *Human Nature* 18: 88–108. In another experiment, University of Michigan undergraduates were given a $10 bonus and told that they could give some of it to their partner in the experiment. Imagine yourself in this experiment for a moment. If you were sitting there making this decision, would you give more if your partner was sitting right next to you, watching you make this decision? Of course you would. The partner in this experiment, however, was nowhere nearby. The only face to be seen was a few well-placed dots on a piece of paper. Those in the "face" condition saw two dots above a single dot—two eyes above a mouth (or nose), as with my chicken coop—whereas those in the control condition saw the same image flipped upside down: one dot above two. These dots are not as powerful as an actual human face, of course, but they produce results in at least the same direction. In the face condition, 40 percent gave money to their partner, compared to only 25 percent in the control condition. This experiment is described in Rigdon, M., et al. (2009). Minimal social cues in the dictator game. *Journal of Economic Psychology* 30: 358–67.

16. Bateson, M., D. Nettle, and G. Roberts (2006). Cues of being watched enhance cooperation in a real-world setting. *Biology Letters* 2: 412–14. Another experiment found that the odds of a person littering in a school cafeteria were cut by more than half—from 36 percent to 16 percent—when posters of eyes were placed along the walls; Ernst-Jones, M., D. Nettle, and M. Bateson (2011). Effects of eye images on everyday cooperative behavior: a field experiment. *Evolution and Human Behavior* 32: 172–78.

17. As quoted in S. J. Gould (1998). Can we truly know sloth and rapacity? In *Leonardo's mountain of clams and the Diet of Worms* (pp. 375–91). New York: Three Rivers Press.
18. On the lack of empathy for plants: Yoon, C. K. (March 14, 2001). No face, but plants like life too. *New York Times*. Retrieved from http://www.nytimes.com/2011/03/15/science/15food.html?pagewanted=all.
19. Morewedge, C., J. Preston, and D. M. Wegner (2007). Timescale bias in the attribution of mind. *Journal of Personality and Social Psychology* 93: 1–11.
20. Sometimes a person's speed of motion can create interesting illusions. Let's take James Harrison as Exhibit A. Harrison, a notoriously vicious defensive player in the National Football League, is known best for his concussion-causing hits, for which he has received significant fines from the NFL. What is surprising to Harrison, and many others, is that many of the hits that result in fines do not incur penalties during the game. The full extent of his malice is obvious only afterward, when league officials can take a game that unfolds at lightning speed and slow it down to almost crawling speed. Only then, when your thoughts can get ahead of Harrison's actions, do the reflexive hits look deliberate, planned, and malicious. Zachary Burns demonstrated, in his PhD dissertation for the University of Chicago, that slowing down videos tends to make actions seem more intentional, including one of the more notorious hits by Harrison. Burns has posted two videos on YouTube, one at regular speed and one in slow motion:

    http://www.youtube.com/watch?v=h1bF8-o52dg
    http://www.youtube.com/watch?v=mfOcHDuZssE

    The stakes are not particularly high for Harrison, who makes money by the millions and is fined by the thousands. The same cannot be said for John "Jordan" Lewis, on trial for murdering police officer Chuck Cassidy in a Philadelphia Dunkin' Donuts. Jordan did not dispute the murder, but he claimed he panicked and acted reflexively. The prosecution claimed the murder was planned and premeditated. The prosecution's key evidence? Three seconds of surveillance video shown to jurors in slow motion. "What can you see," asked Pennsylvania Supreme Court Justice J. Michael Eakin, "in this case only in the slower version that you couldn't see in the fast version?" A more thoughtful, calculating, and rational mind than likely existed, that's what.
    Lewis was convicted of the crime on November 20, 2012. He was given a death sentence.
    This research is described in Z. Burns (2013). "It all happened so slow!": The impact of action speed on assessments of intentionality. (Unpublished PhD diss.) University of Chicago.
21. Nass, C. (2010). *The man who lied to his laptop: What machines teach us about human relationships*. New York: Current.
22. Newman, A., and A. O'Connor (February 17, 2009). Woman mauled by chimp is still in critical condition. *New York Times*. Retrieved from http://www.nytimes.com/2009/02/18/nyregion/18chimp.html.
23. Associated Press (February 11, 2009). Chimp mauling under investigation. CBS News.

Retrieved from http://www.cbsnews.com/stories/2005/03/04/national/main678061.shtml.

Frans de Waal, one of the world's leading primatologists, argues frequently that chimpanzees can at times show compassion and empathy, just as humans do. However, he also notes that many of the best primate researchers are also missing fingers. See also K. Harmon (February 19, 2009). Why would a chimpanzee attack a human? *Scientific American*. Retrieved from http://www.scientificamerican.com/article.cfm?id=why-would-a-chimpanzee-at.

24. American Foundation for Suicide Prevention (2007). American Foundation for Suicide Prevention calls on General Motors to pull advertising. Press release. Retrieved from www.afsp.org/files/Public_Relations//pr_GM.pdf.

25. Clever Apes #19: Godspeed Tevatron. *Clever Apes*. WBEZ, Chicago. September 27, 2011. Radio broadcast.

26. Morewedge, C. (2006). A mind of its own: Negativity bias in the perception of intentional agency. (Unpublished PhD diss.) Harvard University, Cambridge.

27. Waytz, A., et al. (2010). Making sense by making sentient: Effectance motivation increases anthropomorphism. *Journal of Personality and Social Psychology* 99: 410–35.

28. Some of this effect also seems due to the negativity of unexpected events. That is, a negative event is more likely to seem mindful than a positive event. In one experiment, research participants who received an unfair division of a prize were more likely to think that the division was chosen intentionally by a person than randomly by a computer. Generous divisions, in contrast, seemed more likely to be chosen randomly by a computer than intentionally by a person. When a computer or car fails to perform, not only is that unexpected, but it is also negative. These surveys do not allow us to tease apart the two effects. The fair and unfair division experiments are described in C. Morewedge (2009). Negativity bias in the attribution of external agency. *Journal of Personality and Social Psychology* 138: 535–45.

29. Waytz, A., et al. (2010). Making sense by making sentient: Effectance motivation increases anthropomorphism. *Journal of Personality and Social Psychology* 99: 410–35. You can see Clocky here: http://www.nandahome.com/products/clocky/. The owner's manual attests to how easily Clocky is anthropomorphized, reading more like something for new mothers than for clock owners. Mine informs me that "this is a guide for the newest addition to your family" and urges me to "follow these instructions as you welcome Clocky into your home" in order to "reduce the risk of injury" to your new family member. Lovely. The manual refers to Clocky as "he" no less than twenty times in the one-page manual, as in "he can jump from a nightstand up to 3 feet high" and "he can run on wood and most carpeting." These references help explain Clocky's most humanizing feature: when you press "his" snooze button the second time, wheels on the side begin to spin and Clocky starts rolling randomly around your room, so that you have to get up and turn "him" off. He's clearly an alarm clock with your best interests in mind.

30. Heider, F., and M. Simmel (1944). An experimental study of apparent behavior. *American Journal of Psychology* 57: 243–49. You can see the original video here: http://www.youtube.com/watch?v=sZBKer6PMtM.

31. Dennett, D. C. (1987). *The intentional stance*. Cambridge, MA: MIT Press.
32. Luo, Y., and R. Baillargeon (2005). Can a self-propelled box have a goal? Psychological reasoning in 5-month-old infants. *Psychological Science* 16: 601–608.
33. Deborah Blum chronicles the rise and fall of behaviorism more touchingly than you could imagine in her biography of the field's most famous critic, Harry Harlow, in her book *Love at Goon Park: Harry Harlow and the science of affection* (New York: Berkley Books, 2004).
34. Shenhav, A., D. G. Rand, and J. D. Greene (2012). Divine intuition: Cognitive style influences belief in God. *Journal of Experimental Psychology: General* 14: 423–28. Gervais, W.M., and A. Norenzayan (2012). Analytic thinking promotes religious disbelief. *Science* 336: 493–96.
35. Medin, D. L., and S. Atran (2004). The native mind: Biological categorization, reasoning, and decision making in development and across cultures. *Psychological Review* 111: 960–83.
36. Kozak, M., A. A. Marsh, and D. M. Wegner (2006). What do I think you're doing? Action identification and mind attribution. *Journal of Personality and Social Psychology* 90: 543–55.
37. And with animals, too: Sherman, G. D., and J. Haidt (2011). Cuteness and disgust: The humanizing and dehumanizing effects of emotion. *Emotion Review* 3: 245–51.
38. You might think these results just tell us that kids today are especially childish, except that very similar effects emerge in especially adult circumstances. In particular, they emerge among hardened soldiers in the midst of war. Many military units today use warbots—robots designed for battle. And although their engineers will say that they are "just machines," the soldiers who grow connected to them in battle come to think of them very differently. In *Wired for war,* P. W. Singer describes just how humanized these warbots become. They get personalized names. They are given awards. They become, for lack of a better term, *real*. According to one soldier, Frankenstein "was part of our team, he was one of us. He did feel like family." Soldiers working in the warbot machine shops describe their work in language you normally hear from doctors at hospitals. As Singer quotes one machinist: "I wish you all could be here and experience the satisfaction in knowing you saved someone's life today. I wish you could see the fire in their eyes when they first walk in knowing that they could walk out with no robot. I wish you could see the smiles and feel the hugs and handshakes after they leave our shop knowing that their 'little Timmy' is ALIVE." Is this the soldier's version of the Velveteen Rabbit?

    If so, then we have a phenomenon that follows us from birth until death, because social connections seem to make things real at the end of our lives as well. Trying to help the elderly fend off loneliness and depression, some nursing homes are now turning to robots for support, such as Paro, a socially interactive robot made to look like a baby harp seal. Paro has the requisite eyes, movement, and interactive qualities that can trigger the sense of a mind, but it's the connection that builds over time that seems to make Paro come alive for some people. Like the soldiers, the elderly are not confused about Paro. They know it's a machine, but their senses tell them it's real, too. "I love animals," one resident, Lois Simmeth, told a *Wall Street Journal* reporter. Then, turning to Paro, sitting in her lap, she whispered, "I know you're not real, but somehow, I don't know, I love you." Ms. Simmeth is not confused about the nature of Paro, but she, just like all of the rest of us, is confused about how our brains work, in this case how our brains create illusions like a mindful, sentient, and living being out of a mindless, mechanical, and lifeless robot. Tergesen, A, and M. Inada (June 21, 2010). It's not a stuffed animal, it's a $6,000 medical device. *Wall Street Journal.* Retrieved from http://online.wsj.com/article/SB10001424052748704463504575301051844937276 .html/.

39. Broyles Jr., William (2000). *Cast away.* Directed by R. Zemeckis. Twentieth Century Fox.

40. Epley, N., et al. (2008). Creating social connection through inferential reproduction: Loneliness and perceived agency in gadgets, gods, and greyhounds. *Psychological Science* 19: 114–20.

41. Other researchers have reported similar results with belief in God: Gebauer, J. E., and G. R. Maio (2012). The need to belong can motivate belief in God. *Journal of Personality* 80: 465–501; Nilüfer, A., P. Fischer, and D. Frey (2010). Turning to God in the face of ostracism: Effects of social exclusion on religiousness. *Personality and Social Psychology Bulletin* 36: 742–53.

42. Adler, J. (August 29, 2005). In search of the spiritual. *Newsweek* 146: 46–64.

43. Indeed, Binti is the daughter of the famous gorilla Koko, who was taught to use sign language. Binti has never spent even a moment out of captivity.

44. Hare, B., et al. (2002). The domestication of social cognition in dogs. *Science* 298: 1636–39. For more, see B. Hare and V. Woods (2013). *The genius of dogs.* New York: Dutton.

45. Fraser, O. N., and T. Bugnyar (2011). Ravens reconcile after aggressive conflicts with valuable partners. *PLoS ONE* 6: e18118.

CHAPTER 5: THE TROUBLE OF GETTING OVER YOURSELF

1. Others have actually made even more permanent mistakes. DeShawn Stevenson, an NBA basketball player and something of a human billboard, had the letter *P tattooed* on his face to show support for his beloved Pittsburgh Pirates. "That's my favorite team," he explains. When asked by a *Washington Post* reporter why it was drawn—you guessed it—*backward,* he seemed confused. "No, if you're standing [farther away] and looking at me, it looks like a P." Actually, if you're standing farther away it is still every bit as backward.

Others are savvier about this. When Apple made its first laptop, its designers wanted to create the best experience possible for users. They therefore oriented the logo to the user's perspective. The logo was right side up for the user when the lid was closed, but it then appeared upside down to anyone looking at the user when the lid was open. Apple changed the design a few years later, as it got more image conscious. As one Apple engineer noted, "Opening a laptop from the wrong end is a self-correcting problem that only lasts for a few seconds. However, viewing the upside[-down] logo is a problem that lasts indefinitely." Bonnington, C. (May 22, 2012). Former

Apple employee explains "upside-down" logo. CNN. Retrieved from http://www.cnn .com/2012/05/22/tech/gaming-gadgets/apple-upside-down-logo/index.html?hpt=hp _bn11.

2. Diamond, A., and N. Kirkham (2005). Not quite as grown-up as we like to think: Parallels between cognition in childhood and adulthood. *Psychological Science* 16: 291–97. These authors write, "It might be possible that adults do not fully grow out of any of the cognitive or perceptual biases of infancy and early childhood."

3. Lerouge, D., and L. Warlop (2006). Why it is so hard to predict our partner's product preferences: The effect of target familiarity on prediction accuracy. *Journal of Consumer Research* 33: 393–402.

4. Adding insult to injury, the DVDs were also formatted for North American DVD players and would not play on the British versions.

5. Epley, N., et al. (2004). Perspective taking as egocentric anchoring and adjustment. *Journal of Personality and Social Psychology* 87: 327–39; Keysar, B., et al. (2000). Taking perspective in conversation: The role of mutual knowledge in comprehension. *Psychological Sciences* 11: 32–38.

6. *Onion.* (April 13, 2007). Majority of parents abuse children, children report. Retrieved from http://www.theonion.com/articles/majority-of-parents-abuse-children-children -report,2183/.

7. Chambers, J. R., and P. D. Windschitl (2004). Biases in social comparative judgments: The role of nonmotivated factors in above-average and comparative-optimism effects. *Psychological Bulletin* 130: 813–38; Krisan, Z., and P. D. Windschitl (2007). The influence of outcome desirability on optimism. *Psychological Bulletin* 133: 95–121; and Kruger, J. (1999). Lake Wobegon be gone! The "below-average effect" and the egocentric nature of comparative ability judgments. *Journal of Personality and Social Psychology* 77: 221–32.

8. Kruger, J., and J. Burrus (2004). Egocentrism and focalism in unrealistic optimism (and pessimism). *Journal of Experimental Social Psychology* 40: 332–40.

9. Klar, Y., and E. Giladi (1999). Are most people happier than their peers, or are they just happy? *Personality and Social Psychology Bulletin* 25: 586–95.

10. Survey data from Smith, T. W., K. A. Rasinski, and M. Toce (2001). *America rebounds: A national study of public response to the September 11th terrorist attacks.* Chicago: National Opinion Research Center.

11. Ross, M., and F. Sicoly (1979). Egocentric biases in availability and attribution. *Journal of Personality and Social Psychology* 37: 322–36.

12. These data are from J. Kruger and T. Gilovich. "Naïve cynicism" in everyday theories of responsibility assessment: On biased assumptions of bias. *Journal of Personality and Social Psychology* 76: 743–53.

13. Caruso, E., N. Epley, and M. Bazerman (2005). Unpublished data. Harvard University.

14. Gilovich, T., V. H. Medvec, and K. Savitsky (2000). The spotlight effect in social judgment: An egocentric bias in estimates of the salience of one's own actions and appearance. *Journal of Personality and Social Psychology* 78: 211–22.

15. Lest you worry that this spotlight effect is produced by some strange Barry Manilow magic, rest assured that these researchers observed the same results with John Tesh

and Vanilla Ice T-shirts. The spotlight effect also emerges for desirable figures that people were proud to be seen wearing, including Martin Luther King Jr. Others are less likely to notice either our shortcomings or our shining moments as much as we think. The spotlight effect also emerges in less quirky contexts, such as the extent to which others notice the comments you make in conversation or the extent to which others notice when you're lying versus telling the truth. It even emerges in the amount that others notice variability in your performance. You know when you have relatively good days and bad days, making it easy to overestimate how much others attend to these subtle blips. In one experiment, college volleyball players predicted how their performance in practice would be rated by their teammates over a series of days. Players expected significantly more variability in their teammates' ratings than they actually received, assuming that players would notice their good and bad days more than they actually did. And when you're castigating your spouse for not noticing that you were happy or sad or angry or glad, remember that your emotions are far more obvious to you on the inside than they are to others on the outside. Gilovich, T., J. Kruger, and V. H. Medvec (2002). The spotlight effect revisited: Overestimating the manifest variability of our actions and appearance. *Journal of Experimental Social Psychology* 38: 93–99; Gilovich, T., K. Savitsky, and V. H. Medvec (1998). The illusion of transparency: Biased assessments of others' ability to read our emotional states. *Journal of Personality and Social Psychology* 75: 332–46.

16. This quote is frequently attributed to Dr. Seuss. That attribution sounds right, but it appears to be wrong. No published book by Dr. Seuss includes this quote; nor can it be traced to him in any interview I can find. One source suggests that it comes from Bernard Baruch, in his response to a question about how he handled the seating arrangements at dinner parties, as described in Bennett Cerf's book *Shake well before using: A new collection of impressions and anecdotes, mostly humorous* (1948). Baruch's response was "I never bother about that. Those who matter don't mind, and those who mind don't matter." Over the years, this quote seems to have morphed into something both broader and wiser.

17. Research confirms that learning about one particular version of this egocentric bias decreases speech anxiety, just as it did for me: Savitsky, K., and T. Gilovich (2003). The illusion of transparency and the alleviation of speech anxiety. *Journal of Experimental Social Psychology* 39: 618–25.

18. Many people seem to learn this lesson over the long course of their lives. Award-winning journalist Roger Rosenblatt, for instance, wrote a clever little book called *Rules for aging* (Harcourt Books). In the book, he lists what he believes are the fifty-eight most important rules for aging well. I concur completely with Rules 1 and 2: "It doesn't matter" and "Nobody is thinking about you." Now, that's something worth putting on a T-shirt.

19. Babcock, L., and G. Loewenstein (1997). Explaining bargaining impasse: The role of self-serving biases. *Journal of Economic Perspectives* 11: 109–26.

20. Psychologists refer to this consistent bias as the *hostile media effect*. You can read about it here: Vallone, R. P., L. Ross, and M. R. Lepper (1985). The hostile media phenomenon: Biased perception and perceptions of media bias in coverage of the Beirut massacre. *Journal of Personality and Social Psychology* 49: 577–85.

Commentators describe how the media is biased against them every night on the cable news channels; meanwhile, psychologists have documented the hostile media effect in:

—Other aspects of the Middle East conflict: Giner-Sorolla, R., and S. Chaiken (1994). The causes of hostile media judgments. *Journal of Experimental Social Psychology* 30: 165–80; and Perloff, R. M. (1989). Ego-involvement and the third person effect of televised news coverage. *Communication Research* 16: 236–62.

—Military conflict in Bosnia: Matheson, K. and S. Dursun (2001). Social identity precursors to the hostile media phenomenon: Partisan perceptions of coverage of the Bosnian conflict. *Group Processes and Intergroup Relations* 4: 117–26.

—A labor strike: Christen, C. T., P. Kannaovakun, and A. C. Gunther (2002). Hostile media perceptions: Partisan assessments of press and public during the 1997 UPS strike. *Political Communication* 19: 423–36.

—U.S. presidential debate coverage: Dalton, R. M., P. A. Beck, and R. Huckfeldt (1998). Partisan cues and the media: Information flows in the 1992 presidential election. *American Political Science Review* 92: 111–26.

—Opinion news hosts: Feldman, L. (2011). Partisan differences in opinionated news perceptions: A test of the hostile media effect. *Political Behavior* 33: 407–32.

—Coverage of genetically modified food debates: Gunther, A. C., and K. Schmitt (2004). Mapping boundaries of the hostile media effect. *Journal of Communication* 54: 55–70.

—Coverage of animal rights issues: Gunther, A. C., et al. (2001). Congenial public, contrary press and biased estimates of the climate of opinion. *Public Opinion Quarterly* 65: 295–320.

—Coverage of arguments about physician-assisted suicide: Gunther, A. C., and C. T. Christen (2002). Projection or persuasive press? Contrary effects of personal opinion and perceived news coverage on estimates of public opinion. *Journal of Communication* 52: 177–95.

21. Eibach, R. P., L. K. Libby, and T. D. Gilovich (2003). When change in the self is mistaken for change in the world. *Journal of Personality and Social Psychology* 84: 917–31; Eibach, R. P., and S. E. Mock (2011). The vigilant parent: Parental role salience affects parents' risk perceptions, risk-aversion, and trust in strangers. *Journal of Experimental Social Psychology* 47: 694–97.

22. Pinker, S. (2012). *The better angels of our nature: Why violence has declined.* New York: Penguin.

23. Krueger, J. (1998). Enhancement bias in descriptions of self and others. *Personality and Social Psychology Bulletin* 24: 505–16.

24. Ross, L., D. Greene, and P. House (1977). The false consensus phenomenon: An attributional bias in self-perception and social perception processes. *Journal of Experimental Social Psychology* 13: 279–301.

25. Travers, R. M. W. (1941). A study in judging the opinions of groups. *Archives of Psychology* 266: 73; Krueger, J., and R. W. Clement (1994). The truly false consensus effect: An ineradicable and egocentric bias in social perception. *Journal of Personality and Social Psychology* 67: 596–610; Ross, L., D. Greene, and P. House (1977). The false consensus effect: An egocentric bias in social perception and attribution processes. *Journal of Experimental Social Psychology* 13: 279–301.

26. Koudenburg, N., T. Postmes, and E. H. Gordijn (2011). If they were to vote, they would vote for us. *Psychological Science* 22: 1506–10.

27. Alicke, M. D. (1993). Egocentric standards of conduct evaluation. *Basic and Applied Social Psychology* 14: 171–92.

28. Francis Flynn, an organizational psychologist at Stanford University's Graduate School of Business, created this survey to use in his MBA classes and was generous enough to give it to me to use in mine.

29. More precisely, in an online survey of 389 people I conducted, 72.3 percent failed to find six *f*'s. Among those who failed, 61.4 percent reported finding only three. This is similar to the rates reported in published research using smaller samples.

30. If you have kids, I encourage you to give this a try. One afternoon I showed this example to my three sons: our adopted son who had been speaking English for less than a year and my two biological sons, aged six and eleven, who had been speaking English their entire lives. Asked to tell me the number of *f*'s, they found six, five, and three, respectively, right on cue. My eleven-year-old was not happy after being beaten by two kindergarteners.

31. My colleague Linda Ginzel showed this example to me, and her son Ely Keysar used it in a science fair project comparing the performance of younger and older children. I thank Linda for showing this to me, and Ely for pointing me in the direction of research using this example with children, as well as for leading me to try it with my own.

32. Hinds, P. J. (1999). The curse of expertise: The effects of expertise and debiasing methods on predictions of novice performance. *Journal of Experimental Psychology: Applied* 5: 205–21.

33. This story comes from Samson Hsia from the time he worked at Clorox, as told by Malcolm Gladwell in his *New Yorker* article "The Bakeoff" (2005).

34. More details about Newton's tapping study can be found in Pronin, E., C. Puccio, and L. Ross (2002). Understanding misunderstanding: Social psychological perspectives. In Gilovich, T., D. Griffin, and D. Kahneman (eds.), *Heuristics and biases: The psychology of intuitive judgment* (pp. 636–65). New York: Cambridge University Press. Newton's original dissertation, submitted to Stanford University in 1990, was titled "Overconfidence in the communication of intent: Heard and unheard melodies."

35. Kruger, J., C. L. Gordon, and J. Kuban, J. (2006). Intentions in teasing: When "just kidding" just isn't good enough. *Journal of Personality and Social Psychology* 90: 412–25.

36. Chambers, J. R., et al. (2008). Knowing too much: Using private knowledge to predict how one is viewed by others. *Psychological Science* 19: 542–48.

37. Gilovich, T. (1990). Differential construal and the false consensus effect. *Journal of Personality and Social Psychology* 59: 623–34.

38. Kruger, J., et al. (2005). Egocentrism over email: Can we communicate as well as we think? *Journal of Personality and Social Psychology* 89: 925–36.

39. Hagerty, B. B. (April 16, 2012). Christians debate: Was Jesus for small government? National Public Radio. Radio broadcast.

40. To learn more about some of these different interpretations, at least within the Christian religious tradition, see David Myers and Letha Dawson Scanzoni's book, *What God has joined together: The christian case for gay marriage* (San Francisco: HarperSanFrancisco, 2005).

41. This question made the cover of *Time* magazine, September 18, 2006.

42. Dealbook (November 9, 2009). Blankfein says he's just doing "God's work." *New York Times*. Retrieved from http://dealbook.nytimes.com/2009/11/09/goldman-chief-says-he-is-just-doing-gods-work/.

43. Lesher, J. H. (1992). *Xenophanes of Colophon: Fragments.* Toronto: University of Toronto Press.

44. All of the evidence I cite in this paragraph comes from N. Epley et al. (2009). Believers' estimates of God's beliefs are more egocentric than estimates of other people's beliefs. *Proceedings of the National Academy of Sciences* 106: 21533–38.

45. It is worth noting that although fathers and sons often disagree, it appears that Christians are just as egocentric when they reason about Jesus Christ's beliefs as when they reason about God's beliefs. See L. D. Ross, Y. Lelkes, and A. G. Russell (2012). How Christians reconcile their personal political views and the teachings of their faith: Projection as a means of dissonance reduction. *Proceedings of the National Academy of Sciences* 109: 3616–22.

46. This problem hasn't gone away. In 1999, over three centuries after the *Vasa's* sinking, NASA lost its $125 million Mars lander to a similar mistake when Lockheed Martin's engineering team responsible for the approach made its calculations in English units while the NASA team responsible for landing the craft made its calculations in metric units.

47. Savitsky, K., N. Epley, and T. Gilovich (2001). Do others judge us as harshly as we think? Overestimating the impact of our failures, shortcomings, and mishaps. *Journal of Personality and Social Psychology* 81: 44–56. Also Epley, N., K. Savitsky, and T. Gilovich, (2002). Empathy neglect: Reconciling the spotlight effect and the correspondence bias. *Journal of Personality and Social Psychology* 83: 300–12.

48. Hedegaard, E. (February 2012). Mark Wahlberg handles his business. *Men's Journal* 21: 52–56. The quote is on p. 56. In fact, psychologists have a term for this kind of presumed bravado: the "illusion of courage." See Van Boven, L., et al. (2012). The illusion of courage in self-predictions: Mispredicting one's own behavior in embarrassing situations. *Journal of Behavioral Decision Making* 25: 1–12; Van Boven, L., G. Loewenstein, and D. Dunning (2005). The illusion of courage in social predictions: Underestimating the impact of fear of embarrassment on other people. *Organizational Behavior and Human Decision Processes* 96: 130–41.

49. Quotes about Mancow being waterboarded are taken from: http://www.nbcchicago.com/news/archive/Mancow-Takes-on-Waterboarding-and-Loses.html.

Christopher Hitchens subjected himself to the same experience and came to exactly the same conclusion, being haunted by the experience for months afterward. "[If] waterboarding does not constitute torture, then there is no such thing as torture," he concluded. Hitchens wrote of his experience in the August 2008 issue of *Vanity Fair,* in an article titled "Believe Me, It's Torture."

50. Kahn, R. L. (1958). Human relations on the shop floor. In E. M. Hugh-Jones (ed.), *Human relations and modern management* (pp. 43–74). Amsterdam: North Holland.

51. Sometimes, in fact, it can get even more extreme. In one experiment, volunteers participated in an experiment while sitting comfortably indoors or while sitting at a freezing cold bus stop in the dead of winter. They then read a story about either a politically liberal or a politically conservative hiker who got lost on a winter hike and predicted whether hunger, thirst, or cold would be of greatest concern to the hiker. The volunteers were egocentric when predicting the hiker's thoughts and feelings, but only if the hiker shared their own political views. That is, those sitting at the freezing cold bus stop thought the hiker with similar political beliefs would be more concerned about the cold than about food or water, would find the cold to be more unpleasant than hunger or thirst, and would regret not bringing enough warm clothes more than not bringing enough food or water. However, if the hiker had different political beliefs, then the volunteers' own feelings had no effect on their predictions of the person's mental states. Having beliefs that are not "like me" meant having feelings and concerns that are also not "like me."

The experiment about cold bus travelers predicting a hiker's beliefs is described in E. O'Brien and P. C. Ellsworth (2012). More than skin deep: Visceral states are not projected onto dissimilar others. *Psychological Science* 23: 391–96.

CHAPTER 6: THE USES AND ABUSES OF STEREOTYPES

1. Norton, M. I., and D. Ariely (2011). Building a better America—one wealth quintile at a time. *Perspectives on Psychological Science* 6: 9–12.

2. These two pie charts, B and C, reflect the actual wealth distribution from two real countries. Country B is Sweden, and country C is the United States. By very large margins, Americans prefer Sweden.

3. In addition to asking about preferences regarding living in nations with different income distributions, the researchers also asked their respondents to report what they believed was the actual distribution of income in the five wealth quintiles in the United States and what they believed was the ideal distribution. Three interesting effects emerged. First, Americans considerably underestimated the actual amount of wealth inequality. Second, Americans overwhelmingly thought the ideal distribution of wealth would be more equal than the current distribution. Third, liberals, the poor, and women preferred a more equal distribution than conservatives did, but these group differences were relatively trivial compared to the similarity across these groups. The first line of the figure on the next page shows the actual amount of wealth controlled by each quintile in the income distribution. The next seven lines show the estimated amount of wealth inequality for a variety of different groups, all of whom

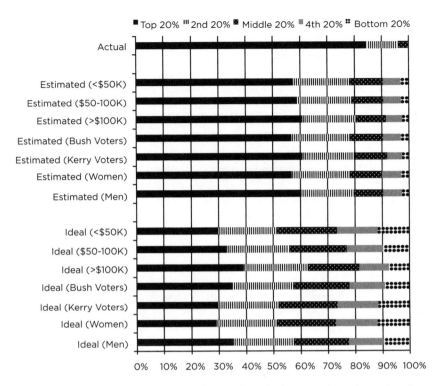

■ Top 20% ⫼ 2nd 20% ▨ Middle 20% ▩ 4th 20% ⁑ Bottom 20%

underestimate the actual amount of inequality. The last seven lines show what these respondents thought was the ideal amount of inequality in the United States; all of them, by large margins, think a more equitable distribution would be more ideal. I thank Mike Norton for sending me these results.

4. I conducted this survey online in the fall of 2012, using Amazon's Mechanical Turk. This is an online crowdsourcing site that coordinates the use of human intelligence for all sorts of tasks that computers are currently unable to perform. It also allows researchers to conduct survey experiments like this one with a reasonably representative sample of respondents.

5. Ashmore, R., and F. Del Boca (1981). Conceptual approaches to stereotypes and stereotyping. In D. Hamilton (ed.), *Cognitive processes in stereotyping and intergroup behavior* (pp. 1–35). Hillsdale, NJ: Erlbaum.

6. This figure comes from D. Ariely (2001). Seeing sets: Representation by statistical properties. *Psychological Science* 12: 57–162.

7. . . . . and over, for a total of 600 trials, if you must know. Groups included 4, 8, 12, or 16 circles, with 15 different configurations of the circles' sizes, with each resulting slide shown 10 different times (4 set sizes x 15 size configurations x 10 replications = 600 trials). Remember this the next time you think it would be fun to participate in a psychology experiment.

8. Other examples: Albrecht, A. T., and B. J. Scholl (2010). Perceptually averaging in a continuous visual world: Extracting statistical summary representations over time.

Psychological Science 21: 560–67; Corbett, J. E., et al. (2012). An aftereffect of adaptation to mean size. *Visual Cognition* 20: 211–31; Choo, H., and S. L. Franconeri (2010). Objects with reduced visibility still contribute to size averaging. *Attention, Perception, and Psychophysics* 72: 86–99.

9. In fact, your brain's statistician looks to be capable of even more impressive feats than calculating an average. Your brain also excludes extremes that might distort the group average, just as a statistician calculating the average salary of a Walmart worker would exclude the CEO who makes millions in order to give a more accurate picture of the average worker's salary. If you had one extremely tiny circle, your brain would ignore it when calculating the average. Just remember these two facts the next time you think you're no good at math. De Gardelle, V., and C. Summerfield (2011). Robust averaging during perceptual judgment. *Proceedings of the National Academy of Sciences of the United States of America* 108: 13341–46.

10. Haberman, J., T. Harp, and D. Whitney (2009). Averaging facial expression over time. *Journal of Vision* 9: 1; Haberman, J., and D. Whitney (2007). Rapid extraction of mean emotion and gender from sets of faces. *Current Biology* 17: R751–53; Haberman, J., and D. Whitney (2009). Seeing the mean: Ensemble coding for sets of faces. *Journal of Experimental Psychology: Human Perception and Performance* 35: 718–34.

11. Diekman, A., A. Eagly, and P. Kulesa (2002). Accuracy and bias in stereotypes about the social and political attitudes of women and men. *Journal of Experimental Social Psychology* 38: 268–82.

12. Hogarth, R. M. (2001). *Educating intuition.* Chicago: University of Chicago Press.

13. For the most comprehensive review available of research on stereotype accuracy, see L. Jussim (2012). *Social perception and social reality: Why accuracy dominates bias and self-fulfilling prophecy.* New York: Oxford University Press.

14. When University of Michigan psychologists Richard Nisbett and Ziva Kunda asked undergraduates to predict their fellow students' typical behaviors and attitudes, they were surprised by the amount of accuracy they observed. "Prior to conducting this research," they wrote, "we thought only of mechanisms that might produce error." Nisbett and Kunda asked these students to estimate behaviors like the percentage of peers who have trouble getting to sleep, routinely get drunk, or attend religious services. Students also estimated attitudes like the percentage who approve of the president's performance, believe a woman should be able to get an abortion on demand, or are in favor of increasing military defense spending. Students were reasonably accurate predicting which behaviors and attitudes were more common than others and were also reasonably accurate predicting the ranges of both behaviors and attitudes. For instance, these students knew that most of their peers got drunk more often than they played pool, were opposed to the current president's conservative policies but were generally in favor of a woman's right to choose, and liked McDonald's hamburgers more than they liked the religious right. These students were not only fairly familiar with one another but were also fairly similar to each other, meaning that they knew the norms of both behavior and attitudes reasonably well. Nisbett, R. E., and Z. Kunda (1985). The perception of social distributions. *Journal of Personality and Social Psychology*, 48: 297–311. Kunda, Z., and R. E. Nisbett (1986). Prediction

and the partial understanding of the law of large numbers. *Journal of Experimental Social Psychology* 22: 339–54.

15. Ryan, C. S. (1996). Accuracy of black and white college students' in-group and out-group stereotypes. *Personality and Social Psychology Bulletin* 22: 1114–27.

16. Epley, N., and J. Kruger (2005). When what you type isn't what they read: The perseverance of stereotypes and expectancies over email. *Journal of Experimental Social Psychology* 41: 414–22.

17. Kring, A. M., and A. H. Gordon (1998). Sex differences in emotion: Expression, experience, and physiology. *Journal of Personality and Social Psychology* 74: 686–703. Van Boven, L., and M. D. Robinson (2012). Boys don't cry: Cognitive load and priming increase stereotypic sex differences in emotion memory. *Journal of Experimental Social Psychology* 48: 303–309.

18. Nelson, L. J., and D. T. Miller (1995). The distinctiveness effect in social categorization: You are what makes you unusual. *Psychological Science* 6: 246–49.

19. Riggs, L. A., and F. Ratliff (1952). The effects of counteracting the normal movements of the eye. *Journal of the Optical Society of America* 42: 872–73.

20. Tajfel, H., and A. L. Wilkes (1963). Classification and quantitative judgment. *British Journal of Psychology* 54: 101–14.

21. Hyde, J. S. (2005). The gender similarities hypothesis. *American Psychologist* 60: 581–92.

22. Actually, in all but one culture. One sample in Spain showed results in the same direction, but it was not statistically significant. Overall, the gender differences were large and consistent. None are in the opposite direction.

23. Hyde, J. S. (2005). The gender similarities hypothesis. *American Psychologist* 60: 581–92. Hyde's main evidence is based on a meta-analysis of as many published reports of studies that tallied results by gender as she could find, assessing gender effects across several different categories: cognitive variables (math, memory, overall intelligence, spatial skills), verbal and nonverbal communication (talkativeness, language ability, smiling), social and personality variables (physical and verbal aggression, leadership style and skill, extroversion), psychological well-being (happiness, anxiety, self-esteem, depression), and motor skills (throwing velocity and distance, running speed, activity level). Across 124 difference variables, 80 percent produced either no gender difference or only small differences. Only 2 of the 124 produced truly large differences: throwing velocity and throwing distance. Men tend to throw a ball faster and farther than women.

24. For a thorough dissection of the true magnitude of gender differences in the brain, see C. Fine (2010). *Delusions of gender: How our minds, society, and neurosexism create difference*. New York: W. W. Norton.

25. Fisher, T., Z. T. Moore, and M. J. Pittenger (2011). Sex on the brain?: An examination of frequency of sexual cognitions as a function of gender, erotophilia, and social desirability. *Journal of Sex Research* 49: 69–77.

26. It gets worse. Joining Brizendine in our Gender Exaggeration Hall of Fame is Leonard Sax, author of *Why Gender Matters*. In "Six Degrees of Separation: What Teachers Need to Know About the Emerging Science of Sex Differences" (*Educational Hori-*

zons, Spring 2006), Sax also begins with good sense at the end of his second paragraph: "As a general rule, the variation within the sexes on those parameters is usually far greater than the small differences between the sexes." Immediately comes the predictable flip to exaggerate the differences in a *new* set of parameters from neuroscience and minimize the similarities, and by the end, Sax is advocating that single-sex schooling is required. Sax himself is not a neuroscientist but is, rather, a popularizer of the research, like Brizendine. The actual neuroscientist Lise Eliot summarizes the existing research findings differently: "Of the various rationales for sex-segregated education, the claim that boys and girls should be taught in separate classrooms because their brains differ is arguably the weakest. Existing neuroscience research has identified few reliable differences between boys' and girls' brains relevant to learning or education. And yet, prominent single-sex school advocates have convinced many parents and teachers that there exist profound differences between the 'male brain' and 'female brain' which support the ubiquitous, but equally unfounded belief that 'boys and girls learn differently.'" Eliot, L. (2011). Single-sex education and the brain. *Sex Roles.*

27. Hyde, J. S. (2005). The gender similarities hypothesis. *American Psychologist* 60: 581–92; Hyde, J. S. (2006). Gender similarities still rule. *American Psychologist* 61: 641–42; Hall, J. A. (1987). On explaining gender differences: The case of nonverbal communication. In P. Shaver and C. Hendrick (eds.), *Sex and gender: Review of personality and social psychology,* vol. 7 (pp. 177–200). Thousand Oaks, CA: Sage.

28. Eyal, T., and Epley, N. (2013). *Exaggerated stereotypes of "essential" gender differences.* Unpublished manuscript. University of Chicago.

29. Briton, N. J., and J. A. Hall (1995). Beliefs about female and male nonverbal communication. *Sex Roles* 32: 79–90.

30. Westfall, J., J. R. Chambers, and L. Van Boven (2012). False polarization among Americans (1970–2004): Partisan identification, attitude extremity, and civic action. Unpublished manuscript. University of Florida, Gainesville.

31. Rutchick, A. M., J. M. Smyth, and S. Konrath (2009). Seeing red (and blue): Effects of electoral college depictions on political group perception. *Analyses of Social Issues and Public Policy* 9: 269–82.

32. Chambers, J. R., R. S. Baron, and M. L. Inman (2006). Misperceptions in intergroup conflict. *Psychological Science* 17: 38–45; Robinson, R. J., et al. (1995). Actual versus assumed differences in construal: "Naive realism" in intergroup perception and conflict. *Journal of Personality and Social Psychology* 68: 404–17; Farwell, L., and B. Weiner (2000). Bleeding hearts and the heartless: Popular perceptions of liberal and conservative ideologies. *Personality and Social Psychology Bulletin* 26: 845–52; Sherman, D. K., L. D. Nelson, and L.D. Ross (2003). Naive realism and affirmative action: Adversaries are more similar than they think. *Basic and Applied Social Psychology* 25: 275–89.

33. Fiorina, M. P., and S. J. Abrams (2008). Political polarization in the American public. *Annual Review of Political Science* 11: 563–88; Seyle, D. C., and M. L. Newman (2006). A house divided? The psychology of red and blue America. *American Psychologist* 61: 571–80.

34. Epley, N., E. M. Caruso, and M. H. Bazerman (2006). When perspective taking

increases taking: Reactive egoism in social interaction. *Journal of Personality and Social Psychology* 91: 872–89.

35. Mallett, R. K., T. Wilson, and D. T. Gilbert (2008). Expect the unexpected: Failure to anticipate similarities leads to an intergroup forecasting error. *Journal of Personality and Social Psychology* 94: 265–77.

36. Masoro, E. J., and S. N. Austad (eds.) (2011). *Handbook of the biology of aging.* Burlington, MA: Academic Press.

37. These data show performance on the Woodcock-Johnson Psychoeducational Test Battery, administered in 1989 and 1990. This figure comes from page 189 of T. A. Salthouse (1999). Pressing issues in cognitive aging. In N. Schwarz, et al. (eds.), *Cognition, aging, and self-reports* (pp. 185–98). Levittown, PA: Psychology Press.

38. Levy, B., and E. Langer (1994). Aging free from negative stereotypes: Successful memory in China among the American deaf. *Journal of Personality and Social Psychology* 66: 989–97.

39. Levy, B. R., et al. (2009). Age stereotypes held earlier in life predict cardiovascular events in later life. *Psychological Science* 20: 296–98.

40. Levy, B. R., et al. (2002). Longevity increased by positive self-perceptions of aging. *Journal of Personality and Social Psychology* 83: 261–70.

41. Levy, B. (1996). Improving memory in old age through implicit self-stereotyping. *Journal of Personality and Social Psychology* 71: 1092–1107.

42. Steele, C. M., and J. Aronson (1995). Stereotype threat and the intellectual test performance of African Americans. *Journal of Personality and Social Psychology* 69: 797–811.

43. Inzlicht, M., and T. Schmader (2011). *Stereotype threat: Theory, process, and application.* New York: Oxford University Press. Also C. Steele (2010). *Whistling Vivaldi.* New York: W. W. Norton.

44. Cohen, G. L., et al. (2006). Reducing the racial achievement gap: A social-psychological intervention. *Science* 313: 1307–10. Cohen, G. L., et al. (2009). Recursive processes in self-affirmation: Intervening to close the minority achievement gap. *Science* 324: 400–403; Walton, G., and G. L. Cohen (2011). A brief social-belonging intervention improves academic and health outcomes of minority students. *Science* 331: 1147–51. Ramirez, G., and S. L. Beilock (2011). Writing about testing worries boosts exam performance in the classroom. *Science* 331: 211–13.

45. Ickes, W., P. R. Gesn, and T. Graham (2000). Gender differences in empathic accuracy: Differential ability or differential motivation? *Personal Relationships* 7: 95–109. See also chapter 6 of W. Ickes (2003). *Everyday mind reading: Understanding what other people think and feel.* Amherst, NY: Prometheus Books.

46. Koenig, A. M., and A. H. Eagly (2005). Stereotype threat in men on a test of social sensitivity. *Sex Roles* 52: 489–96.

47. Baum, C. (July 14, 2010). Throw the bums out as long as my bum stays put. Bloomberg. Retrieved from http://www.bloomberg.com/news/2010-07-15/throw-the-bums -out-as-long-as-my-bum-stays-put-caroline-baum.html.

48. Kunda, Z., et al. (2002). The dynamic time course of stereotype activation: Activation, dissipation, and resurrection. *Journal of Personality and Social Psychology* 82: 283–99.

CHAPTER 7: HOW ACTIONS CAN MISLEAD

1. Kattalia, K. (November 27, 2011). Black Friday shopper collapses, dies. *New York Daily News*. Retrieved from http://articles.nydailynews.com/2011-11-27/news/30445630_1 _black-friday-shopper-early-bird-sales-shopping-center; Kelly, T. (November 27, 2011). Black Friday: Target shoppers step over Walter Vance as he collapses, dies. *Huffington Post*. Retrieved from http://www.huffingtonpost.com/2011/11/27/black -friday-target_n_1115372.html; *Daily Mail*. (November 26, 2011). Not a single Good Samaritan: Frenzied bargain hunters unfazed as they step around and even OVER collapsed man at Target who later died. Retrieved from http://www.dailymail .co.uk/news/article-2066622/Not-single-Good-Samaritan-Frenzied-bargain-hunters -unfazed-step-OVER-collapsed-man-Target-died.html.

2. According to the Centers for Disease Control and Prevention: www.cdc.gov/features/ heartmonth/.

3. Gilbert, D. T., and P. Malone (1995). The correspondence bias. *Psychological Bulletin* 117: 21–38.

4. Before technology allowed people's eyes to fly into space and see roundness through them, you could get a broader perspective only by using identical statues at the same time of day and measuring their shadows in *different* parts of the world. When a statue casts no shadow at the height of the solstice in Athens but still casts a shadow in Alexandria, then roundness is revealed by the shadow's length (at least to mathematicians). Our ancestors, stuck firmly in one place at one time, without the benefit of a far-off friend, accurate rulers, the Pythagorean theorem, or a broader perspective, would never know this.

5. For an accessible version of this argument, see M. Gladwell (July 22, 2002). The talent myth: Are smart people overrated? *New Yorker*. Retrieved from http://www.newyorker .com/archive/2002/07/22/020722fa_fact.

6. Ross, L., T. Amabile, and J. Steinmetz (1977). Social roles, social control, and biases in the social-perception process. *Journal of Personality and Social Psychology* 35: 485–94.

7. All of these are examples of real items that questioners have generated as part of a class demonstration I do with my MBA students at the University of Chicago every year.

8. The Chertoff quote comes from M. Chertoff, interview by M. O'Brien (2005). *American Morning*. Retrieved from CNN Transcripts: http://transcripts.cnn.com /TRANSCRIPTS/0509/01/ltm.03.html.

9. CNN (September 1, 2005). FEMA chief: Victims bear some responsibility. Retrieved from http://articles.cnn.com/2005-09-01/weather/katrina.fema.brown_1_mandatory -evacuation-death-toll-relief-effort?_s=PM:WEATHER.

10. Palazzolo, R. (August 30, 2005). Why do some stay, despite evaluation orders? ABC News. Retrieved from http://abcnews.go.com/Health/Katrina/ story?id=1080873&page=1#.UFCWYY7koZI.

11. These data, and the quotes in this and the preceding paragraphs, are described in N. M. Stephens, et al. (2009). Why did they "choose" to stay? Perspectives of Hurricane Katrina observers and survivors. *Psychological Science* 20: 878–86.

12. Lieberman, R. C. (2006). "The storm didn't discriminate": Katrina and the politics or color blindness. *Du Bois Review* 3: 7–22. For more analysis of those who stayed and left, see Elder, K., et al. (2007). African Americans' decisions not to evacuate New Orleans before Hurricane Katrina: A qualitative study. *American Journal of Public Health* 97: 2122; Eisenman, D. P., et al. (2007). Disaster planning and risk communication with vulnerable communities: Lessons from Hurricane Katrina. *American Journal of Public Health* 97: S109–15; and Sherman, A., and I. Shapiro (2005). Essential facts about the victims of Hurricane Katrina. Washington, DC: Center for Budget and Policy Priorities.

13. ESPN (August 31, 2012). Tyler Hamilton: Lance gave me PEDs. Video file. Retrieved from http://espn.go.com/olympics/cycling/story/_/id/8319041/book-tyler-hamilton -says-lance-armstrong-gave-peds.

14. Choi, I., R. E. Nisbett, and A. Norenzayan (1999). Causal attribution across cultures: Variation and universality. *Psychological Bulletin* 125: 47–63.

15. Krauss, M. W., P. K. Piff, and D. Keltner (2009). Social class, sense of control, and social explanation. *Journal of Personality and Social Psychology* 97: 992–1004.

16. Li, Y. J., et al. (2012). Fundamental(ist) attribution error: Protestants are dispositionally focused. *Journal of Personality and Social Psychology* 102: 281–90.

17. Edelstein, R. S., et al. (2006). Detecting lies in children and adults. *Law and Human Behavior* 30: 1–10; DePaulo, B. M., et al. (1997). The accuracy-confidence correlation in the detection of deception. *Personality and Social Psychology Review* 1: 346–57; Malone, B. E., and B. M. DePaulo (2001). Measuring sensitivity to deception. In J. A Hall and F. J. Bernieri (eds.), *Interpersonal sensitivity: Theory and measurement* (pp. 103–24), Mahwah, NJ: Lawrence Erlbaum Associates; and Vrij, A., and M. Baxter (1999). Accuracy and confidence in detecting truths and lies in elaborations and denials: Truth bias, lie bias and individual differences. *Expert Evidence* 7: 25–36.

18. Risen, J. L, and T. Gilovich (2007). Target and observer differences in the acceptance of questionable apologies. *Journal of Personality and Social Psychology* 92: 418–433.

19. Chan, E., and J. Sengupta (2010). Insincere flattery actually works: A dual attitudes perspective. *Journal of Marketing Research* 47: 122–33. Even flattery from mindless computers is effective: Fogg, B. J., and C. Nass (1997). Silicon sycophants: The effects of computers that flatter. *International Journal of Human-Computer Studies* 46: 551–61.

20. Kelemen, D. (1999). Why are rocks pointy? Children's preference for teleological explanations of the natural world. *Developmental Psychology* 35: 1440–53.

21. Kelemen, D., and E. Rosset (2009). The human function compunction: Teleological explanation in adults. *Cognition* 111: 138–43; Rosset, E. (2008). It's no accident: Our bias for intentional explanations. *Cognition* 108: 771–80.

22. Gilbert, D. T., B. W. Pelham, and D. S. Krull (1988). On cognitive busyness: When person perceivers meet persons perceived. *Journal of Personality and Social Psychology* 54: 733–40.

23. Steblay, N., et al. (2006). The impact on juror verdicts of judicial instruction to disregard inadmissible evidence: A meta-analysis. *Law and Human Behavior* 30: 469–92.

24. Kassin, S. M., and H. Sukel (1997). Coerced confessions and the jury: An experi-

mental test of the "harmless error" rule. *Law and Human Behavior* 21: 27–46; Kassin, S. M., D. Bogart, and J. Kerner (2012). Confessions that corrupt: Evidence from the DNA exoneration case files. *Psychological Science* 23: 41–45; Wallace, D. B., and S. M. Kassin (2012). Harmless error analysis: How do judges respond to confession errors? *Law and Human Behavior* 36: 151–57.

25. Gilbert, D. T., and E. E. Jones (1986). Perceiver-induced constraint: Interpretations of self-generated reality. *Journal of Personality and Social Psychology* 50: 269–80; Hansen, E. M., C. E. Kimble, and D. W. Biers (2001). Actors and observers: Divergent attributions of constrained unfriendly behavior. *Social Behavior and Personality* 29: 87–104; Napolitan, D. A., and G. R. Goethals (1979). The attribution of friendliness. *Journal of Experimental Social Psychology* 15: 105–13; Ross, L., M. R. Lepper, and M. Hubbard (1975). Perseverance in self-perception and social perception: Biased attributional processes in the debriefing paradigm. *Journal of Personality and Social Psychology* 32: 880–92.

26. For the rest of the list, see http://voices.yahoo.com/falling-love-movie-set-1267023 .html.

27. Zimbardo, P. (2007). *The Lucifer effect: Understanding how good people turn evil.* New York: Random House.

28. Fama, E. F., and K. R. French (2010). Luck versus skill in the cross-section of mutual fund returns. *Journal of Finance* 65: 1915–47.

29. Thaler, R. H., and C. R. Sunstein (2008). *Nudge: Improving decisions about health, wealth, and happiness.* New Haven: Yale University Press.

30. Willis, L. E. (2008). Evidence and ideology in assessing the effectiveness of financial literacy education. *San Diego Law Review* 46: 415–58.

31. Mullainathan, S., and E. Shafir (2013). *Scarcity: Why having too little means so much.* New York: Times Books.

32. Wansink, B., and J. Kim (2005). Bad popcorn in big buckets: Portion size can influence intake as much as taste. *Journal of Nutrition Education and Behavior* 37: 242–45. For a description of many more experiments of this kind, read B. Wansink (2006). *Mindless eating: Why we eat more than we think.* New York: Bantam Dell.

33. Geier, A. B., P. Rozin, and G. Doros (2006). Unit bias: A new heuristic that helps explain the effect of portion size on food intake. *Psychological Science* 17: 521–25.

34. Van Ittersum, K., and B. Wansink (2012). Plate size and color suggestibility: The Delboeuf illusion's bias on serving and eating behavior. *Journal of Consumer Research* 39: 215–28.

35. Latané, B., and S. Nida (1981). Ten years of research on group size and helping. *Psychological Bulletin* 89: 308–24.

36. One of the most famous experiments in psychology shows just how easy it is to miss an unexpected event happening right before your eyes, in plain view, when your attention is focused elsewhere. The experiment involved watching two basketball teams, one in white shirts and one in black shirts, pass a basketball back and forth. Roughly midway through the video, a man in a gorilla suit walks through the scene from right to left, pounds on his chest in gorilla-like fashion, and then walks off. If you're simply watching the video, the gorilla is obvious. But if you're counting the passes

made by the white-shirted team, the gorilla is all but invisible. Only 8 percent of perfectly sighted viewers in the original experiment noticed. You can read about this experiment and many others like it in *The invisible gorilla: and other ways our intuitions deceive us,* by Daniel Simons and Christopher Chabris.

37. The inherent ambiguity of a serious emergency was brought into the full view of a nation in 1993 when two-and-a-half-year-old James Bulger was kidnapped at a shopping center near Liverpool, England, by two ten-year-old boys, who later tortured and killed him. So deeply troubling in this tragedy was not only what would lead two ten-year-olds to kidnap and kill but, more important, what would lead so many observers who saw the trio walking around town to do absolutely nothing to stop it. The reason at trial became clear. Thirty-eight bystanders testified in court that they saw the three boys but did not sense from anyone else that the situation was an emergency, and thus concluded that the three must be brothers. You can read more about this case here: Levine, M. (1999). Rethinking bystander nonintervention: Social categorization and the evidence of witnesses at the James Bulger murder trial. *Human Relations* 52: 1133–55.

38. For more on this particular idea from psychologist Phil Zimbardo, see http://heroicimagination.org/.

39. Calibrating your sixth sense to recognize the power of context also helps you understand how to bring out the heroism in others, should you ever find yourself suffering a public emergency someday. Instead of waiting for a Good Samaritan, look into the eyes of just *one* bystander—anyone—and say loudly that you are in a real emergency. Say that you need help. Say what help you need. And then say please. Calibrating common sense helps you understand others more accurately, but it still pays to be polite.

CHAPTER 8: HOW, AND HOW NOT, TO BE A BETTER MIND READER

1. Obama, B. H. (September 21, 2011). Remarks by President Obama in address to the United Nations General Assembly. New York. Retrieved from http://www.whitehouse.gov/the-press-office/2011/09/21/remarks-president-obama-address-united-nations-general-assembly.

2. Quoted in Porter, S., L. ten Brinke, and B. Wallace (2012). Secrets and lies: Involuntary leakage in deceptive facial expressions as a function of emotional intensity. *Journal of Nonverbal Behavior* 36: 23–37.

3. This comes from the book description of *Body Language 101.* Lambert, D. (2008). *Body language 101: The ultimate guide to knowing when people are lying, how they are feeling, what they are thinking, and more.* New York: Skyhorse.

4. Other researchers report similar results. These experiments also demonstrate more accuracy in guessing another's emotions when you can hear the person than when you can only see them: Gesn, P., and W. Ickes (1999). The development of meaning and contexts for empathic accuracy: Channel and sequence effects. *Journal of Personality and Social Psychology* 77: 746–61; Hall, J. A., and M. Schmid Mast (2007). Sources of accuracy in the empathic accuracy paradigm. *Emotion* 7: 438–46; Reinhard, M. A.,

et al. (2011). Listening, not watching: Situational familiarity and the ability to detect deception. *Journal of Personality and Social Psychology* 101: 467–84.

5. Blanch-Hartigan, D., S. A. Andrzejewski, and K. M. Hill (2012). The effectiveness of training to improve person perception: A meta-analysis. *Basic and Applied Social Psychology* 34: 483–98.

6. Lopata, C., et al. (2008). Effectiveness of a manualized summer social treatment program for high-functioning children with autism spectrum disorders. *Journal of Autism and Developmental Disorders* 38: 890–904; McKenzie, K., et al. (2000). Impact of group training on emotion recognition in individuals with a learning disability. *British Journal of Learning Disabilities* 28: 143–47; Moffatt, C. W., C. Hanley-Maxwell, and A. M. Donnellan (1995). Discrimination of emotion, affective perspective-taking and empathy in individuals with mental retardation. *Education and Training in Mental Retardation and Developmental Disabilities* 30: 76–85; Silver, H., et al. (2004). Brief emotion training improves recognition of facial emotions in chronic schizophrenia: A pilot study. *Psychiatry Research* 128: 147–54.

7. Blanch-Hartigan, D., S. A. Andrzejewski, and K. M. Hill (2012). The effectiveness of training to improve person perception: A meta-analysis. *Basic and Applied Social Psychology* 34: 483–98.

8. Frank, T. (September 25, 2007). Airport security arsenal adds behavior detection. *USA Today*. Retrieved from http://usatoday30.usatoday.com/travel/flights/2007-09-25 -behavior-detection_N.htm.

9. Weinberger, S. (2010). Airport security: Intent to deceive? *Nature* 465: 412–15.

10. Gilovich, T., K. Savitsky, and V. H. Medvec (1998). The illusion of transparency: Biased assessments of others' ability to read one's emotional states. *Journal of Personality and Social Psychology* 75: 332–46.

11. Porter, S., and L. ten Brinke (2008). Reading between the lies: Identifying concealed and falsified emotions in universal facial expressions. *Psychological Science* 19: 508–14.

12. In the microexpressions study I just described, there was some evidence of more inconsistent emotional expressions when people were trying to mask their emotions that lasted longer than a brief flash, just not very much. When researchers looked at the upper part of people's faces, there was no significant difference in the expression of emotions between those showing genuine versus concealed emotions. A significant difference emerged only when analyzing the lower face, and even there the effect was surprisingly small. When showing genuine emotion, volunteers nevertheless showed inconsistent emotional expressions 31 percent of the time. When they were concealing genuine emotions, their inconsistent expressions rose to 40 percent. That 9 percent increase in accuracy is the gain you could get by learning to spot inconsistent emotions as accurately as a frame-by-frame analysis.

13. Porter, S., and L. ten Brinke (2010). The truth about lies: What works in detecting high-stakes deception? *Legal and Criminological Psychology* 15: 57–75. The quote is on p. 59.

14. Schmidt, M. S., and E. Lichtblau (August 11, 2012). Racial profiling rife at airport, U.S. officers say. *New York Times*. Retrieved from http://www.nytimes.com/2012/08/12/us /racial-profiling-at-boston-airport-officials-say.html?pagewanted=all&_r=0.

15. One study suggested a problem that may come from exaggerated claims about body language and emotional expressions. Although the show with the most dramatic claims, *Lie to Me,* is fictional, the consequences of its exaggerated messages could have real consequences. One study asked volunteers to watch an episode of the show. Doing so did not increase their ability to detect lies compared to volunteers in a control condition who did not watch the episode, but it did increase their tendency to identify true statements as lies. Like the sophomore who learns a little and presumes to know everything, the little that can be learned from studying the "tells" can lead to more confidence than actual ability. Levine, T. R., K. B. Serota, and H. C. Shulman (2010). The impact of *Lie to Me* on viewers' actual ability to detect deception. *Communication Research* 37: 847–56. See also Lord, C. G., et al. (1997). Leakage beliefs and the correspondence bias. *Personality and Social Psychology Bulletin* 23: 824–36.

16. For the distinction, see the story by Helen Kennedy in the *Daily News:* BP's CEO Tony Hayward: The most hated—and most clueless—man in America (June 2, 2010). http://www.nydailynews.com/news/national/bp-ceo-tony-hayward-hated-clueless -man-america-article-1.178007#ixzz2KzfYiYdS.

17. One series of studies demonstrates this clearly. The more partisan people were in a dispute, the more negative their attitudes toward the opposition became, but only after being asked to adopt the opposition's perspective. Tarrant, M., R. Calitri, and D. Weston (2012). Social identification structures the effects of perspective taking. *Psychological Science* 23: 973–78.

18. Epley, N., E. M. Caruso, and M. H. Bazerman (2006). When perspective taking increases taking: Reactive egoism in social interaction. *Journal of Personality and Social Psychology* 91: 872–89.

19. Todd, A. R., et al. (2011). When focusing on differences leads to similar perspectives. *Psychological Science* 22: 134–41.

20. See Experiment 3a of Eyal and Epley (2010). How to seem telepathic: Enabling mind reading by matching construal. *Psychological Science* 21: 700–705.

21. Vorauer, J. D., V. Martens, and S. J. Sasaki (2009). When trying to understand detracts from trying to behave: Effects of perspective-taking in intergroup interaction. *Journal of Personality and Social Psychology* 96: 811–27; Vorauer, J. D., and S. J. Sasaki (2009). Helpful only in the abstract? Ironic effects of empathy in intergroup interaction. *Psychological Science* 20: 191–97; Vorauer, J. D., and S. J. Sasaki (2010). In need of liberation or constraint? How intergroup attitudes moderate the behavioral implications of intergroup ideologies. *Journal of Experimental Social Psychology* 46: 133–38.

22. Lerouge, D., and L. Warlop (2006). Why it is so hard to predict our partner's product preferences: The effect of target familiarity on prediction accuracy. *Journal of Consumer Research* 33: 393–402. Sadly, I didn't know about these results a few years ago when getting my wife's Christmas present. Economists find that gift receivers are willing to sell their gifts for roughly 20 percent *less* than what gift givers paid for them, a clear sign that I'm not the only one who gives bad gifts when they rely on guessing rather than asking directly. Couples getting married often try to reduce the number of bad gifts they get by providing gift registries, where they list, very specifically, the things they want most. Wedding attendees, however, routinely fail to listen

to the couples, instead buying gifts not on the list. It's easy to understand why. Just as I did with my wife, when you think you know someone, you don't need to ask what they want; nor do you even need to listen when they tell you. This is a mistake. When researchers at Harvard and Stanford asked married couples about the gifts they received at their wedding, they reported that they were more grateful for the gifts they received from their gift registry list than the gifts they received that had not been on the list. They also said the gifts from their registry were more thoughtful than the other ones. When your friends tell you they want dishes for their wedding but you're sure this sculpted ashtray you found is so much better, put down the ashtray and get the dishes. Despite what the cliché says, it's not really the thought that counts for gift receivers; it's the gift that counts. Give your loved ones what they want, not what you think they will want. They will thank you later.

23. Gino, F., and F. J. Flynn (2011). Give them what they want: The benefits of explicitness in gift exchange. *Journal of Experimental Social Psychology* 47: 915–22. Zhang, Y., and N. Epley (2012). Exaggerated, mispredicted, and misplaced: When "it's the thought that counts" in gift exchanges. *Journal of Experimental Psychology: General* 141: 667–81.

24. Gilbert, D. *Stumbling on happiness.* New York: Vintage. The quote is on p. 213.

25. Ickes, W., et al. (2000). On the difficulty of distinguishing "good" from "poor" perceivers: A social relations analysis of empathic accuracy data. *Personal Relationships* 7: 219–34.

26. The actual correlation between the number our participants believed they answered correctly and the number they actually predicted correctly was .25. This is fairly typical of experiments that compare confidence and accuracy. The correlation is typically greater than 0, but far less than perfect.

27. I had an experience very similar to this one, but much more mundane, on the very morning I was writing this section of the book. I suspect you've had instances like it. My lesson came during an infuriating time trying to get an identification card replaced. The agency had one official phone number. Call it before 8:30 a.m. and you'd receive a message to call back between 8:30 and 5:00. Call during that time, as I did for a solid week, and you'd get a busy signal. Call at 5:00 and you'd be told to call back again at 8:30. The personnel there also never returned my e-mails. I tried to imagine the scene inside the office: my mind envisioned an empty room waiting for the lazy bureaucrat to come back from a long run to Starbucks. My mind panned back and forth between the coffee shop and the empty office, only making me angrier. Why on earth aren't they answering my phone call? How could a state impose a law that they then don't enable people to follow? I imagined their perspective, and it only made matters worse.

I finally dug up the phone number for a private office within the agency. A day after leaving a message, I got a call back. This officer apologized profusely for how long it had taken to get back to me and said that the entire office was up in arms about the phone line I—and everyone else—had been trying to call. He explained that the state had eliminated the positions that used to answer the phone lines, and this office now got fifteen hundred calls a day on that number, with only one person left to answer that line. He said their phone system was antiquated, and that as far as he knew, there was not even a way to leave an outgoing message on the system when the line was busy, explaining the situation. The perspective I got from him bore little relation to the perspective I'd imagined—or taken—from him. The workers there weren't lazy or indifferent, as my perspective-taking attempt had suggested. They were desperately trying to implement a law imposed on them without being given sufficient resources to do it. My mistake.

28. Mearsheimer, J. J. (2011). *Why leaders lie: The truth about lying in international politics.* New York: Oxford University Press.

29. Even if they don't tell you the truth under these circumstances, research suggests that your ability to detect a lie increases substantially if you've asked someone a direct question than if you've asked a vague or indirect question. If you want to know the truth, ask about it directly. Levine, T. R., A. Shaw, and H. Shulman (2010). Increasing deception detection accuracy with strategic questioning. *Human Communication Research* 36: 216–31.

30. Pelley, S. (2008). Interrogator shares Saddam's confessions. *60 Minutes.* New York: CBS News. A report about George Piro's interrogation from the FBI is also here: http://www.fbi.gov/news/stories/2008/january/piro012808.

31. You can watch Daniel Gilbert talk about this study on this website: http://www.wjh.harvard.edu/~wegner/wegstock.html. The data are reported in B. Burum, D. T. Gilbert, and T. Wilson (2013). Unpublished manuscript. Department of Psychology, Harvard University, Cambridge, MA.

32. In contrast, it also explains why people *are* able to tell how much status they have within a group. Detecting how much someone likes you is hard, but you get better feedback about how prominent, respected, and influential you are in a group. More important, if you act as if you have more status than you actually do, then you get shot down quite quickly by other group members. As a result, people know their status within a group better than almost any other aspect of their reputation in the eyes of others. Anderson, C., et al. (2006). Knowing your place: Self-perceptions of status in face-to-face groups. *Journal of Personality and Social Psychology* 91: 1094–1110.

33. Johnson, S. D., and C. Bechler (1998). Examining the relationship between listening effectiveness and leadership emergence: Perceptions, behaviors, and recall. *Small Group Research* 29: 452–71; Ames, D. R., L. Benjamin, and J. Brockner (2012). Listening and interpersonal influence. *Journal of Research in Personality* 46: 345–49.

34. Markman, H. J., S. M. Stanley, and S. L. Blumberg (2001). *Fighting for your marriage: Positive steps for preventing divorce and preserving a lasting love.* San Francisco: Jossey-Bass.

35. One example of such an activity is progressive storytelling, where each student adds a sentence to a developing story, repeating each preceding sentence before adding his own. There are many others. Adele Diamond describes some of the research on the effectiveness of these activities, designed by a company called Tools of the Mind, in this article: Diamond, A., and K. Lee (2011). Interventions shown to aid executive function development in children 4 to 12 years old. *Science* 333: 959–64.

36. Srivastava, S., et al. (2009). The social costs of emotional suppression: A prospective study of the transition to college. *Journal of Personality and Social Psychology* 96: 883–97.

37. Human, L. J., and J. C. Biesanz (2011). Target adjustment and self-other agreement: Utilizing trait observability to disentangle judgeability and self knowledge. *Journal of Personality and Social Psychology* 101: 202–16.

38. Aron, A., et al. (1997). The experimental generation of interpersonal closeness: A procedure and some preliminary findings. *Personality and Social Psychology Bulletin* 23: 363–77.

39. Urbina, I. (July 21, 2010). Workers on doomed rig voiced concern about safety. *New York Times*. Retrieved from http://www.nytimes.com/2010/07/22/us/22transocean.html ?pagewanted=all.

40. Kachalia, A., et al. (2010). Liability claims and costs before and after implementation of a medical error disclosure program. *Annals of Internal Medicine* 153: 213–21.

41. Chen, P. W. (August 19, 2010). When doctors admit their mistakes. *New York Times*. Retrieved from http://www.nytimes.com/2010/08/19/health/19chen.html ?pagewanted=all.

AFTERWORD: BEING MINDWISE

1. Much of this information comes from Arthur Schlesinger's foreword to Kennedy's autobiographical account of the Cuban Missile Crisis, *Thirteen Days*. Many other books cover the crisis in considerably more detail.

2. The full set of letters sent between Khrushchev and Kennedy, from both before and after the Cuban Missile Crisis, can be found here: http://www.state.gov/www/about _state/history/volume_vi/exchanges.html. The opening letter I'm referring to is from October 26, 1962.

3. Kislyakov, A. (2003). Hotline: 40 years of building up trust. *CDI Russia Weekly* 263: article 12.

4. Cited in Schlessinger's foreword to *Thirteen Days*.

5. Fish, S. (October 3, 2011). When Harry should avoid meeting Sally. *New York Times*. Accessed July 26, 2013; http://opinionator.blogs.nytimes.com/2011/10/03/when-harry -should-avoid-meeting-sally/?_r=0.

INDEX

Page numbers in *italics* refer to illustrations.

ABC News, 145
abortion, 110, 132
actors, acting
  costar romances and, 150
  typecasting and, 148–9
acupuncture, 47
Addis Ababa, Ethiopia, xi
adoption, xi–xiii, 163
Afghanistan, 51, 53, 59
  Guardians of Peace program and, 176
Africa, 110
  ubuntu concept and, 51
African Americans, 61
  racism and, 40
  stereotypes and, 134, 137
aging
  cognitive function and, 134–6, *135*
  stereotypes and, 134–6, *135*
AIDS (acquired immune deficiency
    syndrome), 12
Alexander, Matthew, 178
Al Qaeda, 91
  in Iraq, 178
ambiguity, egocentrism and, 106–9, *108*
Amharic, 163
Andon cords, 56
anesthesia, infant surgery without use of,
    41–2
animals, anthropomorphism and, 62,
    63–4, 65, 68, 69, 70, 75, 76, 79–81,
    82, 203n–4n, 205n–6n, 208n
anthropomorphic selection, 82
anthropomorphism, xvi, 61–82
  animals and, 62, 63–4, 65, 68, 69, 70,

    75, 76, 79–81, 82, 203n–4n, 205n–6n,
    208n
  automobiles and, 62, 63, 64–5, 70, 71–2,
    75, 76–7
  children and, 76
  chimpanzees and, 63, 70, 75, 82,
    203n–4n
  dehumanization as opposite of, 64
  disasters and, 61–2, 65, 71, 75–6
  explanation of the unpredictable and,
    66, 70–6, 206n
  eye mimicry and, 66–9, *66*
  "gray minds" debate and, 63–6
  intention for actions and, 73–4
  liking and, 76–80, 207n–8n
  mere-presence effect and, 78
  musical instruments and, 79
  perception and, 66–70
  pets and, 62, 63–4, 65, 79–80, 203n
  random video experiment in, 73
  religious beliefs and, 61–2, 63, 65, 71,
    75–6, 80, 110–11
  robots and, 68, 69–70, 71, 72, 75, 79,
    207n–8n
  sense of being watched and, 68,
    204n–5n
  September 11, 2001 terror attacks and,
    62, *62*, 65, 68, 201n, 202n–3n
  social connections and, 66, 78–9, 80–1,
    207n–8n
  social isolation and, 79–80, 207n–8n
  speed of motion and, 69–70
  three triggers for, 65–6
anti-Semitism, 39

apologies, 149
Apple, 208*n*–9*n*
Aristotle, 57
armed forces
   "don't ask, don't tell" policy and, 172–3
   turnover and, 55, 175
Armstrong, Lance, 147
Asians, stereotypes and, 137
associative networks, 24–8
atheism, atheists, 115
Atran, Scott, 201*n*
attention, "invisible gorilla" experiment
   and, 222*n*–3*n*
attitudes, xvii, xviii
attractiveness, 7, 105–6, 114, 170–1
   associative networks and, 25–6
   bilateral symmetry and, 25–6
   introspection and perception of, 27–8,
     28, 31–2
authority, Milgram's research on obedience
   to, 16–17, 29
autism, 164
automobiles, anthropomorphism and, 62,
   63, 64–5, 70, 71–2, 75, 76–7
Avery, Mary Ellen, 41–2

Bacall, Lauren, 150
Bachmann, Michele, 114
Bailey, Cristina, 75
banking system, poverty and, 153
Baron-Cohen, Simon, 42, 130–1
Baruch, Bernard, 210*n*
baseball, xii, 12, 99, 208*n*
basketball, 208*n*
Bauer, André, 49
Bay of Pigs invasion (1961), 185
Bazerman, Max, 94
Beatty, Warren, 150
behavior
   consciousness and, 24–6
   habits and, 26–7
   "help requests" study of, 26–7
   sense of being observed and changes in,
     68, 204*n*–5*n*
behaviorism, 74–5, 207*n*

beliefs, xvii
Bible, 109
bigotry, 14–16, 28–9
bilateral symmetry, perception of
   attractiveness and, 25–6
Bill of Rights, U.S., 163
Binti Jua, 80–1, 208*n*
Biomimicry Institute, 67
birds, aversion to visual contrasts of, 67
Blackie (guitar), 79
Blankfein, Lloyd, 109–10
blindness, egocentrism and, 111–12
blogs, 187
blue states, stereotypes and, 132
Blum, Deborah, 207*n*
body language, 161–7, 183, 223*n*–4*n*, 225*n*
   autism and, 164
   microexpressions and, 164–7, 224*n*
Bogart, Humphrey, 97, 150
Bonds, Barry, 99
Boothman, Richard, 183
Boston Children's Museum, 87
Bourdain, Anthony, xiv, xix
brain, xix
   acupuncture and, 47
   associative networks and, 24–8
   cerebral cortex of, xviii
   circle test experiment and, 120–2, *121*,
     124, 125
   color perception and, 33
   evolution and, 25, 26
   frontal lobes and, 22
   group assessments and, 121–2, 216*n*
   insight into others' minds as greatest
     skill of, xiii–xx
   medial prefrontal cortex (MPFC) of,
     47–9, 54
   neurons and, 24
   number of possible states of, 24
   predictable malfunctions of, xvii
   synapses and, 24
   thoughts and behavioral responses and,
     24–6
   vision and, 21–4, *22*, 32–3
   visual cortex of, 22

brainoscope (fictitious device), 5
British Petroleum (BP), 168
Brizendine, Louann, 129–30, 218*n*
Brookfield Zoo, 80
Brown, Gordon, 90
Brown, Michael, 145, 151
Broyles, William, Jr., 79
brut sauvage, 41
Buddhism, Buddhists, 80
Buffon, Georges, 69
Bulger, James, 223*n*
Burns, Zachary, 205*n*
Burton, Richard, 150
Bush, George W., 3–4, 8, 23, *23*, 109
business
    context of success in, 143
    dehumanization and, 54–7
    egocentrism and ethics in, 101–2, *102*
    motivation perception and, 115–16
bystanders, crowd behavior and, 141–2,
    154–6, 223*n*

cable news media, 162
California, gay rights and, 65
California State Police, racism and, 40
Cambridge, University of, 67
Camp David Accords (1978), 132–3
Canada, Afghan war and, 51
cancer, 147
capital punishment, 110
Capone, Al, 20
Carlin, George, 33
Carnegie, Dale, 167, 171
carrots, 65
Car Talk, 72, 76
Caruso, Eugene, 94
Casablanca, 96–7
Cassidy, Chuck, 205*n*
Cast Away, 79
Castro, Fidel, 185
cell phones, 65, 103, 176
Center for Military Readiness, 172
Central Intelligence Agency (CIA), U.S.,
    185
cerebral cortex, xviii

Cerf, Bennett, 210*n*
Chabris, Christopher, 223*n*
Chamberlain, Neville, 8
champagne, 41
Chaplin, Charlie, 70
Chertoff, Michael, 145
Chicago, Ill., 57, 59
    Brookfield Zoo in, 80
    Fermilab in, 71, 72
    Shedd Aquarium in, 171
Chicago, University of, 54
chickens, 68
children, 184
    anthropomorphism and, 76
    association of actions and intentions by,
        149
    egocentrism and, 86–9, *88*, *89*, 103, 212*n*
    knowledge and, 103, 212*n*
    language and raising of, 163–4
    social testing of, xviii–xix, 195*n*
chimpanzees
    anthropomorphism and, 63, 70, 75, 82,
        203*n*–4*n*
    testing of social abilities of, xviii–xix,
        195*n*
China, revering of elderly in, 135
Christie, Julie, 150
cigarettes, 58
circle test experiment, 120–2, *121*, 124,
    125
Citibank, 55
Civil War, U.S., 109
    dehumanization and, 46
clairvoyance, xiii
Clapton, Eric, 79
Clinton, Bill, 33
Clippy (Microsoft avatar), 70
Clocky (alarm clock), 72, *73*, 79, 206*n*
Clorox, 103–4, 114
CNN, 85, 129
codfish, 169–70
cognitive function, aging and, 134–6, *135*
College Republican National Committee,
    85
color perception, 33

combat
    dehumanization and, 45–6, 52, 200*n*,
        202*n*
    shock and awe strategy and, 52, 53
    warbots and, 71, 72, 207*n*
commuting, social engagement and, 57–9
computers, anthropomorphism and, 63,
        70, 72, 75
conflict resolution, stereotypes and, 132–3
Congress, U.S., 139
    "don't ask, don't tell" policy and, 172
    TSA and, 166
conservatives, 106–7, 109, 115, 118, 119
consideration, experiments on perception
        of, 5
Constitution, U.S., 111
cooperation, xv
Cornell University, 67
corporations, anthropomorphism and, 63
correlation, psychological testing and, 5–6,
        7, 196*n*–7*n*
correspondence bias, 142, 145, 147,
        149–50, 176
couples
    egocentrism and, 93–4
    gift giving and, 225*n*–6*n*
    perspective getting and, 173–5, *174*, *175*
    perspective taking and, 170–1, 173–5,
        174, *175*, 225*n*–6*n*
coworkers, assessment of attitudes of, 5–6
cows, 65, 76
Crook, George, 38, 40, 46, 60
crowds
    attention limitation in, 155, 223*n*
    behavior and, 141–2, 154–6
Crowe, Russell, 150
Cuba
    Bay of Pigs invasion and, 185
    missile crisis and, 185–6, 187–8
"curse of knowledge," 103
Czechoslovakia, 8

Daily Show, 188
Darwin, Charles, 110, 162, 164
dating, 78–9

death penalty, 110
deception, 8, 11–12
Decorno, 95
Deepwater Horizon disaster, 168, 182
deer, 65, 76
Defense Department, U.S., "don't ask,
        don't tell" policy and, 172–3
defensiveness, experiments on perception
        of, 5
dehumanization, xvi, 37–60
    African Americans and, 40
    ancient Greeks and, 40, 199*n*
    anthropomorphism as opposite of, 64
    armed forces' turnover and, 55, 175
    business and, 54–7
    combat and, 45–6, 52, 200*n*, 202*n*
    essence of, 41
    football and, 41
    homeless people and, 49
    immigrants and, 40
    "lesser mind" assumption and, 49–51
    Native Americans and, 37–9, 40, 46, 51,
        59–60
    physical distance and, 45–6
    psychological distance and, 42–3,
        48–9, 60
    racism and, 37–40
    social engagement and, 51–9
    social isolation and, 57–9
    Standing Bear trial and, 37–9, 40, 46,
        51, 59–60
Del Giorno, Mark, 71
DeMint, Jim, 34
Democrats, 119–20, 131–2
Descartes, René, 13
developmental psychology, 86–9, *88, 89*
devil, Satan, 62, *62*, 65, 68, 202*n*–3*n*
Diamond, Adele, 227*n*
disasters, 145, 151, 168, 182
    anthropomorphism and, 61–2, 65, 71,
        75–6
diseases, xi, 11–12, 147
    social isolation and, 58
doctors, desensitization to patients of,
        41–2, 47, 200*n*

Dodge Charger, 62
dogs, 82
   anthropomorphism and, 63–4, 203*n*
   "guilty look" and, 63–4, 203*n*
dolphins, 171
Donnelly, Elaine, 172
"don't ask, don't tell" policy, 172–3
Dreams from My Father (Obama), 52, 201*n*
drones, 46, 52, 53
ducks, 70
Dundy, Elmer, 38, 59–60
Dylan, Bob, 110

earthquakes, 76
education
   emotional transparency and, 181–2
   perspective getting and, 181, 227*n*
   student performance and, 151, 152
   teacher course evaluations and, 7
ego, 19
egocentrism, xvi, 82, 85–116, 156, 162,
      167, 180
   ambiguity and, 106–9, *108*
   blind and, 111–12
   children and, 86–9, *88*, *89*, 103,
      212*n*
   couples and, 93–4, *94*
   developmental psychology and, 86–9,
      88, *89*
   emotions and, 92–3
   groups and, 94–5, 113, 115–16, 214*n*
   happiness and, 92–3
   illusion of courage and, 113–14, 213*n*
   interpretation ("lens problem") and, 91,
      99–116, *102*, *108*
   knowledge and, 102–6, 212*n*
   media bias and, 34, 100, 210*n*–11*n*
   parent perceptions and, 100
   personal perspective ("neck problem")
      and, 90–8, 109, 112–13, 114
   personal responsibility and, 93–5
   politics and, 101, 106–7, 109, 111,
      115
   religious beliefs and, 106, 109–11
   speech anxiety and, 97, 98, 210*n*

   spotlight effect and, 95–9, 113, 165,
      209*n*–10*n*
   timing and sufficiency of corrections for,
      88–90, *89*
Egypt, 132–3
Eisner, Thomas, 67
elections
   of 1936, 124
   of 2008, 85, 200*n*–1*n*
   egocentrism and, 101
   incumbent advantage and, 139
   polling and, 179–80
   snap judgments and, 4
Eliot, Lise, 218*n*
e-mail
   egocentrism and, 107–8, *108*
   stereotypes and, 125
emotions
   autism and, 164
   body language and, 161–7, 223*n*–4*n*,
      225*n*
   egocentrism and, 92–3
   microexpressions and, 164–7
   physical mimicry and empathic
      understanding of, 45
   transparency in expression of, 181–3
empathic accuracy, 173
empathy, 131, 137–8
   eyesight and, xv, 43–6
   physical actions and, 44–5
   physicians and, 47–8
   terrorists and, 52–3
   verbal intelligence and, 173
environmentalism, 151–2
Essential Difference, The (Baron-Cohen),
      130–1
ethics, egocentrism and, 101–2, *102*
Ethiopia, xi, xvi, 59, 184
ethnicity, stereotypes and, 136–7
evolution, 25, 26
*Expression of the Emotions in Man and
      Animals, The* (Darwin), 162
extrasensory perception (ESP), xiii, 161
Eyal, Tal, 131
eye mimicry, 66–9, *66*

eyesight
  brain function and, 21–4, *22*, 32–3
  deafness compared with loss of, 163,
    223*n*–4*n*
  empathic responses and, 43–6

fake eyes (eye mimicry), 66–9, *66*
Fascists, 45
Federal Bureau of Investigation (FBI), 178
Federal Emergency Management Agency
    (FEMA), U.S., 145
feedback, 167, 179–81, 227*n*
  parroting and, 181
  progressive storytelling and, 227*n*
feelings, xvii
Female Brain, The (Brizendine), 129
feminism, 129
Fermilab, 71
fetuses, mind debate and, 63
Fighter, The, 113
financial literacy programs, 151, 153
first impressions, 4
Fish, Stanley, 188
fishing industry, 169–70
flat-earth thinking, 142, 144, 146, 220*n*
flattery, 149, 150
floods, 76
fMRI scanners, 47, 48–9, 72, 110–11
Fodor, Jerry, xv
football, 70
  dehumanization of players in, 41
  speed of motion and, 205*n*
forgiveness, xv
For Love of Insects (Eisner), 67
Fox News, 85
France, dehumanization of British by, 41
Francis of Assisi, Saint, 80
free will, 49–51
Fremont, Calif., GM-Toyota intrinsic
    motivation experiment at, 56–7
friendliness, experiments on perception
    of, 5
friendly-fire incidents, 51
frontal lobes, 22
Fryer, Roland, 152

Galilei, Galileo, 86
Gates, Robert, 173
gay rights, 65, 109, 110
  "don't ask, don't tell" and, 172–3
Geller, Uri, 19–20
gender
  exaggeration of differences in, 129–30,
    137–8, 217*n*, 218*n*
  similarities and, 129–31
  stereotypes and, 123, 125–6, 128–31,
    134, 137–8, 217*n*, 218*n*
General Dynamics Robotic Systems, 71
General Motors (GM), 70
  intrinsic motivation experiment and,
    56–7
General Social Survey, 123
gift registries, 225*n*–6*n*
Gilbert, Daniel, 173
Gilles, Ralph, 62
Gilovich, Thomas, 97
God
  anthropomorphism and, 61–2, 63, 65,
    71, 75–6, 80, 111
  egocentrism and, 106, 109–11
Goldman Sachs, 109
gorillas, 80–1, 208*n*
Gould, Stephen Jay, 61, 138
Government Accountability Office (GAO),
    U.S., 166
Grandin, Temple, 100
Gray, John, 131
Great Britain, French dehumanization
    of, 41
Greeks, ancient
  anthropomorphism and, 110
  dehumanization and, 40, 199*n*
Grossman, Dave, 200*n*
groups
  brain assessment of, 121–2
  differences and defining of, 126–8, *127*,
    129–30, 131, 133–9, *135*, 170
  egocentrism and, 94–5, 113, 115–16, 214*n*
  feedback and, 179, 227*n*
  stereotypes and, 120–2, *121*, 124, 126–8,
    127, 215*n*–16*n*

Guardian, 69
Guardians of Peace program, 176
gun rights issue, 113

habits, 26–7
Haiti, 75
Hall, G. Stanley, 19
hallucinations, 79
Hanks, Tom, 79
happiness, 92–3
Harlow, Harry, 207*n*
Harrison, James, 205*n*
Harry Potter, 161
Harvard University, 152
  faculty well-being survey and,
    175
  group responsibility experiment at,
    94–5, 113
Hayashi, Patrick, 99
Hayward, Tony, 168
heart disease, 141
Heath, Chip, 55
Hebb, Donald, 74–5
help, requests for, 26–7
Herodotus, 199*n*
Hidden Valley Ranch Dressing, 103–4
Hitchens, Christopher, 214*n*
Hitler, Adolf, 8
Hoare, Philip, 69
Homeland Security Department,
  U.S., 145
homeless, dehumanization of, 49
honesty boxes, 68
hostile media effect, 34, 100, 210*n*–11*n*
House of Representatives, U.S., 139
How to Break a Terrorist (Alexander), 178
How to Win Friends and Influence People
  (Carnegie), Principle 8 of, 167, 171
human immunodeficiency virus
  (HIV), 11
human rights, dehumanization and, 40
Hume, David, 76
hummingbirds, 69
humor, sense of, experiments on
  perception of, 5

hunters, anthropomorphism and, 65
hurricanes, 61–2, 65, 71, 75, 145,
  151
Hussein, Saddam, 8, 178
Hutus, 39
Hyde, Janet, 129

Ickes, William, 9, 173
illusion of courage, 113–14, 213*n*
immigration, immigrants, dehumanization
  and, 40
Indian Territory, 37, 38, 39
inference, xvii, 46–9
  MPFC and, 47–9, 54
  neuroimaging experiments and, 48–9,
    200*n*–1*n*
inhibition hypothesis, 164
intelligence, experiments on perception
  of, 5, 6
intentions, xvii, xviii
interrogations, 178
intrinsic motivators, 54–7, 202*n*
introspection, xvi, 12–13
  bigotry and, 14–16, 28–9
  limitations to understanding of self
    through, 14–34
  planning fallacy and, 18–19
  shoppers' preferences and, 30–1
*Invisible Gorilla, The: and Other Ways Our
  Intuitions Deceive Us* (Simons and
  Chabris), 223*n*
Iraq
  Al Qaeda in, 178
  U.S. invasion and occupation of, 52,
    53, 61
Islam, Muslims, 115
Israel, 132–3, 162, 168–9

Jahoda, Gustav, 40
James, William, 14, 32
Japan, U.S. firebombing of, 202*n*
job interviews, 7
Johnson, Todd, 71
Jolie, Angelina, 150
Jung, Carl, 28

juries
  inadmissible evidence instructions and,
    150
  personal attendance of witnesses before,
    162

Katrina, Hurricane, 61–2, 145, 151
Keaton, Diane, 150
Keller, Helen, 161
Keller, Maryann, 57
Kennedy, John F., 92
  Cuban missile crisis and, 185–6, 187–8
Khrushchev, Nikita S., 185–6, 187–8
kidnappings, 223n
King, B. B., 79
King, Martin Luther, Jr., 210n
  assassination of, 40
Kismet (MIT robot), 68
knowledge
  "curse" of, 103
  egocentrism and, 102–6, 212n
  others as main source of, 173
  self and, xvi, 12–13, 14–34, 179
  stereotypes and, 124–6, 139–40
Koop, C. Everett, 12
Kruger, Justin, 107
Kunda, Ziva, 216n–17n

Landon, Alfred M., 124
language
  child-rearing and, 163–4
  knowledge and, 173
LaPiere, Richard, racial bigotry experiment
  of, 14–16, 28–9
leadership, experiments on perception of, 5
"legilimency," 161
Leibniz, Gottfried Wilhelm von, 13
LeMay, Curtis, 202n
Lenny (guitar), 79
lens problem (interpretation) 91, 99–116,
  102, 108
Lepidoptera, 66–7, *66*
lesbians, "don't ask, don't tell" policy and,
  172–3
Lewis, John "Jordan," 203n

Lewis, Ray, 41
liberals, 106–7, 109, 115, 118, 119
Lie to Me, 165, 225n
Lincoln, Abraham, 109
Lippmann, Walter, 117
Literary Digest, 124–5
lithops, 66
littering, context and reduction of, 151–2
Little League baseball, xii
Lockheed Martin, Mars Lander loss and,
  213n
Lorre, Peter, 96–7
*Love at Goon Park: Harry Harlow and the
  Science of Affection* (Blum), 207n
Lovett, Debbie, 34
Lucille (guitar), 79
lying, 149, 162, 225n, 227n
  microexpressions as predictor of, 165–6
  perspective getting and, 177–9

Madonna, 150
Maine, 124
"Majority of Parents Abuse Children,
  Children Report" (*Onion*), 91
Male Brain, The (Brizendine), 129
Manilow, Barry, 96, 209n–10n
Marist Institute for Public Opinion,
  superpowers poll by, xx, 195n
Markman, Howard, 181
marriage
  egocentrism and, 93–4
  gay rights and, 109, 110
  gift giving and, 171, 225n–6n
  speaker-listener technique and, 181
Mars Lander, 213n
Masood, Talat, 53
Masoro, Edward, 134
Massachusetts Institute of Technology
  (MIT), 68
mass media, 85
  "nonverbal analysts" and, 162
  perceived bias in, 34, 100, 210n–11n
McCain, John, 85, 200n
mealworms, 67
Mearsheimer, John, 177

media bias, 34, 100, 210*n*–11*n*

medicine

  infant surgery without anesthesia and, 41–2

  malpractice liability and, 182–3

  physician empathy and, 47–8

Memphis, Tenn., King assassination in, 40

men

  emotions and, 125–6, 164

  frequency of sex thoughts of, 130

  see also gender; women

Merchant of Venice, The (Shakespeare), 39

mere-presence effect, 78

Michigan, University of, 216*n*–17*n*

Microsoft Word, 70

Milgram, Stanley, obedience to authority study of, 16–17, 29

Miller, Elaine, 95

mind, human

  associative networks and, 24–8

  conscious versus unconscious functions of, 19–21

  ego and, 19

  free will concept and, 49–51

  habits and, 26–7

  house metaphor for, 19–21

  iceberg metaphor for, 19–20, 21

  naïve realism and, 33–4, 99

  psychics misrepresentation of, 19–20

mind reading (insight)

  actions' context importance to, 141–57

  anthropomorphism and, *see* anthropomorphism

  attractiveness perception and, 7, 25–8, *28*, 31–2, 105–6, 114, 170–1

  blindness versus deafness as limitation to, 163, 223*n*–4*n*

  body language and, 161–7, 183, 223*n*–4*n*, 225*n*

  bystander and crowd behavior and, 141–2, 154–6, 223*n*

  cerebral cortex and, xviii

  cooperation and, xv

  correspondence bias and, 142, 145, 147, 149–50, 176

  cultural influences and, 147–8

  dating and, 78–9

  deception and, 8, 11–12

  dehumanization and, *see* dehumanization

  egocentrism and, *see* egocentrism

  empathy and, xv, 43–8, 52–3, 131, 137–8, 173

  feedback and, 167, 179–81, 227*n*

  first impressions and, 4

  flat-earth thinking and, 142, 144, 146, 220*n*

  forgiveness and, xv

  friends and relatives and, 9

  inference and, xvii, 46–9

  interpretation ("lens problem") and, 91, 99–116, *102*, *108*

  intrinsic motivators and, 54–7, 202*n*

  limitations to, xv–xvii, 14–34

  lying and, 149, 162, 165–6, 177–9, 225*n*, 227*n*

  Marist "superpowers" poll and, xx, 195*n*

  microexpressions and, 164–7

  misunderstanding causes of behavior and, 150–6

  motivation perception and, 115–16

  observing others' gaze and, 43–4, 67

  others' impressions of you measured by, 4–9

  overconfidence in skill at, 3–13

  performance appraisals and, 176–81

  personal perspective ("neck problem") and, 90–8, 109, 112–13, 114

  perspective getting and, 172–81, *174*, *175*, 188, 227*n*

  perspective taking and, 161–2, 167–71, 173–5, *174*, *175*, 183, 225*n*–6*n*

  Quiz Bowl experiment and, 143–5, 146, 147

  reasoning and, xviii

  romantic partners and, 9–12, *11*, 196*n*

  self-knowledge and, xvi, 12–13, 14–34, 179

  self-worth perception and, 10

  sensing minds of others and, 43–6, 199*n*–200*n*

mind reading (insight) *(continued)*
  shortcomings in, xx, 3–34, 41,
    196*n*–7*n*
  sixth sense nature of, xi–xx
  snap judgments and, 4
  social interactions and, xiv, xviii–xix,
    51–9, 78–9, 207*n*–8*n*
  speed of motion and, 69–70, 205*n*
  stereotypes and, *see* stereotypes
  talking stick and, 180–1
misunderstanding, overconfidence and,
  3–13
monkeys, 69
Morse code, 104
Muller, Erich "Mancow," 114–15
musical instruments, anthropomorphism
  and, 79
mutual fund managers, context of success
  of, 150–1

Nagin, Ray, 61–2, 75
naïve realism, 33–4, 99
Napoleon I, Emperor of France, 141,
  142
National Aeronautics and Space
  Administration (NASA), 213*n*
National Basketball Association (NBA),
  208*n*
National Football League (NFL)
  dehumanization of players by owners
    in, 41
  slow-motion replays of tackles in, 205*n*
National Public Radio (NPR), 34, 72
Native Americans, 37–9, 40, 46, 51,
  59–60, 180
Nazis (National Socialists), 39
Nebraska, 37
neck problem (personal perspective), 90,
  91–5, 112–13
Nelson, Willie, 79
neuroimaging
  inference and, 48–9, 200*n*–1*n*
  religious beliefs and, 110–11
neurons, 24
Nevada, drone operations in, 46

Newcastle, University of, 68
Newlywed Game, 9
New Orleans, Hurricane Katrina and,
  61–2, 145
Newton, Elizabeth, 104, 212*n*
New York City, 59, 92
New York Times, 182, 188
NHI (No Humans Involved), 40
Nimoy, Leonard, 148–9, 150
Niobrara River, 37
Nisbett, Richard, 216*n*–17*n*
Noland, Chuck (char.), 79
nonverbal analysts, 162
North Atlantic, 169
Northwestern University, 145
Nudge (Thaler and Sunstein), 151
NUMMI (New United Motor
  Manufacturing, Inc.), 56–7

Obama, Barack, 52, 90, 109, 162, 200*n*,
  201*n*
obedience to authority, Milgram's research
  on, 16–17, 29
obesity
  context and campaign against, 151,
    153–4
  portion size and, 154
Obesity Action Coalition, 153
oil industry, Deepwater Horizon disaster
  and, 168, 182
Oklahoma, 37
Omaha, Nebr., 38
Omaha Indians, 38
Onion, 91, 163
*On Killing: The Psychological Cost of
  Learning to Kill in War and Society*
  (Grossman), 200*n*
opinion polls, xx, 109, 179–80, 195*n*
Orwell, George, 45
owl butterflies, 66–7, *66,* 68

Pain in Neonates (Avery), 41–2
Pakistan, 53
Palestinians, Palestine, 162, 168–9
Palin, Sarah, 33–4

paranoia, 95
parents
    perception of danger and, 100
    see also children
Paro (robot), 207*n*–8*n*
parochial altruism, 53, 201*n*
parroting, 181
payday loans, 153
performance appraisals, 176–81
perspective
    deception and, 177–9
    egocentrism and, 90–8, 109, 112–13,
        114
    getting of, 172–81, *174*, *175*, 188, 227*n*
    getting of, barriers to, 176–81
    gift selection and, 171, 225*n*–6*n*
    interracial interactions and, 171
    taking of, 161–2, 167–71, 173–5, *174*,
        175, 183, 225*n*–6*n*
    talking stick and, 180–1
    transparency and, 181–3
pets, anthropomorphism and, 62, 63–4,
    65, 79–80, 203*n*
Philadelphia, Pa., 59
Phillips, Mark D., 202*n*–3*n*
physicians
    desensitization to patients of, 41–2, 47,
        200*n*
    empathy and, 47–8
    malpractice issue and, 182–3
Piaget, Jean, 86–9, 98
pigs, 65, 76
Piro, George, 178
Pitt, Brad, 150
Pittsburgh Pirates, 208*n*
planning fallacy, 18–19
politics
    egocentrism and, 101, 106–7, 109, 111,
        115
    incumbent advantage and, 139
    inferential brain function and, 48,
        200*n*–1*n*
    lying and, 177
    naïve realism and, 33–4
    snap judgments and, 4

stereotypes and, 118, 119–20, 131–2,
    139–40
polls, polling, xx, 109, 179–80, 195*n*
Ponca Indians, 37–9, 40, 46
popcorn, 154
Popov, Alex, 99
poverty
    banking system and, 153
    context and reduction of, 151, 152–3
praying mantises, 66
preferences, xvii, 30–1, 129
Principles of Psychology (James), 14
prisoners, anthropomorphism and, 79
progressive storytelling, 227*n*
Proust, Marcel, xi, 185
psychics, 19–20, 161
psychological distance, 42–3, 48–9, 60
psychological experiments, correlation
    and, 5–6, 7, 196*n*–7*n*
psychology
    attention limitation experiment in,
        222*n*–3*n*
    behaviorism and, 74–5, 207*n*
    correspondence bias and, 142, 145, 147,
        149–50, 176
    curse of knowledge and, 103
    Newton's "tapping study" and, 104,
        212*n*
    Piaget and, 86–9
    Quiz Bowl experiment and, 143–5, 146,
        147
public speaking, egocentrism and, 97, 98,
    210*n*
Putin, Vladimir, 3–4, 8

Quiz Bowl experiment, 143–5, 146, 147

racial profiling, 166
racism, 14–16, 28–9
    dehumanization and, 37–40
    profiling and, 166
    stereotypes and, 136–7
Ramachandran, V. S., 24
ravens, 82
red phone (U.S.-USSR hotline), 186

red states, stereotypes and, 132
religious beliefs, 161
    anthropomorphism and, 61–2, 63, 65,
        71, 75–6, 80, 110–11
    egocentrism and, 106, 109–11
    mind-action context and, 148
    neuroimaging experiment on,
        110–11
Republicans, 119–20, 131–2
reputation, experiments in perception of,
    5–6
research polls, xx, 109, 179–80,
    195*n*
robots, anthropomorphism and, 68,
    69–70, 71, 72, 75, 79, 207*n*–8*n*
Roomba, 75
Roosevelt, Franklin D., 124
Rosebud Creek, Battle of (1876), 46
Rosenblatt, Roger, 210*n*
Rubens, Michael, 188
Rules for Aging (Rosenblatt), 210*n*
Rwanda, 39
Ryan, Meg, 150

saccades, 126–7
Sacks, Oliver, 111–12
same-sex marriage, 109, 110
savings accounts, 153
Savitsky, Ken, 97
Sax, Leonard, 216*n*
Schroeder, Juliana, 58
science fiction, 161
scientific method, xv
Screening of Passengers by Observation
    Techniques (SPOT) program, 165,
    166
Sea of Cortez, 79
self-knowledge, xvi, 12–13, 14–34, 179
    associative networks and, 27–8
self-worth, 10
September 11, 2001 terror attacks, 52,
    62, 62, 65, 68, 91, 92, 113–14, 201*n*,
    202*n*–3*n*
    anthropomorphism and, 62, 62, 65, 68,
        201*n*, 202*n*–3*n*

Seuss, Dr., 210*n*
"Sex Differences in Human Male
    Preferences" (study), 129
sexism, 16
Shakespeare, William, 39
*Shake Well Before Using: A New Collection
    of Impressions and Anecdotes, Mostly
    Humorous* (Cerf), 210*n*
Shaw, George Bernard, 37
Shedd Aquarium, 171
shock and awe strategy, 52, 53
shopping preferences, 30–1
Shylock, 39
shyness, 182
Sierra Leone, 59
silk moths, 66
Simmeth, Lois, 207*n*–8*n*
Simons, Daniel, 222*n*–3*n*
Sinai Peninsula, 132–3
Singer, Peter, 52, 202*n*, 207*n*
Six-Day War, 132
sixth sense, mind reading or insight as,
    xi–xx
Skin Horse, 77, 78
sloths, 69
Small Plate Movement, 154
Smith, Adam, 44
smoking, 58
snap judgments, 4
social interactions, xiv, xviii–xix, 51–9, 66,
    78–9, 80–1
social isolation, 57–9, 79–80, 207*n*–8*n*
solitary confinement, 79
songs, "tapping study" on recognition of,
    104, 212*n*
South, Clay, 114
South Carolina, 49
Soviet Union, 185–6, 187–8
Spanish Civil War, 45
speaker-listener technique, 181
speech anxiety, 97, 98, 210*n*
speed dating, 7
spicebush swallowtail caterpillar, *66, 67*
Spock (char.), 146, 148–9
sports, context of success in, 143

spotlight effect, 95–9, 113, 165, 209n–10n
Standing Bear, 37–9, 40, 46, 51, 59–60
Stanford University, 14, 55
Star Trek, 148–9
Steffel, Mary, 5
stereotypes, xvi, 115–16, 117–40, 156, 167,
    168–9, 187, 214n
  accuracy and error of, 117–24
  African Americans and, 134, 137
  aging and, 134–6, *135*
  Asians and, 137
  circle test experiment and, 120–2, *121,*
    124, 125
  conflict resolution and, 132–3
  differences and, 126–8, *127,* 129–30,
    131, 133–9, 170, 217n, 218n
  expectations and self-fulfillment of,
    137–8
  explanation and, 133–8, *135*
  gender and, 123, 125–6, 128–31, 134,
    137–8, 217n, 218n
  groups and, 120–2, *121,* 124, 126–8, *127,*
    215n–16n
  knowledge and, 124–6, 139–40
  line length experiment and, 127–8, *127*
  politics and, 118, 119–20, 131–2,
    139–40
  race and ethnicity and, 136–7
  reality and, 122–4
  visible facts versus invisible states and,
    125, 126, 216n–17n
  wealth inequality and, 118–20, *119,* 132,
    214n–15n
Stevens, Martin, 67
Stevenson, DeShawn, 208n
stock market, anthropomorphism and, 62,
    71, 75
students, stereotype study of, 125,
    216n–17n
Stumbling on Happiness (Gilbert), 173
Stutesman, John, 145
suicide bombers, 52, 53
Sunstein, Cass, 151
Super Bowl, 70
Supreme Court, Canadian, 162

Sweden, *Vasa* disaster and, 112, 213n
synapses, 24

"Take Five to Live Light" campaign, 153
Taliban, 176
talking stick, 180–1
Talking to the Enemy (Atran), 201n
Target, 141
taxes, taxation, 118
taxicabs, 58–9
Taylor, Elizabeth, 150
teasing, 105
telepathy, xiii
telephones, 65, 103, 176, 226n
  egocentrism and, 107–8, *108*
television, anthropomorphism and, 78
terrorism, terrorists, 51, 52–3, 62, *62,* 65,
    91, 92, 113–14, 178, 201n, 202n–3n
  parochial altruism and, 53, 201n
Tesh, John, 209n–10n
Tevatron, 71, 72, 75
texting, 108, 125
Thaler, Richard, 151
Theory of Moral Sentiments, The (Smith), 44
Titchener, Edward, 13
tobacco, 58
Todd, Ashley, 85–6, 90, 91, 113
toddlers, social testing of, xviii–xix, 195n
Tools of the Mind, 227n
torture issue, 114–15, 214n
Tour de France, 147
Toyota, GM intrinsic motivation
    experiment and, 56–7
Transportation Security Administration
    (TSA), U.S., 165, 166
travel, social engagement versus solitude
    and, 57–9
Trigger (guitar), 79
T-shirt experiment, 96, 209n–10n
Tutsis, 39
Twitter, 29, 108, 109, 125, 187
typecasting, 148–9

ubuntu concept, 51
United Nations (UN), 162

United States of America
  Afghan war and, 53, 176
  Cuban missile crisis and, 185–6, 187–8
  Iraq invasion and, 52, 53, 61
  September 11, 2001 terror attacks and,
    52, 62, *62*, 68, 91, 201*n*, 202*n*–3*n*
  stereotyping of aging in, 135–6
  World War II and, 45–6, 202*n*
Universal Declaration of Human Rights
    (1948), 40
University of Michigan Hospitals,
    182–3

vacuum cleaners, 75
Vance, Walter, 141–2, 154
Vanilla Ice, 209*n*–10*n*
Vasa, 112, 213*n*
Vaughan, Stevie Ray, 79
vegetarianism, anthropomorphism and,
    65, 69
Velveteen Rabbit, The (Williams), 77
Vermont, 124
Vietnam War, 79
vision
  brain function and, 21–4, *22*, 32–3
  color perception and, 33
  deafness compared with loss of, 163,
    223*n*–4*n*
  defining groups and, 126–8, *127*
  saccades and, 126–7
visual cortex, 22

Wahlberg, Mark, 113–14, 213*n*
Wallace, David Foster, 85
Wall Street Journal, 207*n*–8*n*
Walt Disney Company, 70, 76
Wansink, Brian, 154
wants, xvii

warbots, 71, 72, 207*n*
Washington, D.C., 59
waterboarding, 114–15, 214*n*
waving, 59
wealth inequality, 118–20, *119*, 132,
    214*n*–15*n*
weather, anthropomorphism and, 61–2,
    63, 71
wedding gifts, 225*n*–6*n*
Weiner, Anthony, 29
whales, 69
Whitchurch, Erin, 27–8, *28*
Why Gender Matters (Sax), 218*n*
Why Leaders Lie (Mearsheimer), 177
Williams, Juan, 34
Williams, Margery, 77
Wilson, Timothy, 28
Wilson (anthropomorphized
    volleyball), 79
Wired for War (Singer), 52, 202*n*, 207*n*
"With God on Our Side" (Dylan), 110
women
  emotions and, 125–6
  frequency of sex thoughts of, 130
  see also gender; men
Wood, Natalie, 150
World Health Organization (WHO), xi
World Trade Center attack, 62, 65, 68, 91,
    113–14, 202*n*–3*n*
World War II
  dehumanization and, 45–6, 202*n*
  U.S. firebombing of Japan in, 202*n*

Xenophanes, 110

Yerkes laboratories, 75

Zarqawi, Abu Musab al, 178

Nicholas Epley is the John Templeton Keller Professor of Behavioral Science at the University of Chicago Booth School of Business. He received his PhD in psychology from Cornell University in 2001 and was an assistant professor in the Department of Psychology at Harvard University until 2005. His research has produced more than fifty publications appearing in over two dozen journals and has been funded continuously since 2002 by the National Science Foundation and the John Templeton Foundation. He has written for *The New York Times* and the *Chicago Tribune,* been named a "professor to watch" by the *Financial Times,* and is the winner of the 2008 Theoretical Innovation Prize from the Society for Personality and Social Psychology. In 2011, he was awarded the Distinguished Scientific Award for Early Career Contribution to Psychology from the American Psychological Association. He lives on the South Side of Chicago with his wife and their four children.

A NOTE ON THE TYPE

This book was set in Adobe Garamond. Designed for the Adobe Corporation by Robert Slimbach, the fonts are based on types first cut by Claude Garamond (c. 1480–1561). Garamond was a pupil of Geoffroy Tory and is believed to have followed the Venetian models, although he introduced a number of important differences, and it is to him that we owe the letter we now know as "old style." He gave to his letters a certain elegance and feeling of movement that won their creator an immediate reputation and the patronage of Francis I of France.

Composed by North Market Street Graphics, Lancaster, Pennsylvania

Printed and bound by Berryville Graphics, Berryville, Virginia

Designed by Maggie Hinders